THE STARTUP'S GUIDE
TO CUSTOMER SUCCESS

THE STARTUP'S GUIDE TO CUSTOMER SUCCESS

HOW TO CHAMPION THE CUSTOMER AT YOUR COMPANY

JENNIFER CHIANG

NEW DEGREE PRESS

THE STARTUP'S GUIDE TO CUSTOMER SUCCESS

How to Champion the Customer at Your Company

ISBN   978-1-64137-188-9   *Paperback*

          978-1-64137-189-6   *Ebook*

For the past, present, and future members of
the customer success community

CONTENTS

INTRODUCTION

———

"We innovate by starting with the customer and working backwards. That becomes the touchstone for how we invent."

– Jeff Bezos, CEO of Amazon

In the early 2000s, Amazon was struggling with a problem: how do you keep people engaged and – more importantly – loyal to Amazon?

Customers would only go to Amazon to buy the item that they were looking for and went along their way. There had to be a way to keep customers engaged and shopping the site.

In 2004, Amazon's fourth quarter profit was $346.7 million, or 85 cents a share.[1] This was below Wall Street's expectations. Coupled with announcements in further investments in marketing and technology, their stock price tumbled – even down 14.6% in one day.[2]

Amazon tried lowering prices of their goods to become more competitive and a promotion where there was free shipping with orders over $25 in exchange for slower delivery.[3]

Except by now, Wall Street started to become skeptical of whether Amazon was solving the core issue. They noted that while these things helped, they questioned whether these initiatives would reduce profits too much. "There's a cost related with a lot of things they are doing," said McAdams Wright Ragen analyst Dan Geiman.[4] "Presumably they will pay off somewhere down the road."

Amazon really needed something to bring their company to the next level.

Traditionally, to solve the problem that they were having, a business would look into creating a loyalty program, such as one where customers could rack up points they could later redeem for credits or other perks.

---

1   Soto Ouchi, Monica. 2005. "Wall Street Slaps Amazon On Costs". *The Seattle Times*, 2005.
2   Ibid.
3   Marcus, Wohlsen. 2014. "Amazon Prime Was Too Good To Be True After All". *Wired*, 2014.
4   Soto Ouchi,"Wall Street Slaps Amazon On Costs".

Amazon took a different approach. Their culture is notoriously focused on customer obsession. In fact, according to Jeff Bezos, the CEO of Amazon, it's their most important leadership principle.

"Even when they don't yet know it, customers want something better, and your desire to delight customers will drive you to invent on their behalf," Bezos wrote in a letter to stakeholders.[5]

In November 2004, after years of testing and searching for the right loyalty program, a software engineer by the name of Charlie Ward submitted an idea through the internal suggestion box.[6] The suggestion was to offer a free shipping service. Ward noticed how shipping costs and delivery times were big concerns for Amazon customers, and thought some customers would use Amazon more (and spend more per checkout) if they were part of a "buying club that offered rapid shipping."[7]

Bezos was "immediately enchanted by the idea," and on a Saturday evening, he gathered a group of his executives in the boathouse of his Medina, Washington home to crank out the logistics.[8] They brainstormed a free two-day shipping

5   Temkin, Bruce. 2017. "Customer Obsession Lessons From Amazon. Com's Bezos". Blog. *Experience Matters.*
6   Bishop, Todd. 2015. "10 Years Later, Amazon Releases Every Prime Number – Except The One Everyone Cares About". *GeekWire*, 2015.
7   Greene, Jay. 2015. "10 Years Later, Amazon Celebrates Prime's Triumph". *The Seattle Times*, 2015.
8   Seward, Zachary. 2014. "The Very Unscientific Tale Of How Amazon First Set The Price Of Prime". *Quartz*, 2014.

concept. Bing Gordon, a board member at Amazon, came up with a name for it all: "Prime."[9]

They worked fast; Bezos wanted this to be out and ready within two months – in time for the next earnings call in January 2005.

"We knew we were building something that was going to be new and different," said Amazon Vice President Greg Greeley about the planning meeting.[10] "We knew we were onto something."

With that, Amazon Prime was born – pay an annual flat fee and receive unlimited two-day shipping.

It was a program that would cost them in the short term, but they knew it had potential. Prime members initially behaved differently and explored the site more (and in turn, bought more) to justify their annual fee. Over the years, Amazon added more benefits, such as unlimited video streaming or Amazon Music, to Prime membership to further promote customer loyalty and satisfaction.

The effort paid off. Looking at the data, they saw Amazon Prime members spent $1,500 a year on Amazon, which is a whopping 250% more than the non-Prime Amazon user.[11] Furthermore, Prime users represented two-thirds of the retail revenue. It's no wonder that even when Amazon

---

9   Carpenter, Hutch. 2010. "Model For Employee Innovation: Amazon Prime Case Study". Blog. *Cloudave.*

10   Greene, "10 Years Later, Amazon Celebrates Prime's Triumph".

11   Duryee, Tricia. 2015. "Amazon's 40 Million Prime Members Spending $1,500 A Year On Average". *GeekWire*, 2015.

Prime raised their annual fee over 25% back in 2014, their membership grew 53%.[12]

"In all my years here, I don't remember anything that has been as successful at getting customers to shop in new product lines," says Robbie Schwietzer, VP of Amazon Prime and an eight-year veteran of the company.[13]

The program now boasts 100 million members in 2018 and continues to grow.[14]

***

So what happened at Amazon?

Amazon focused on their *customers'* success – understanding what their customers' pain points were and what customers needed from Amazon to become successful long-term.

In fact, there is now a whole practice around **customer success**.

Like a growth stage startup, the customer success industry is at a hockey stick moment. It has become a new fad within companies to become more customer-centric and to create customer success (CS) verticals – whether established properly or otherwise – and new customer success

---

12   Greene, "10 Years Later, Amazon Celebrates Prime's Triumph".
13   Siu, Eric. 2016. "5 Things Digital Marketers Can Learn From Amazon Prime's 35 Percent Growth". *Entrepreneur*, 2016.
14   Reilly, Katie. 2018. "Amazon Has More Than 100 Million Prime Subscribers, Reveals Jeff Bezos". *TIME*, 2018.

roles. Some companies have begun to reap the benefits of having a customer success team and are sharing that Kool-aid with their peers.

This industry, which started to gain momentum in 2010, now has over 3+ million profiles show up when I typed "customer success" into the LinkedIn search bar in 2018.

Customer success is no longer a nice-to-have, but rather an imperative for every company – subscription based or otherwise – to compete in today's economy. Customers are becoming more accustomed to top notch support and experience, and every company – whether you're an old traditional behemoth or a new scrappy startup – must adhere to those customers' expectations and standards or else go down the drain.

The idea of customer-centricity isn't new. What is new is the *emphasis* within companies on customer-centricity. Customer success has gone from fancy customer support or account management to a *company philosophy*. Other teams, from marketing to production to operations, have realized the positive, multiplicative impacts of having a customer success team within their company. By working more cross-functionally, companies have adapted a more customer-centric approach to their business model. It's no longer about 'how do I get the customer satisfied now?' But also about 'how do I get the customer satisfied with the product, to a point where they are super excited tell their friends about us?'

***

I wanted to write this book for one reason: **When I first started in customer success, I was lost and overwhelmed.** As I've learned over the past year plus writing this book, I'm not alone in that feeling.

I felt lost in the dark about what customer success was, what best customer success practices would be for a company like mine (you know, non-B2B and with a very lean team), and how to even get started. Overwhelmed by the number of resources, I did not know who or what to trust. Different sources oftentimes contradicted each other and there seemed to be no true consensus.

A bit about me, I work at an education technology startup. While I was excited by the mission and the team when I was introduced to the role, I did not fully understand what I was doing or what exactly I was striving for in customer success.

The company that I work for offers 24/7, on-demand homework help via a student's smartphone or tablet. Essentially, if a student is stuck on a homework problem late at night, early in the morning, or whenever really, all they had to do was open the app, take a photo of their homework problem, and they would be connected to a real live person who would help them with their problem.

At the time, my company had just started a program where we initially worked with schools to bring our product to underserved, under-resourced populations. We knew we had a product that would benefit all students, so we wanted to figure out how best to access to quality, one-on-one support to those students who may not normally have access to these kinds of resources.

From this program, we worked with a bunch of teachers and school administrators, and quickly realized we needed to do more than just sell our product well. We realized that in order to succeed, we needed to keep our key stakeholders happy and informed about their students' activity with our service. We needed to streamline the onboarding experience, so that we could sign-up more students, remotely, at once without compromising effectiveness. We needed to be three steps ahead so that when the school asked for something, we were already there with an answer.

Due to this process, customer success was born – albeit not called customer success yet by name.

I was excited by this new journey and I was honored to be at the helm. There were so many great articles and ideas I could implement for our customers – we could implement a dashboard, so schools would be able to see everything in real time. We could host onboarding webinars and check-in calls to make sure administrators, teachers, and staff members were set up for success. We could send swag to every school, so students would be more excited about learning.

However, the honeymoon phase quickly faded. People, articles, and books recommended large investments just to get some of the basic things accomplished.

"Have a score for every customer so that you can monitor their health and write out a playbook for how to address a customer when they get into x health category." Great idea – but at the time we operated off a Google sheet and maybe some scribbles on the side of my notebook. We didn't have time to write a playbook. Heck, we didn't even know what problems we would face. Every client had a different school system and a different demographic of student and technology use. Due to the strong seasonality of our product, we didn't have time to finish quarterly business reviews, let alone write playbooks.

"Invest in these third party apps to help monitor and manage your clients." Would love to, but we don't have the money nor the headcount for it. I have been on multiple demo calls where I tell them "So, I'm a team of one and would like to learn more about your product" and the salespeople would just say (and correctly so) "Sorry, we can't help you because our minimum contracts are $10,000 and even that's on the low side. Reach back out to us again when you have at least five people on your team." So how do I get to five when I can't even succeed at being a team of one?

This was an incredibly frustrating time for me and I do not want others to go through the same thing that I did. Now that I'm further along, I've realized that I didn't need those huge investments to build a customer success organization. I just needed to know the basics, create a strategy, get buy-in, and execute.

I wanted to create a resource that was tailored toward people like me back then – lost in the sea of information, and overwhelmed by sorting through all of them to see what piece of advice would work well for your company's business model. After all, because more and more smaller companies are investing in customer success, we need a customer success model which works for all of us – not only those who can shell out the big bucks for large integrations and consultants.

***

Customer success can no longer be just "another function" within a company.

Nearly every growth-stage software or technology business has its own story where the customer success team pulled some rabbit out of a hat with a key customer or customer segment.

I've spent the past year talking to dozens of industry leaders, researching core principles of the highest performing customer success teams and managers, and looking inward at what our small team was doing – both well and terribly – to offer a framework to success in customer success. This book is a reflection of that journey.

Part I of this book will review the background of customer success and on a high level, how it could potentially look at your company. Part II will cover how to create a customer success team successfully, from getting management buy-in to hiring. Part III will dive into the core functions of customer success: four phases of the customer journey as well as how culture and feedback play a key role. Lastly, in Part IV, we will look ahead to what a maturing customer success team looks like and what the future looks like for customer success.

In a nutshell, by understanding your Product Complexity and your User Complexity, which we'll dive into more in the Framework chapter, you'll be able to better determine whether your company's customer success function's core focus should be to 1) revolutionize, 2) delight, 3) automate, or 4) simplify. From there, you can better understand how the lessons shared in this book can best be applied to your organization.

We're beyond the phase of "this is cool" to "this is vital." Going forward, the success of customer success (pun intended) will require deliberate, smart, and strategic thinking for companies to execute and reap the benefits. Customers are more discerning now, so the bar has been raised for everyone – even for those companies who are just months old.

Inside this book, you'll hear unique and insightful stories including:

- How Tim Raftis used his product manager background to approach retention and feedback as a young customer success leader at Affinity.
- The four main attributes Shreesha Ramdas found to be must-haves when hiring your first customer success team.

- How Jamey Jeff reevaluated and reimagined the quarterly business review process at his company to derive more value for his customers with less work.
- How Jennifer Walker connects teams with customers to facilitate productive product feature discussions.
- How Jesse Scharff created a system of agent/customer feedback within his company not only to better understand the customer, but also to improve team morale, stakeholder happiness, and revenue numbers.
- How Maranda Dziekonski manages her time wisely to not only get everything done, but also fight fires and plan ahead.

Companies should empower their customer success teams to flourish – to truly represent the customer inside the company, the company to the customers, and become the defining factor that really differentiates your company from the competition. To accomplish this, companies need to adopt a brutally rigorous customer-centric mindset.

***

This isn't easy.

There is an abundance of resources that can tell you what customer success could look like at your company. However, just like our customers, every company is different, every team is different, and every person's budget is different. You might be running a SaaS company or company that deals with physical products; you might be at a company that has a five thousand headcount or just five.

However, what doesn't differ in customer success is the mindset and the drive. There are the basics of customer success that you'll need to know to get started and this book will cover that; but what will take your customer success team – and ultimately, your company – to the next level is the mindset that you bring to the table and the passion that you share with your colleagues to champion your customer.

PART I

BACKGROUND AND FRAMEWORK

To start, let's understand how customer success came about and its rise as a company mindset. Furthermore, customer success at every company will look a bit different. Some companies have more complex products, and some have more complex users. Learn about how each of these levers can influence your customer success function and how you can best champion the customer at your company.

CUSTOMER SUCCESS
AS A MINDSET

———

"Today's B2B customers feel empowered. They demand a whole new level of customer focus, expecting companies to know them personally, recognize their challenges, and cater to their needs."

— Dana Niv, Strategic Customer Success Manager at WalkMe

For the past decade, everywhere you turned you would hear that customer success was the next big thing. In fact, since 2009, the popularity of customer success has increased 726%.[15]

———

15 Google Trends. 2019. "Explore: "Customer Success"". *Google Trends.*

Customer success has been *the* orthogonal strategy that companies implemented to get a leg up over their competition. A 2016 Forrester study noted that almost 3 out of every 4 businesses named customer experience and success as their top priority.[16] In 2017, the number of companies with dedicated customer success teams increased 225%.[17]

Why this trend? Customers no longer just buy things, they require an *experience*.

A 2013 study by Walker found that 86% of buyers would choose a better customer experience, even if it meant paying a bit more.[18] [19] That same study also forecasted that by 2020 customer experience will surpass price and product as a key brand differentiator. Not surprisingly with findings like this, 89% of companies, according to a 2014 Gartner study, reported that they expected to compete mostly on the basis of customer experience going forward.[20]

What does customer experience mean? It means that nowadays customers are expecting:

---

16 Forrester Research, Inc. 2016. "72% Of Businesses Name Improving Customer Experience Their Top Priority". *Media Center*.

17 Goodbary, Brooke. 2017. "Hiring For Customer Success Teams". Blog. *Medium*.

18 Basu, Tyler. 2019. "The Top Customer Success Strategies Used By Successful Companies (Complete Guide)". Blog. *Thinkific*. Accessed January 2.

19 Walker Information, Inc. 2013. "Customers 2020: A Progress Report".

20 du Toit, Gerard, Rob Markey, Jeff Melton, and Frédéric Debruyne. 2017. "Running The Business Through Your Customer's Eyes".

1. **Flawless onboarding**: Customers want to get started at their pace and on their signal.

2. **Quick signal of a positive and non-trivial return on investment**: Customers want to know early on that the product is worth their time in the long-run.

3. **Easy-to-find and easy-to-understand help when they need it**: If customers have any problems, they want an easy answer right then and there.

4. **A top of the line customer service experience**: If customers need any additional assistance, it should be seamless and flawless. They should be treated as if they are royalty.

However, all of this takes years for even the most successful and straightforward companies to develop; this is where customer success can come in to fill the gap. Customer success can help streamline experiences, grow product engagement and loyalty, and help to bring in and more importantly – *keep* – business.

Five years ago, companies could just focus primarily on customer experience – what customers see and feel and the user interface that they experience. Now, things are moving quickly and more companies are adopting customer success or customer-success-like functions into their companies to not only optimize customer experience, but also to make sure that customers are reaching their goals. Previously, a good customer experience didn't necessarily have to align with customer goals, but with customer success, helping customers succeed is the centerpiece.

In 2018, what makes the difference now is not whether you have a customer success function, but rather how much you enable your customer success function to flourish within the company.

As Nick Mehta, CEO of Gainsight, puts it, "The biggest barrier to customer success is that CEOs [are] not making it an important part of the culture."[21]

To flourish, customer success must become the company mindset to unlock the biggest opportunity in business.

Because customer success comes into play toward the end of the revenue funnel, when some cash and investment from the clients are already in, companies – particularly startups – sometimes push it off as second priority.

This is absolutely incorrect. If customer success is secondary, then you've placed the customer as secondary and customers will realize that quickly.

To achieve this, customer success needs to exceed expectations in all three foci – external, internal, and multiplicative.

Customer success's focus externally is to create champions of both the product and brand. To create a champion of a product, customer success must help the customer maximize their return on investment. To create a champion of a brand, customer success must create an emotional

---

21 Ganapathy, Shankar. 2016. "The Power To Delight: Inspiring Quotes On Customer Success". Blog. *Mindtickle!*.

experience branded through stellar customer experience and customer service.

Customer success's focus internally is to establish and empower a customer-centric mindset within the company. To establish this mindset, customer success needs to beat the drum around customer centricity to prove value. To empower this mindset, customer success needs to provide continuous feedback (which includes creating a good relationship between the company and clients to get constructive, continuous feedback) to enable other verticals to be customer focused.

If done correctly, customer success can then oil a good machine and have multiplier effects for every department within the company. Marketing will have testimonials, good content, and a deeper understanding of customers. Sales will have more sales because of a better brand and more referrals. The product, engineering, and operations teams will better understand customer needs and requests. Furthermore, customer success can spearhead improvements in overall company morale and team synergy.

If this all sounds exciting to you and you want to make your customer success team flourish at your company, then you are in the right place.

HISTORY OF CUSTOMER SUCCESS

———

For a very long time, business has been very *transactional.* A customer bought a product and each company had some form of implementation function to get you started and a support team to answer any questions that you may have afterwards. While companies would want customers to have a great experience with the product, they had more or less considered your purchase as complete by then. After all, the lifetime value that they receive from you, more often than not, is already paid in full.

With the rise of the subscription economy and SaaS industries, business now has to become more *experiential.*

What this means is that each product represents an experience that extends far beyond just the product. It now also includes brand recognition and proactive customer support, among other things to make sure that you have the best experience possible with the company as a whole.

Once you purchase something, that first purchase only represents a small fraction of the lifetime value of the customer. This puts a lot of pressure on the company to make sure that you are having a good customer experience throughout your time, that you are maximizing your value derived from the service, and that you will therefore stay and renew the subscription.

After all, as Bessemer Venture Partners puts it, "The most important part of SaaS isn't software. It's service."[22]

RISE OF THE INTERNET

Prior to the Internet, customer interactions post-sales were slower in nature.[23] Think call centers and switchboards. With this limitation, it is understandable how customer centric verticals weren't a high priority back then. After all, to get in touch with someone was already quite a challenge and the technology just wasn't there yet.

Then, in 1991, the World Wide Web opened many doors for the customer. Customers could now quickly communicate with companies even after business hours

---

22 Zorzi, Stefano. 2015. "Service As A Software". Blog. *Medium.*
23 "Customer Success: A Brief History | Customergauge". 2015. *Customergauge.*

and companies could more easily distribute information. First, came email customer support and, not long after, live chat support. With the rapid innovation in communication technology, more sophisticated customer relationship management (CRM) tools allowed companies to track their customers more efficiently and scale their business. By the 2000s, the rise of online help desks and self-serve help allowed customers to get support faster and on-demand, which saved time for both the customer and the company.

However, as the internet became more accessible and common, customers could compare companies more effortlessly and make the switch to another company just as quickly. It became far too easy for customers to switch between companies in the SaaS model, which meant that revenue – particularly that which was supposed to come from renewals and upsells – tanked. This was serious and companies needed a way to respond.

Alongside this technological transformation was the rise in customer advocacy organizations who noticed new business opportunities in customer experience. Most notably documented by Joseph Pine and James Gilmore with their article "Welcome to the Experience Economy" in 1998 and the book *Experience Economy* in 1999, companies started to notice that in the age of the service economy, it was no longer enough just to have a good product and good support to make it big, companies now had to step back and reevaluate and optimize the whole customer journey – from beginning to end.[24]

Previously, there was no need for teams or even performance metrics to take into consideration customers' experiences and the value that they've derived from the product. Now, there was definitely a need. Retention was vital for the subscription economy. For business to grow, senior management teams started to recognize that they needed a new function within the company to address this.

THE FIRST CUSTOMER SUCCESS TEAMS EMERGE

While there were a number of companies trying to solve these issues with teams that may have not been called "customer success," the first customer success department recorded was in 1996 at – surprisingly enough – a non-SaaS company called Vantive.[25]

Though they collected all of the money from the sale upfront, Vantive was a CRM company whose business model relied heavily on referrals. They would often walk into sales pitches, throw down a list of Vantive customers in front of a potential client, and invite them to call any of the customers on the list to hear about Vantive. This meant that each of those customers on the list had to be satisfied at all times;

---

24 Pine, B. Joseph, and James Gilmore. 1998. "Welcome To The Experience Economy". *Harvard Business Review*, 1998.

25 Customer Success Association. 2019. "The History Of Customer Success – Part 1". *Customer Success Association*. Accessed January 2.

a failed implementation or any dissatisfaction among these customers would be unacceptable and potentially fatal.

To make sure that this was never an issue, John Luongo, Vantive's CEO at the time, hired Marie Alexander, former Director of Product Management and VP of Services and Support at Harbinger, in 1994 to craft an innovative approach in customer retention. By 1997, Marie had created a new department called "customer success" and introduced them during the sales handoff, "This is the customer success team that's going to ensure that you're successful in using Vantive. And their compensation is based on your success."[26]

Vantive then used this department to better understand how success with Vantive was defined in each of their customer's eyes and to better manage customer expectations. Every six months, the client would meet with their assigned customer success team and they would discuss whether Vantive had met the previously mentioned expectations and bring up any concerns. Vantive found success in this customer retention strategy and the customer success department grew to include customer support, documentation, and training.

This was starting to catch on. In 2004, Bruce Cleveland was a new General Manager at a subsidiary of Siebel, a CRM company.[27] While learning the ropes at his new job, he noticed a disturbing trend. After the initial sale, no one

---

26 Ibid.
27 Ibid.

was responsible for the retention and expansion of the customer. He also observed that those customers who derived the most value from the product were also the ones that were least likely to churn. To address this, he created an organization within his company to specifically focus on increasing usage of the product (and therefore the derived value) which he called the "Customer Success Management team."

Then, in 2005, Salesforce was growing as an up and coming sales platform company and was rapidly acquiring customers.[28] However, customers were also rapidly leaving and discontinuing service. With this leaky bucket problem, Salesforce realized that the only way to stay afloat would be to create a team focused on driving adoption and improving retention. While they were not the ones to create the idea of customer success, Salesforce stood on the shoulder of the Marie, Bruce, and the others before, and they went on to build one of the largest customer success teams in the industry, which is still called to this day, "Customers for Life."

***

In the past, customer success-like roles did exist in some capacity, but were not necessarily called "customer success" nor empowered as they are now. They may have been called customer experience, account management, project

---

28   Ibid.

management, or customer support. While those roles also still exist today, customer success takes cues from each of them to become an even better advocate for and an advisor to the customer.

Customer success is a relatively new industry, roughly only a decade old. There has since been an explosion of content, thought leadership, and ideas. This is all very exciting, however, because customer success has almost grown somewhat organically within every organization with a subscription-based business model, each customer success organization comes in with a very different perspective. This, combined with a general lack of time, has made it difficult for the customer success industry to absorb all of the learning so that we can adequately train the next generation of customer success hires and leaders.

With the rise of the subscription economy roughly twenty years ago, customer success emerged as the answer to low product adoption and declining retention. Twenty years later, customer success has been established as a necessity for successful businesses and it is not going anywhere. In the next section, we will review how you can better understand how to build a customer success function that will suit *your* company's needs.

FRAMEWORK

This book is about understanding how you, as the reader, can get your feet wet in customer success. You may already have a customer-success-like function or none at all and want to figure out how to create one.

When I was just starting out and trying to figure out how to best create and establish customer success at my company, I remember thinking:

"The product that I'm working with isn't some huge software platform meant to be used by thousands of employees; it's actually the complete opposite. It's an app where one student has one account and that's it. However, I hear – particularly when it comes to direct to consumer businesses – that tech-touch, aka pure automation, is the way to go for a company like mine because a customer success team just simply wouldn't have enough bandwidth – time, resources, or manpower – to cover all of the accounts and *still* justify the cost of having a customer success team."

"However, the product that I work with is also very emotion-based. After all, we're dealing with children's education here! Automation isn't something that can replace human touch, but we only had one person. Therefore, it is difficult to staff one customer success person to so many accounts and still make sure that each account is getting the attention that it needs. Does this mean that customer success isn't something for my company at all? How exactly would it work here?"

The answer – it's all about focus.

At the beginning, there is no way one can start out in customer success and absorb all of the information – the best practices on how to run a quarterly business review, how to implement in-app NPS surveys with intricate logic, or even the basics of mapping the customer journey. There's too much to learn and handle all at once and you don't want to burn out.

So, *focus*.

Understand how your product is seen through your customers' eyes, and then understand where the customer is coming from emotionally. Once you truly understand that, not only will you be able to better and more intelligently prioritize which resources to sort through, but you will also be able to make more informed strategic decisions as you learn more about the customer success industry.

***

Every product is different and every product's users are different. As the customer success industry expands and becomes more socialized within all companies – big or small, old or just started yesterday – , there is a need to better understand how customer success can help a business like *yours*.

There are two main factors that play into how a customer success function would operate in a company: *Product Complexity* and *User Complexity*.

Everything has its nuances, but what customer success ultimately boils down to is the relationship between the company and the customer. Product Complexity represents the intricacies behind the company, while User Complexity represents the idiosyncrasies behind whom you serve. Some are simpler than others are, so as you develop your customer success function and strategy, you should keep these two factors in mind.

By understanding these two, you can better understand how customer success will play into your business strategy long-term. Furthermore, you will have a better understanding of how to use the lessons and takeaways throughout this book.

WHAT IS PRODUCT COMPLEXITY?

Simply put, Product Complexity is how complex your product is for your customer to use. Here, we want to understand how your users derive value from your product and how much effort it takes to get there. This also includes how intuitive your product is to use.

Having a simpler product doesn't mean that the customer success role is easy, and similarly, having a very intricate product doesn't mean that the customer success role is impossible. It just means that the customer success strategy for these two products will look very different. A simple example is that to onboard a new user, simpler products may use in-app tool tips to get the customer started, whereas more complex products may connect the customer with a professional services team.

For example, Salesforce is a clear example of a complex product. It has many functions and features, from allocating leads to your sales team, to generating data reports to check on sales metrics, to hosting a community page where your customers can interact with you. Furthermore, working with Salesforce requires a lot of engineering to properly set up within an organization. After all, that's why the job market now lists specifically for dedicated "Salesforce Engineers", "Salesforce Product Managers", and "Salesforce Administrators." Lastly, it takes months before the end user can even start to get to know the product, and even more months, if not years, after that for the teams to be fully ramped up and see the value from the initial investment.

On the flip side, UberEats is a good example of a less complex product. Note that this does not mean that the product isn't complex behind the scenes, but rather that the user-facing functionality is not as complex. On UberEats, customers choose the restaurant they want to order from, what they want to eat, click a button and their order arrives at their doorsteps within an hour (and sometimes less!). To use UberEats, the customer just needs to download the app and voila – they can start browsing all of their meal options. Not long after, the customer will have freshly made food at their doorstep ready to be consumed; the value is derived!

WHAT IS USER COMPLEXITY?

User Complexity here refers to how deeply or emotionally your product impacts your customers. Here, we want to understand how your product integrates into the end users' lives and the impact that it has on those lives. Companies often forget how emotional (or apathetic) customers can be when deciding to purchase a new product or service, but it is nevertheless a critical component to how customer success teams should approach their role and build out their strategy.

With this reflection, we also want to wean out user expectations of the product. For example, it may be a simple product, but if the user has high expectations for the product versus "if it does the bare minimum that's fine," you would want to treat each of these the customer's experiences differently because they see you differently.

Products in industries that are very personal or close to home tend to have more complex users. For example, Rover, the online marketplace where people can get dog sitters and dog walkers, may not be a very complex product, but is an emotional one. People love their pets and want to make sure that they are getting services from a reputable source that treats their dogs well. If the dog comes back hurt or unhappy in anyway, the owners will become extremely sensitive.

On the other hand, products with very specific use cases, particularly at the workplace, have relatively lower User Complexity. For example, DocSend is a service that provides document tracking functionalities so that you can see how often a document that you send out is opened, viewed, or downloaded by users. While it may dissolve some regular frustrating inconveniences, if a document link failed momentarily, there would not be as much panic as there would be for a disappointed Rover customer. Customers purchase DocSend as a solution to a business need to learn more about their customers' document habits and the business' document effectiveness; but it will not elicit as much of an emotional roller coaster as Rover.

How does this fit together?

By understanding your company's Product Complexity and User Complexity, you can better understand how to focus your customer success team – how the team defines success and how they can bring success to your customers.

When you plot Product Complexity and User Complexity on a two by two matrix, it charts out four customer success team focuses – revolutionize, delight, automate, and simplify.

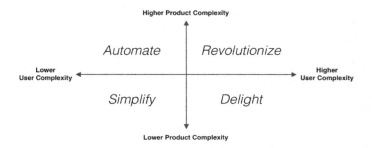

Let's break this down a bit more and delve deeper into what each of these mean.

Revolutionize: For companies that are high in both Product and User Complexity, the customer success team's focus is to "revolutionize" – revolutionize the way that think about the problem that your product will help them solve and help guide them throughout that journey. Your user will have to make significant changes to their day-to-day life to either better understand how their product works with yours or to even use your product properly. By doing so and if it all goes successfully, they will feel the impact at their core and be incredibly triumphant and thankful.

However, because these users are also very emotionally invested, if something goes wrong, they will feel defeated. They will have invested a lot of effort in something that isn't providing them the value that they wanted to see and they will need heavy support from the customer success team to get them to become product evangelists.

Customer success teams that are focused on "revolutionizing" should focus heavily on the onboarding experience. Not only may they have to introduce something rather radical and perhaps face some opposition from stakeholders, but also they need to cradle the users' expectations and emotional investments to make sure that the users – both key stakeholders and end users – are indeed set up for success. If things go awry, Customer Success Managers (CSMs) here will need to employ a highly empathetic and helpful attitude to hear out the customer and help them address the issue at hand.

Delight: For companies that are not high in Product Complexity but have high User Complexity, the customer success team's focus is to "delight" – delight your customers so that they feel valued and taken care of. Your users are trusting you with something dear to them – for example, a pet, their email, or their finances – and so while your product is easy to use and doesn't need a lot of hand holding, customers here will be extremely sensitive if anything goes awry. On the flip side, users here will also be very receptive and enthusiastic when things go well – for example, a new feature was released, a new product was added to the service, or even that your startup raised another round of funding!

Here, Customer Success Managers will be more focused on the engagement phase of the customer's journey. It is imperative that you hear out the customers and each of their stories and feedback and demonstrate to them that they are indeed heard. You are dealing with something that is important to them, so they will have suggestions and thoughts (sometimes to the point where you can't please everyone!).

Automate: For companies that are high in Product Complexity but have low User Complexity, the customer success team's focus is to "automate" – automate processes that had been headaches for your customer so that they can be more efficient. The user has clearly indicated that there is a significant need for your services and is therefore willing to put in the effort. Your service is most likely going to help free up a lot of time for your customers to do more high priority tasks.

Here, Customer Success Managers will be focused on the onboarding phase of the customer journey. We want to make sure that the customer is all set up and ready to go. Once they are all set and things are in motion, the customer will not need to manage the service as closely as long as it works as planned. They appreciate new updates and functionalities, but primarily want to solve a specific business issue. Customer success managers here will also want to focus on making the renewals process as straightforward and easy as possible for these customers.

Simplify: For companies that have low Product Complexity and low User Complexity, the customer success team's focus is to "simplify" – simplify your customer's lives by making things easy to understand and process. Demonstrate value early and then "get out of the way." Because your product isn't that complex, you won't need a lot of upfront effort to get started. However, because you also most likely aren't the most important vendor of theirs, they won't spend nor do they want to spend too many brain cycles on your company and your product. While that can be a good thing at times, it also presents a challenge to maintain engagement.

Here, Customer Success Managers will be focused initially on onboarding to ensure clean adoption, but eventually shifting the primary focus to engagement. At times, this will seem more similar to a customer experience focused team where you focus more on product flow enhancements to guide the user instead of working directly with the customer one by one. Customers here tend to use products in this area for a specific purpose, which means that once they've derived the first value; if the pain point doesn't come up again or has mostly been resolved, customer success will have the challenge of maintaining engagement, keeping customers educated on underutilized features, and exciting customers to become advocates for their company.

Regardless if your company is primarily B2B (business to business) or primarily B2C (business to consumer), this framework holds true for either at the beginning of your journey. There is a slight correlation here between Product/

User Complexity and whether a company is B2B or B2C, however it is definitely not a rule. For example, B2C companies' users tend to be higher in User Complexity because you are more likely dealing with something that they will personally benefit from and because they are using their own money. Another example is the B2B companies' products tend to be higher in Product Complexity because they typically serve more users per account and therefore will need to accommodate more use cases.

As your customer success function grows, whether your company is B2B, B2C, or something else will become a factor in how your customer success team functions and grows. This will be primarily dictated by the amount of resources available to you and the resources that your customers will expect you to have and provide.

QUIZ: WHERE DOES YOUR COMPANY FALL?

If you are still stuck on understanding where your company falls in terms of the Product Complexity or User Complexity scales, take this short quiz. Keep track of what score you put for each of the questions.

PRODUCT COMPLEXITY

PC1. How quickly can a customer start using your product at its fullest capacity?

Instantaneous magic 1 2 3 4 5 A year plus long integration

PC2. How intuitive do you feel your product is to use?

As natural as it can be 1 2 3 4 5 Takes some time to learn where everything is

PC3. How much technical support does your customer need from your team?

A three year old could figure it out without help 1 2 3 4 5 It's required to work with one of our company's employees to even start

PC4. How many layers it is from the person who signs the check to the end user?

The person who pays is the person who uses it 1 2 3 4 5 It's hard to count, but quite a bunch – and it varies by customer too

PC5. Is the industry standard's product similar to yours?

Basically the same with a small strategic differentiation 1 2 3 4 5 There is nothing like us out there

PC6. How many core – as you define it – features does your product have?

Just one core feature 1 2 3 4 5 Over ten core features

PC7. How many different use cases are there for your product's core functionality?

Just one use case 1 2 3 4 5 There are a bunch of use cases

PC8. What are you helping your customers solve?

Just one well-defined problem 1 2 3 4 5 Killing multiple birds with one stone

PC9. How easy is it for a person not from your company to describe your product to their friend?

Super easy – one sentence 1 2 3 4 5 Definitely tricky – easier with a live demonstration

PC10. How often are customers coming from a similar product to yours?

Never, they've never had a third-party solution to this pain point before 1 2 3 4 5 Most customers have used some sort of competitor (whether direct or not) before

USER COMPLEXITY

UC1. How is success determined by your customer for your product?

The bare minimum is delivered 1 2 3 4 5 When they reach their larger business/personal goals

UC2. How personal does your product get with your users?

I don't think they'd notice if we were down for a day 1 2 3 4 5 It affects something that they would drop everything for

UC3. How would your rate your users expectation of your product?

Pretty low expectations 1 2 3 4 5 Impossibly high expectations

UC4. How emotionally invested is the user when they buy your product?

Decision purely based on logic 1 2 3 4 5 Very emotional decision

**UC5. What are they thinking about in those
moments when they pay the bill?"**

"One less thing to deal with" 1 2 3 4 5 "I hope this works
otherwise there will be more headaches"

**UC6. If the customer is successful with your product,
what is their emotional response?**

"Oh, that's nice" 1 2 3 4 5 "You've done the impossible – thank you!"

**UC7. If the customer encounters a minor bug, how
do they respond?**

"Hi, I think I found an error – could you help me get to
the next step?" 1 2 3 4 5 "This is obviously not working
– I want a refund immediately"

**UC8. How well-defined is the customer's pain
point(s)?**

The pain point(s) is extremely well-defined 1 2 3 4 5
The pain point(s) is more nebulous / a feeling

**UC9. How important are testimonials to your sales
pitch/marketing content?**

The product speaks for itself 1 2 3 4 5 Vital, they
wouldn't trust us otherwise

**UC10. How often would your customer like to be
notified post-implementation?**

"Just alert me when there's outages" 1 2 3 4 5 "I want
to know everything. Keep me posted as much as possible"

Add up your scores for both the Product Complexity section and the User Complexity section. In general, the higher your Product Complexity score is, the more complex your product is; and the higher you are on the User Complexity score, the more complex your user base is.

Product Complexity score: 5 – 25; User Complexity score: 5 – 25

→ **Customer Success Team's Focus:** Simplify

Your product is intuitive and your customers are typically looking for a quick solution for their pain points. Your focus is to simplify the customer journey for your customer and make sure that it is easy for the customer to get the help and solutions that they need and move on.

Product Complexity score: 5 – 25; User Complexity score: 26-50

→ **Customer Success Team's Focus:** Delight

Your product is easy to use, but your customers are putting a lot of trust in you. Focus on delighting your customer and keeping them in the loop whenever anything good or bad happens.

Product Complexity score: 26-50; User Complexity score: 5 – 25

→ **Customer Success Team's Focus:** Automate

There may be a lot going on with your product, but your users have a specific business need and you're perfect. They don't have a lot of time to spare, so focus on helping them automate their processes and making the overall customer experience seamless.

Product Complexity score: 26-50; User Complexity score: 26-50

→ **Customer Success Team's Focus:** Revolutionize

Change isn't easy and your product may be hard to adopt at first from a conceptual standpoint – your customers are sensitive and committing to you is big. Focus on revolutionizing their world but in an empathetic way; support them throughout the process and be there when things don't go as expected and when big milestones are reached!

HOW TO USE THIS BOOK

By reflecting on where your company stands in Product Complexity and User Complexity, you can better understand your role and impact as a customer success team not only internally for your company, but also externally for your customers.

Now that you understand better 1) how complex your product is, 2) how complex your users are, and 3) what your customer success's team should be focused on, you can have a better framework of where your team fits as you head into the next parts and chapters.

PART II

HOW TO GET STARTED

Before you can get started creating a customer success function within your team, let's first review the minimum requirements of what it takes to understand when, how, and who to start a customer success function. Once we understand those factors and determine that this is something that you think is right for your company, we will dive into what customer success will be doing at your company.

WHEN TO START
CUSTOMER SUCCESS

———

"We over-invested in customer success early, and we used that to differentiate ourselves as a company."

– Zakir Hemraj, Co-Founder and CEO of Loopio

In 2014, Zakir Hemraj was laser focused on the product side of Loopio.[29]

As Co-Founder and CEO, he wanted to make sure his company could create the best tool for other businesses to streamline their response processes for requests for

———

29   Augustin, Mathilde. 2017. "Inside Customer Success: Loopio". Blog. *Amity.*

proposals (RFPs), requests for information (RFIs), and security questionnaires.

He always had the customer top of mind, whether regarding his business strategy or the culture he was trying to create at Loopio, but he didn't think that he'd eventually serve in customer success.

"With the help of my team, we are responsible for building a repeatable and methodical framework to ensure our customers stay customers."

However, he quickly realized that for him to lead his company to achieve that goal of high retention, he needed to focus on the customer and build a customer-centric team at Loopio.

"The path to my current role in customer success was very unexpected. I started my career as a developer, I also worked in sales for a couple of years. When we started Loopio, my Co-Founder Matt and I were building the product, and our third Co-Founder Jafar was selling and getting initial traction in the market. It wasn't until we closed some deals that a couple of our customers started to ask about implementation, onboarding, and best practices. Being the keener that I was, I volunteered to work out an implementation plan, and that's how customer success was born at Loopio."

"For a while, I was working in those two worlds: coding features for the product and managing customer relationships. A mentor once told me a terrible, but effective, analogy

– 'you can't sit on two toilets at the same time.' Eventually, that's what happened. It got to a point where nothing I was doing was at the level of quality that I wanted it to be. I did a bit of soul-searching, talked to a few mentors, and I realized that the best thing for me personally, and for the future of Loopio, was to focus on customer success."

"So three years ago, the team didn't really exist. It was a team of one! We're still a pretty small team of five. We've seen the structure evolve slightly, but not drastically, over the years."

"We over-invested in customer success early, and we used that to differentiate ourselves as a company."

"In retrospect, nothing was more valuable than understanding the pains and needs of our customers. It helped us make better decisions for the business. As a CEO, having the ability to speak to customers every single day, especially in those early stages, helped us lay the foundation for a feedback-driven culture."

***

To lead Loopio toward customer-centricity, Zakir knew he needed a team dedicated to customers. However, it didn't come easy. As with any large business decisions, it should take some thought.

Understanding when to start a customer success function within your team is important. While the company as a whole should always be cognizant of the customer, having a dedicated function to it is a big step.

Investing too early may be disheartening to the customer success team's morale because they won't have enough early wins, and investing too late may be fatal to your customers' perception of your brand.

You might be asking yourself at this point, "I sort of – kind of – have a customer success function that lives nebulously within product and customer support. We're pretty customer-centric already – do I still need customer success at my company?" or "I just built out a sales team, does that mean that I have to have a customer success team?"

While every company is different, this decision doesn't become any less critical. Every company will eventually need to develop a customer success function as they grow and acquire more customers (and want to retain them).

First, understanding when is the right time to dedicate a person or a team to customer success is delicate, but a strategic step in the process.

The first time that I was told I would lead the customer success efforts at my startup, it was a lot to take in, but I knew I had to step up to the plate.

We had just formed an official sales team, and as someone who had been working with current customers up to this point as an unofficial Customer Success Manager, I knew that caring for customers after they joined was essential for the customer's success, and therefore our success as well. Our customers had always appreciated when we took extra special care of them, so why couldn't we formalize that process?

I knew we needed a customer success team – someone to advocate for the customer inside the company; someone to look out for the customer journey.

Even if I wasn't able to articulate why for my company at that time, we were perfectly ripe for a customer success team.

Working in the education space, our customers had many expectations of our product, needs to be addressed, and questions to be answered. We needed a team not only to guide them, but also to learn and synthesize their feedback that they may provide throughout their time with us.

Furthermore, at the time, we didn't have anyone at the company whose primary focus was the customer. With so many critical decisions being made, such as pricing, marketing strategies, and product focus, it was important that someone representing the customer was at the table.

Given these signals, it was indeed a good time for us to start a customer success function.

To understand if you are ready for a customer success organization, you need to understand three things about your company:

1. **Your customer's journey:** How complex is your customer experience?
2. **Your team's bandwidth:** Can your current team focus on the customer to the standard that you want or do you need support?

3. **Your company's customer champion:** Do you have someone within the company who can sincerely vouch for the customer during tough discussions?

By first reflecting on these three things, you can get a better sense of what customer success would look like at your company and better determine whether it's the right time to begin building that function.

THE CUSTOMER'S JOURNEY

In just the first month of officially taking the helm of customer success at my startup, I was stopped three separate times by three separate people in three separate coffee meetings.

"Jen – stop what you are doing and map out the customer journey. If you don't map out the customer journey, you won't have a clear picture of what to do next or what to work on."

"Jen – what do you mean you don't know what happens before they come to you? What material have they already seen? Where are these customers coming from – marketing wise and emotionally?"

"Jen – you can't figure out the later stages until you figure out the earlier ones. Set those up properly first, otherwise you'll have a leaky bucket problem."

They were all completely right; to start off on the right foot, I needed to understand my customers' journey.

As Russel Lolacher, Host of the CX Storytime Podcast, said, "You're not 'customer-first' if you don't understand their paths to you."[30]

From the moment your customer hears about your product to the time they renew (or move on), comprehending your customer's full journey is important. It is also imperative the company as a whole – and not just customer success – understands the mindset, the emotions felt throughout the customer journey, and the hoops they make the customer jump through.

Therefore, by understanding the complexity of your customer's user experience – in conjunction with understanding your Product and User Complexity – you will be better informed about your decision to create a customer success function.

User Experience Complexity is the level of customization and/or handholding required for your customer to see success with your product. This represents a key subset of the intersection between Product Complexity (how complex your product is by itself) and User Complexity (how complex or emotional is your user with respect to your value proposition).

For example, if you have a low Product Complexity score, – if your product just requires a customer to press a button and your customer sees success – you may not

30 Johnson, Eric. 2019. "17 Strategies From Customer Success Experts". Blog. *Typeform*. Accessed January 2.

need a customer success team, as it seems like your customers can see value easily enough from your product without your help. If your product has a high Product Complexity score, having a team dedicated to guiding and supporting customers will be more necessary for your customers to see success. Having a customer success team here will help users avoid becoming overwhelmed at the start and help them feel as though they are supported throughout their experience.

The most common exercise to make this assessment is mapping out the customer journey.

To start, follow these simple instructions:

1. *Determine the timeline:* This can be a month, a year, or over multiple years. This period should encompass your customer's journey with your company from end to end in a linear fashion starting the moment the customer first sees your company's marketing material and ending around when the contract renews. For example, if your product requires a 6-month implementation period, you would want to make sure that your timeline is at least a year.

2. *List key milestones:* You can do this on your medium of choice – on paper, with sticky notes, or on the computer. Jot down the key moments that your customer experiences during the timeline determined in step one. These milestones should also reflect "moment of truth" events, such as the renewal date, and may be closely tied

with your business metrics. For example, if your company offers a weeklong trial, the date that the trial ends is a great example of a key milestone. After compiling a list, rearrange them in chronological order and map them onto your timeline.

3. *Add in customer touch points:* When is your company reaching out to the customer? What are common times the customer reaches out to you? Jot them down and add them to your map. For example, do you have a receipt email that goes out after the sale? Do you require customers to attend an onboarding webinar? Are there any touch points that are designed so that the customer must reach out to you? For example, are they supposed to ask to expand their contract?

4. *Add in customer emotions:* This is optional, but highly recommend especially for those with high User Complexity scores. What are your customers feeling at each stage? For example, does the invoice stress them out because they don't know how much they would be charged? Or are they super ecstatic because they are seeing early benefits post-implementation?

It may seem tedious, but this is an important exercise for not only understanding the lay of the land but also maintaining alignment throughout the company. In 2017, 90% of marketers agree that designing a successful customer journey and working at close quarters with customer success represents their top priority.[31]

This is a beautiful and powerful exercise, as Jack Gerli, one of the two members of the client success team at Delighted, reflects: "What's cool about the function that I'm in is realizing what our customer's journey is and understanding at every point where the success team can add the value."

"We are the face, We are the voice, We are the content behind the product."

"When we think about onboarding and educating the customer, the customer's product knowledge comes through us and the content that we develop and publish online. We've got great product documentation here at Delighted, spanning from the basics of a feature to how you – as a specific type of user – should be using the feature. And since our core metric is retention, we're focused on reducing our churn to zero which means that we need to understand the silent majority: Why are they churning? How can we get a better pulse before they churn? How can we engage them to get more value from the product?"

"It's great being in client success and overseeing the whole customer journey. You are the judge, jury and executioner by helping customers upgrade, implement, and expand. It's ridiculously stressful, but rewarding."

---

31 Mura, Andy. 2018. "The Status Quo Of Customer Success In SaaS: Stats, Facts, Data, And Japanese Restaurants". Blog. *Userlane.*

Dan Steinman, General Manager of Gainsight EMEA, shares how useful the customer experience mapping exercise is in determining customer success's strategy and figuring out what is best (and scalable) for customers.[32]

"We no longer want to understand the journey retroactively in order to improve it for the next customer. Instead, we want to proactively intervene in the process to improve it in real-time for each customer. In fact, that is the basic definition of customer success."

"To this end, the activity is no longer to map out the optimal customer journey. It is to *create and then operationalize* the customer lifecycle so that it delivers the desired outcome for your customers and, ultimately, the financial results for you."

In fact, by operationalizing the customer lifecycle and making sure that it is customer centric, a 2017 McKinsey report has found that this exercise raises customer satisfaction scores by 15 to 20 points (out of 100), reduces costs to serve by 15% to 20%, and boosts employee engagement by 20%.[33]

Dan further notes two important considerations when completing this exercise. The first is the types of customers that your company may serve and how different tiers of

32 Steinman, Dan. 2018. "How To Map The Customer Journey With Engagement Models". Blog. *Gainsight*.
33 McKinsey & Company. 2017. "Customer Experience". McKinsey & Company.

customers may warrant different attention. The second is the type of events that can trigger a customer success response.

As much as we love all of our customers, when we map the customer journey – either in reflection or in a strategic planning meeting – we need to keep in mind how we may be treating different customer segments.

"All customers are not created equal. We may wish they were and we may even pretend that we're going to treat them all the same. Ultimately, some customers are bound to get special treatment, often based simply on the amount of money they spend. At some point, especially in a recurring revenue business, segmenting your customers becomes a financial necessity. You just can't spend as much time (money) managing a £1,000 customer as you do a £1,000,000 customer."

We will continue to talk more about customer segmentation in the Onboarding chapter.

The second thing to note when completing this exercise is whether the events are triggered proactively or reactively. For example, there are scheduled events, such as weekly sync meetings or annual on-site visits, or unscheduled events, such as a large drop in usage or an overdue invoice.

Dan adds how it is important not only to map out the healthy customer's experience, but also the unhealthy customer's experience and build events and strategies around addressing those warning signs.

"Over time and with the right systems in place, you'll be able to analyze these behaviors and questions mathematically, but it's often a very good start just to approach it anecdotally. The right people in your business have a pretty good sense of what makes for a healthy or unhealthy customer."

Your first customer journey map may not be large, but the process of creating this map will enable you to reflect on what the experience is currently like for your customers. From here, you can see how it differs from where you want it to be for both your first few customers when you first start out and your different segments of customers as you scale. Perhaps there are events in your map, which are not necessary or missing events, which could be added to drive more value. By seeing the lay of the land, you can better understand whether or not you need someone at the helm owning the customer experience, championing the customer to other internal teams, and being the face of your company to customers as they embark on their journey with your company.

BANDWIDTH

"I believe the biggest fallout of the 'digital age' for businesses is that while we can now communicate with others faster and more efficiently than ever before, we are doing so with less *care*," said Christian York, the Director of Client Success at Kira Talent, a startup in Toronto, Canada which helps higher-ed admissions find the best students.[34]

---

34   York, Christian. 2017. "Client Success 101: Building Strong, Personal Relationships". Blog. *Amity*.

"If you want to stand out from the 83 other people your client interacts with on a day-to-day basis, then ... you must maintain a high level of geniality even in the most insignificant of interactions."

The sentiment he brings shows how easy it is to fall into the trap that automation can replace the human touch and how, to combat this, a thoughtful effort into developing customer relationships could be a differentiator for your product.

While automating everything is a solution for some teams, particularly those whose focus is to Automate (low Product Complexity/low User Complexity), it is not a solution for everyone. The bandwidth saved may not outweigh the value derived from the human touch a customer success team could provide.

With your customer experience map in hand, let's talk about bandwidth. Ask yourself these two questions: 1) Who currently owns each part of the user journey, and 2) Does that department have the bandwidth to handle this part of the user's journey to a high enough caliber in your opinion?

This is another exercise also around focus.

While you want to stay lean, you also want to make sure every department within your company is focused on their primary charter and isn't stretched too thin. Furthermore, when you want to add, expand, or double down on a function within a department, you must also be cognizant of whether that department can actually handle the workload.

Throughout this exercise, it's easy to get wound up in the "what ifs" of the company – "what if we had the sales team own this part of the customer experience and product owning this other part of the customer experience?" "What if we had marketing automate everything instead of hiring someone?" When these thoughts come up, bring it back and think about the customer. What would they want and how can you best serve them given your constraints?

"When you, the company, start being concerned about customer retention or know that customer retention, or expansion might be an issue that you would want to focus on, that's when you should start to build a customer success organization."

Jim Jones, VP of Customer Success at ISI Telemanagement Solutions, has been working with multiple organizations over the years to create and grow their customer success teams and solutions. Over the years, he has focused on improving efficiency and retention metrics, achieving 95% customer retention rates or higher.

"Another time to consider creating a customer success team is when you get to the point where, for example, if you have a product that does x and five other people also have a product that does x. However, if you become a trusted advisor and give your customer thought leadership in your industry or in the customer's industry, then automatically you're offering more than your competitors."

"So when you need to differentiate your product by providing that thought leadership, that is when you might start thinking about getting a customer success team as well."

Thinking about customer success teams is exactly what most companies start gravitating toward when they are confronted with this question. Many customer success teams actually stem from bandwidth issues.

Lauren Frye, now a graphic designer at Marketo, recounts the early days at Bizible, a marketing performance management software.[35] Back then, having just one customer interfacing team proved to be too much, so they invested in customer success.

"During the early stages of Bizible, as deals were consistently closing, all seemed well in the land of sales. After their product demo, system installation, and onboarding process was complete, customers seemed satisfied. However, while our sales team was paying attention to our current pipeline of leads and opportunities, we also needed to support our current customers."

"But we had a problem. Our customer support team was also our sales team. We were pulled in two directions, unable to fulfill either one of these roles proficiently. At the end of the day, we realized that we weren't dedicating enough resources to be able to serve our current clients well and move them along in their understanding of Bizible's role in their marketing. This was very concerning."

"As we sought out a solution, we began to design a new division within Bizible. It wasn't long before we concluded

---

35 Frye, Lauren. 2015. "What Our Customer Success Team Taught Us About Referral Marketing". Blog. *B2B Marketing Blog.*

that merely solving technical issues wasn't the only service we wanted to provide. We actually didn't need a 'support' team. Instead, we needed a team that would identify with the customer's marketing goals and help them achieve those objectives. So, we formed our customer success team."

Similarly, Perry Monaco, Head of Customer Success at LinkedIn Canada, recalls how a customer education need was the seed to customer success.[36]

"When I first started at LinkedIn, the concept of customer success existed but the label did not. We've always wanted our customers to feel successful, see a return on their investment, and have a very positive relationship with our organization."

"When I first started, I was primarily an educator, in terms of working with our customers and showing them how to recruit passive candidates and how to engage with our tools. We've evolved significantly since then, but the ultimate goal has always remained consistent."

However, sometimes this exercise isn't about reacting to a particular need that your customers have, but rather looking ahead and preparing for upcoming needs as your company gets more and more customers.

---

36 Augustin, Mathilde. 2017. "10 Leaders Share Their Customer Success Career Paths". Blog. *Amity.*

Oleg Rogynskyy, Founder and CEO of People.ai, reflects on how he should have invested in customer success earlier on at his previous company, Semantria.[37]

"I didn't hire a customer success professional early enough, and that impeded Semantria's early growth."

"Without a dedicated customer success professional we lacked the internal resources to properly nurture the large number of accounts we onboarded. ... We weren't able to support and retain all of the accounts that we had onboarded in our first stage as company."

"The problem was that as a small startup we didn't have enough people to give each account the attention they deserved. I'm confident that if we had had someone who was 100% focused on customer success this could have been avoided."

Becoming customer-centric is a tough journey, but when considering whether you should make an entire team dedicated to just the customer, your current team's bandwidth – in conjunction with your own standard of how you think the customer should be treated – is an important factor.

CUSTOMER CHAMPION WITHIN THE COMPANY

"Successfully leading a customer success organization requires leaders to recognize that the ultimate success or failure of customers is more than just the responsibility of the customer

---

37 Rogynskyy, Oleg. 2016. "Why You Need Customer Success Early". Blog. *Gainsight.*

success team. It's the customer success leader's responsibil-
ity to ensure that the marketing team is producing content
that drives the right sort of conversations, that the engineer-
ing team is building a product or platform that meets every
need of your ideal customers, and that the sales team is set-
ting the right expectations with prospects before they ever
become customers."

– Sam Brennand, Director of Customer Success at Uberflip

Finally, similar to team bandwidth – but perhaps more important – is understanding whether or not your organization has a customer champion within the company. A customer success team is like a conductor making sure the internal teams are in sync and harmonizing with the customers' needs. In fact, a 2013 study of primarily marketing and IT executives found the biggest challenge to becoming more customer-centric was "functional silos prevent customer data sharing."[38] There has not yet been a team to help connect everything together!

To understand whether you have a customer champion within the company, break down how your team views the customer:

---

38   MacDonald, Steven. 2018. "How To Create A Customer Centric Strategy For Your Business". Blog. *Superoffice.*

- Is your company truly customer-centric, or will internal teams need reminders about the customers' needs and goals?
- Which vertical is the customer champion within the company?
- Most critically, who will fight the tough battles on behalf of the customer within the company when decisions get dicey?

As the customer base grows and the product and user experience becomes more complex, you will need someone who works with customers and understands their pain points and what their goals are. Someone must go out and talk with the customers to learn this. In the early days, this may be someone from marketing, a salesperson, or even the CEO.

Determining customer pain points is much more than just saying, "The customer wants x," but rather "The customer is experiencing x problem which is making them feel y." These pain points can encompass both those that stem outside the product and those within.

For example, "I am always anxious about whether or not I locked my door" is a customer pain point that stems from external factors; but "I fear that I will lock myself out because I keep forgetting the code to my newly install door lock" is a customer pain point which stems from the product.

However, as the business grows, someone needs to keep a pulse on the customer; after all, the human touch really matters.

Allison Pickens, COO at Gainsight, elaborates on how a customer champion can help bridge the gaps between customer needs and the product so that both sides are satisfied.[39]

"Our business is one where human touch really matters. Our executive team is actually staffed on some of our biggest clients, which is abnormal since we should be focusing on things that scale and not a single customer. However, I've found it to be a great learning experience and allows me to bring in more stories into the strategic conversations that I'm having."

"You want a product that can adopt itself and prove value on its own. However, there will always be gaps with what your product can do and what your customers want. If there aren't any gaps, you should take another look at your total addressable market. Anyway, you want to fill these gaps with a customer relationship."

"For example, there was a client who had very high churn rate; in that they had a very low renewal rate. And the inclination of the team was product-focused and, therefore, they wanted to address this issue with product changes. However, it takes a couple of quarters to do that! And with that decision comes a lot of long-term consequences – your reputation is

---

39 Pickens, Allison, and Julia DeWahl. 2018. "#Techtalks: All About The Customer". Presentation, Opendoor, 2018.

damaged and not to mention, you're still losing customers because of a high churn rate."

"The balance here and the question becomes – do we optimize for fixing product now or investing in building customer relationships to fill in these gaps?"

To make sure the customer's voice is always at the table, leaders, most famously Jeff Bezos, leave a chair empty at board meetings to represent the customer.[40] But sometimes, you need lend an actual voice to the conversation.

Ellie Wilkinson is the Senior Digital Marketing Manager at Highspot and former Manager of Customer Success at Moz, and she speaks about how it's not easy to balance business interests with customer pain points and how she, as a Customer Success Lead, can help keep beating the customer drum.[41]

"As a customer success leader, you need courage to advocate for both customers and your customer success team. It takes strength to speak up about what's not working or what could be better. Sometimes, you'll encounter conflict. But you owe it to your team and to customers to push for improvement."

Championing the customer starts by having a customer champion within to orchestrate it all; reflecting on whether

40 Thompson, Bob. 2016. "Take A Tip From Bezos: Customers Always Need A Seat At The Table". *Entrepreneur*, 2016.

41 McLaren, Matthew. 2016. "14 Quotes On Succeeding In Customer Success Leadership". Blog. *Amity*.

your company already has this or not can help you determine whether you need to create a customer success function at your company.

***

If your customer journey is complex, your team's bandwidth can't address customer needs appropriately, and your company doesn't have that customer champion, then you are ready for a customer success function for your team! In the next chapter, we will go over how to get that started.

KEY TAKEAWAYS

To best determine whether your company is ready for a customer success function, or not, focus on these things:

1. **Understand your customer's journey**: Map out your customer experience – both the healthy and unhealthy experience. Given your customer success focus, as determined by your Product Complexity and User Complexity scores, reflect on whether a human-touch (or a human-designed-touch) experience would benefit your customer.

2. **Understand your team's bandwidth**: While one team having more responsibilities can drive alignment, it can also spread them thin and reduce the quality of output. After mapping out your customer's journey, determine which functions own what, the work needed to get all of the projects done, and their current bandwidth. If they

are spread so thin it is no longer feasible to champion your customer, you should consider adding a customer success function to take ownership.

3. **Understand who your customer champion is within the company**: Figure out which team (or realizing the lack of a team) can champion the customer; even when business strategy gets tough. This will be a key input in determining whether you need a customer success organization at your company!

By first understanding the three above aspects, you can better determine whether it is the right time for you to start a customer success function.

HOW TO GET BUY-IN
FOR CUSTOMER
SUCCESS

___

"Show your executive how it could've been different, if only someone had been paying closer attention. Don't just focus on the loss. Show the potential."

— Emily Hayes, VP of Client Success at Access Development

In 2012, a SaaS marketing automation software called RD Station had its public launch to address a gap in marketing technology within the Latin American market. Guilherme

Lopes, one of the five founders and Head of Product at the time, was super excited about the launch.[42] [43]

"I think that every other young engineer that starts a company thinks that you will write the code, publish your software, and get rich. I too thought that it would work like that, but it didn't."

"When we launched our software, we were really successful from a sales perspective. We sold like 20 accounts in one month and that was like a big win for us. We celebrated that. Then we discovered that customers, especially in the SaaS world, could pay for one month and not for the other. How come?!"

That's when they realized there needed to be a team to address this.

"Those were the early days of our startup, we began studying about that awful thing called churn when we discovered customer success."

From there, his partner and CEO, Eric Santos saw the value in establishing a customer success function and tasked Guilherme to be at the helm. Eric wanted this function to "help our customers be successful."

"At first I thought he was kidding, I hated that name 'customer success.' It seemed like a fancy term to make the

---

42 Lopes, Guilherme. 2017. "Sharing Customer Success Experiences". Blog. *Medium.*
43 Corthout, Jeroen. 2018. "Guilherme Lopes Of RD Station". Blog. *Founder Coffee.*

traditional software post-sale operations a cool thing. But then I started studying it."

"Now, I've been running our customer success division for more than six years now and I am totally passionate about it."

He currently runs a 200-strong customer success team in a 600 person company.

***

Guilherme and his team learned quickly churn was going to be a huge problem from the start. The founders and CEO realized the value in investing in customer success early and made the call.

So, knowing you need to start a customer success function, as we discussed in the previous chapter, is step one; however, once you know your team is ready for a customer success function, you still need to get the relevant stakeholders involved and their buy-in. You cannot spearhead this alone, especially if you need resources – financial or strategic – from company leadership.

"If you don't have the full support of management, it can be frustrating to get everything you need – and get everyone else what they need – because you're working in and between so many departments. But I don't know how to do the job any other way than holistically. When you get results though, that's when you can prove your worth and name your price," says Nichole Elizabeth DeMeré, Co-Founder of Purposebe-yondproduct.com.[44]

- Fortunately, over the years, research has proven investing in customer success pays significant dividends.
- Increasing customer retention rates by 5% increases profits by 25% to 95%. – Bain & Company[45]
- 80% of your company's future revenue will come from just 20% of your existing customers. – Gartner Group[46]
- Attracting new customers will cost your company 6 to 7 times more than keeping an existing customer! – Bain & Company[47]
- Companies with a customer centric culture have a higher valuation as compared to their competitors. – Forrester's Customer Experience Index 200[48]
- Probability of selling to an existing customer is 60% to 70%. For new prospects, it's just 5% to 20%. – *Marketing Metrics: The Definitive Guide to Measuring Marketing Performance*[49]

44 Nica, Irina. 2018. "6 Pieces Of Career Advice From Women In Customer Success". Blog. *HubSpot*.
45 Reichheld, Fred. 2019. "Prescription For Cutting Costs: Loyal Relationships". Bain & Company, Inc.
46 Lawrence, Alex. 2012. "Five Customer Retention Tips For Entrepreneurs". *Forbes*, 2012.
47 MacDonald, Steven. 2018. "The Secret Ingredient To Increasing Revenue". Blog. *Superoffice*.
48 Burns, Megan. 2013. "The Customer Experience Index". Forrester Research, Inc.
49 Farris, Paul, Neil Bendle, Phillip Pfeifer, and David Reibstein. 2014. *Marketing Metrics: The Definitive Guide To Measuring Marketing Performance*. Upper Saddle River, N.J.: Pearson Education.

You would think that with statistics like these behind it, customer success would sell itself.

However, it is not that easy.

Being customer centric maybe on a lot of executive's minds, but that doesn't mean they are willing to put in the resources to make sure that is the case. In 2017, 72% of businesses say improving the customer experience is their top priority but only 20% of businesses actually deliver great customer experience. Furthermore, only 23% of companies focus on a customer-centric strategy instead of dealing with channel or product-centric structures, despite their executives already agreeing on the value of a customer success program.[50]

For a while, customer success was seen as a cost center because a lot of what customer success does is hard to quantify and are mostly long-term plays. However, attitudes are slowly starting to shift and more and more companies see their customer success teams mature. In fact, a 2015 Preact survey shows that 70% of CEOs are now in support of customer success and that number is continuing to grow.[51]

When I proposed establishing a customer success function at my company, it took some time to get full buy-in. They were down to have the function, but wanted to adjust what

50   Mura, "The Status Quo Of Customer Success In SaaS: Stats, Facts, Data, And Japanese Restaurants".
51   Preact, and Service Excellence Partners. 2015. "2015 Customer Success Priorities Survey". Presentation, LinkedIn, 2015.

the function's focus was. Due to not fully understanding what customer success represented at the time, I had focused more efforts on getting referrals in hopes of reaping the "negative churn" benefits. (Negative churn is where the customer expands their contract and or brings in more customers.)

While generating referrals is a very exciting part of the role, it felt premature. Something was off.

Looking at the research, this focus on renewals and advocacy wasn't abnormal. In a TSIA Customer Success Baseline Survey, 66% of companies cited "Renewals" or "Expansion" as either their primary or secondary charter, whereas only 34% of companies cited "Adoption."[52]

I had a gut feeling that our customer success strategy at the time – especially for a high Product Complexity, high User Complexity service like ours – needed to be more customer centric and not so focused on generating more revenue. After all, the customer doesn't care about referring their friends until they are satisfied with the product themselves. If I was going to be the customer champion, I wanted to make sure the customer was taken care of and heard.

This wasn't easy. After crunching numbers, heated negotiations between what is good for the business and what is good for the customer, and consulting advisors and other customer success leaders, the company chose to be customer-centric from the top down.

---

52 Nanus, Phil, and Allison Pickens. 2016. "Building A Business Case For Customer Success". Presentation, 2016.

To formalize this, we introduced a new team value: "Put Our Families First." It remains one of our core values to this day.

***

There are two approaches to driving this conversation within your management team:

1. **With numbers**: Showing the impact a customer success team could have, particularly on revenue, is a powerful way to get executive buy-in.

2. **Without numbers**: There are many unquantifiable ways a customer success team can add value to both the customer and the company. Share with your team how having a customer success function could also help make their jobs easier as well.

Ideally, you do a combination of both. However, keep in mind whom your audience is and tailor your proposals accordingly. Is your CEO more wary about finances right now or whether the company has product market fit? How could a better relationship with the customers specifically benefit each department? These sorts of distinctions will help you better tailor your pitch.

PRESENTING THE CASE FOR CUSTOMER SUCCESS WITH NUMBERS

"In the initial development phase of a business, we often focus on customer acquisition with less attention given to renewals and retention... even as a known pitfall, many still stumble," said Daniella Degrace, former VP of Customer Success at Radian6.[53]

She recommends crunching the numbers to show the impact. "Focusing on a lightweight renewal straw model from day one will ensure you avoid the unpleasant surprise of waking up one day to find a leaking recurring revenue bucket... then having to incur costs to tune your sales organization to sell more just to stay even on your sales projections. You just can't win that battle."

It's tough. Executives will naturally look at a company vertical and ask – how will this department improve our bottom line? After all, this is a business!

The truth is customer success does not hurt the bottom line; in fact, it can help it a lot! The Temkin Group, a customer experience consulting firm, found that on average, a typical $1 billion company can gain $775 million over three years through modest customer experience improvements (e.g. streamlining the support ticket submission process).[54] For software companies, the gain goes up to $1.1 billion. That's

---

53   Philip, Paul. 2016. "The Why, What and How of Customer Success". Blog. *Amity.*
54   Temkin, Bruce. 2018. "ROI Of Customer Experience". Temkin Group.

just modest improvements – and customer success does so much more.

Furthermore, an executive briefing report from McKinsey confirms, "Armed with advanced analytics, customer experience leaders gain rapid insights to build customer loyalty, make employees happier, achieve revenue gains of 5% to 10%, and reduce costs by 15% to 25% within two or three years. But it takes patience and guts to train an organization to see the world through the customer's eyes and to redesign functions to create value in a customer-centric way."[55]

The customer success community in the past has been quite defensive about being a cost center. While the sentiments are changing, the caution prevails. To ease fears and drive the conversation forward, we can paint the picture with numbers.

Brooke Goodbary is a customer success consultant currently at dataxu, formerly at Intercom and Thunder.[56] She notes that particularly for medium to enterprise B2B companies, you typically need to have more of a business case.

"I see SaaS companies with 50 to 100 employees as being in the sweet spot for establishing a customer success team. Companies at this stage usually have enough ARR on the line to justify an investment in customers' success, and are

55   McKinsey & Company. 2016. "The CEO Guide To Customer Experience". McKinsey & Company.
56   Goodbary, Brooke. 2015. "Dissecting Preact's Customer Success Priorities Report". Blog. *Medium.*

growing fast enough that it makes sense to establish a dedicated customer advocate."

However, Jim Jones, VP of Customer Success at ISI Telemanagement Solutions, breaks it down more for us.

"Strictly from a numbers perspective, it's harder to take a seller or an account manager and put them in a customer success role because then you're going to be losing that quota coverage that you had. Whereas for customer support, the general philosophy there is that we can take one person out of the pool and everybody else just takes more tickets."

He recalls one of the times when he had to pitch to an executive team at one of the companies that he worked with in Chicago, and the discussions that they had to push to reengineer a customer success team.

"What we did was to look at the financial model and say, 'Here is what we're going to have to invest, but here's the upside to that investment. We took a major dip in renewals because we lost some big customers we shouldn't have lost.'"

"And so – and I'm just making up numbers right now – but I could say, 'The cost of investing in the customer success team is going to be $250,000 a year. And people can be a bit taken aback by this high number."

"But I'd go on, 'However, we lost XYZ company that was worth a million dollars in ARR (annual recurring revenue). Not that I'm saying we're going to have perfect renewals with a customer success team, but with this team, one – you will reduce your customer churn number and – two – by cross-selling and doing upsells, you could go into negative churn territory.' And that was the 'Aha moment' for them. It's always about numbers."

"This is a really hard business to make happen just on gut feel. I was a consultant for a couple years in Chicago and what I tried to do was to help a company build and improve their customer success teams. What I found was that there were a lot of CEOs saying, 'I hear you and I get that this is important, but I can't spend any money on it.' My thought was, 'Well, you can't afford to not spend money.' But in a lot of cases that ended up being a losing argument."

"A lot of these companies that I was called in on or involved with were smaller companies, so you would say – 'You lost this amount in renewals and therefore you need to invest this amount.' They would respond, 'Sorry, I don't have that money to invest.'"

"There is enough material that's out there on the web that CEOs and leaders of sales can peruse to get a general idea of what they need to do in lieu of creating a customer success team. But two years later down the road, they come to me and say, 'We don't completely get it and we're not seeing the results that we want.' To ask somebody to spend money to improve retention, oddly enough, is not always an easy sell."

While not foolproof, laying out the numbers case for customer success helps to set the stage for a productive discussion about starting customer success at your company.

After all, human beings are biased. One key bias is loss aversion. That is, if you lose $100,000, that feels worse than winning $1 million, even if it's not logical. Another bias is the recency bias. If you lose $100,000 today to prevent losing $1 million in 3 years, you just don't care – because the $100,000 today is more heavily weighted in your emotional assessment.

Therefore, in our next section, we'll talk you through how to argue emotionally as well, because the numbers are compelling but they won't do the job themselves.

PRESENTING THE CASE FOR CUSTOMER SUCCESS WITHOUT NUMBERS

"The best time to bring up customer success is when you've lost a key customer or account," says Emily Hayes of Access Development.[57]

"Even the most new business-obsessed executive will wince after seeing a major customer depart. Their first instinct will be to go hunting for more new customers to replace those who churned."

"You can present another option, though. A way to stop this from happening again. It isn't enough to just point out that key customers are bailing. Spend some time with the 'why.' Customer success pros are the ones who watch for these signs and proactively create a plan to address them."

---

57 Hayes, Emily. 2017. "How To Save The Day And Convince Your Executives To Adopt Customer Success". Blog. *Access Development*.

"Show your executive how it could've been different, if only someone had been paying closer attention. Don't just focus on the loss. Show the *potential*."

"Loyal, engaged customers are highly profitable on many levels. Customer success isn't just about securing revenue. It's about your reputation as a company and the value you place on your own products, services, employees, and customer relationships."

Emily is spot on. While numbers can help make the case for customer success more concrete, the true value of customer success extends beyond just the dollar signs and into brand and multiplicative effects throughout the company.

According to KPMG, 88% of CEOs are concerned about customer loyalty, realizing that understanding the customer agenda is essential.[58] After all, dissatisfied customers whose complaints are taken care of are more likely to remain loyal, and even become advocates. Furthermore, research shows that a dissatisfied customer will tell 9 to 15 people about their poor experience.[59]

Maranda Dziekonski, VP of Customer Success at Pared and frequent contributor to Amity's Customer Success Blog, elaborates on how you can show the executive team the potential customer success can bring to the table.

---

58 KPMG International. 2017. "Customer First: How To Create A Customer-Centric Business And Compete In The Digital Age". KPMG International.

59 Khan, Jawad. 2019. "7 Signs That Your Customer Regrets Choosing You". Blog. *Hiver*. Accessed January 3.

"I've been lucky where both the CEO and the executive team always saw true value in customer success. However, when it comes down to it, it is all about tying revenue to customer success."

"Putting things in numbers usually speaks to the majority of the executive team, but you'll have different partners in the executive team that will want to see different things."

"For example, the marketing team needs case studies! Even when you're a small company, the marketing team needs stories that they can tell to reel in more customers. Customer success can help provide those stories, which then helps provide content for marketing to be able to publish. The sales team want referrals, such as customer references. Customer success can also provide that if they are doing their job in a proactive manner. Product needs feature recommendations especially from the highest value customers."

In fact, according to a Content Marketing Institute and MarketingProfs report, nearly two-thirds of B2B marketers say that customer case studies are effective tools in their arsenal.[60] Garrett Moon, Founder of Todaymade, also touted, "When our number one goal is to help our customers succeed, we may have already designed all of the sales strategy we really need."[61]

---

60 Odden, Lee. 2013. "100+ B2B Content Marketing Statistics For 2013". Blog. *Top Rank Marketing.*
61 Moon, Garrett. 2019. "There's Only One SaaS Sales Strategy You Really Need". Blog. *Neil Patel.* Accessed January 3.

Maranda continues about how if your team needs more convincing, ask to run an experiment.

"If the executive team isn't bought in and is focused on revenue, run A/B studies. Say, 'This is a managed group of accounts and this group isn't managed.' Then after some time, compare the upsell rates between the two groups. What are the renewals rates like between the two? How about the churn rate or the net promoter score? Tie all of the numbers together. Even in a small team, you should be looking at customer sentiment and churn between your control group versus your managed group."

"Let's say you have ten high value customers, right? – and that very well could be the case that a small organization. Then you need to show what value customer success adds to those ten accounts – from what product feedback we've received from them, intel on how we can and are going to retain those customers, and then add more information like that to get more executive buy-in."

Lastly, sometimes you need to educate your team what customer success truly is, just as I did to get full executive buy-in.

"CEOs in particular are often risk-averse. It's important for them and others to know that customer success is not a new, risky idea. It's existed in various forms for many years, and recently has become dialed in thanks to the efforts of technology companies," says Emily Hayes of Access Development.[62]

---

62 Hayes, "How To Save The Day And Convince Your Executives To Adopt Customer Success".

"Take an executive to a customer success event and learn together. Introduce them to some of the established professionals in the space. Besides educating themselves, they'll likely feel comforted knowing that there's a community built around the idea. It doesn't remove all the risk, but it shows that the concept isn't radical at all."

Kaiser Mulla-Feroze, Chief Marketing Officer at Totango, summarizes this sentiment well, "The profile of the customer success profession is clearly on the rise. More teams are reporting directly into the CEO, and companies are investing heavily in growing the ranks of their customer success teams – from CSMs (Customer Success Managers) all the way to VPs and Chief Customer Officers."[63]

Showing and describing to the executive team the power and potential behind customer success, you will help them see what a customer success team can bring to both the company and the customers.

***

Negotiating for a customer success function at your company can be tough. Perhaps your executive team is swayed more by numbers or perhaps they would like to know how focusing on the customer could tangibly help other departments.

---

63 Crandell, Christine. 2015. "2015 State Of The Customer Success Profession". *Forbes*, 2015.

Either way, it is important that you will present a combination of both a numbers case and a case for the bigger picture to show positive returns on investment. After all, both cases will materialize once customer success goes live at your company!

However, once you get the go ahead, remember the pitch doesn't stop there. You will continually need to make the case for customer success to continue existing at your company by showing progress. This is showing progress through data such as number of renewals or an increased net promoter score (NPS) score, but also through a more customer-centric culture and a more beloved brand.

KEY TAKEAWAYS

Once you have determined that customer success is something your company needs, get buy-in from the executive team. To do so, leverage a *combination* of both of these tactics:

1. **Present a case with numbers**: Business is business. Executives want to know what their return on investment will be if they were to invest in customer success. Present them with how customer success can affect the bottom line – whether that is through renewals and expansions, or preventing of churned accounts!

2. **Present a case without numbers**: Focus on how customer success can positively affect other departments (ex. giving marketing more testimonials or product better user testing channels). The potential here is enormous!

Furthermore, if your executive team is still shy, educate them about customer success by showing them how much the industry has grown and the vibrant community around it.

Only with their buy-in can you properly start a customer success function that can best cater to your customers' and company's needs.

WHO TO START
CUSTOMER SUCCESS

"Give one person responsibility for listening to your customers and authority to act on what they hear."

> – Guy Letts, Co-Founder of Customersure

"It takes a special type of person to work in customer success. They must be built to serve. They must thrive in an environment of helping other people. They must derive success from watching *other people succeed*. They must focus on *other people's problems*."[64]

---

64 Vinje, Nils. 2017. "Hiring That First Customer Success Manager". Blog. *Glide Consulting.*

Nils Vinje runs Glide Consulting, and he has worked with both venture-backed startups and Fortune 1000 companies to boost customer success at their organizations. He knows how hard finding the right person to start customer success can be and how important starting early is.

"If you hire early and pick the right candidate, your customer success program will take off, giving you a boost of retention, and ultimately growth."

"Hire your first Customer Success Manager as early as possible. You *definitely* need one by the time you hit about $2 million in annual recurring revenue, or as soon as you have one customer that represents 20% or more of your income (because you don't want to lose that one)."[65]

"In an ideal case, one of the first customer success hires would be in the leadership position. However, the demand for customer success leaders is way ahead of the supply right now which makes finding the right hire tricky."

"So, knowing that the ideal case doesn't happen very often, having someone in the seat doing the work is what is most important when getting started. The early leader could come from another part of the organization. If he/she can't come from within your organization, you should start with your personal network."

"The key however is that there is a concerted effort around customer success. In other words, it doesn't just become

---

65   Vinje, Nils. 2019. "The Importance Of Hiring For Customer Success Early". Blog. *Glide Consulting*. Accessed January 3.

someone's 10th job. When your organization has less than twenty people, your culture is still malleable. You need people who think and work according to your values. It's possible to find a quality hire through a recruiter or job search platform, but they aren't likely to fit."

"However, you need to cast your nets wide. Like I said, CSMs aren't common, so make it clear that you're looking for someone who hasn't necessarily worked customer success before, but has the appropriate skills. Search for strengths, not titles."

Dave Blake, Founder and CEO of ClientSuccess and former VP of Strategic Accounts at Omniture, also notes how the first customer success person to start your team can come from anywhere, but what is most important is not their titles, but what they bring to the table.[66]

"There is no standard professional background that CSMs commonly come from."

"This role is so new that it's hard to find talent with many years of direct experience as a Customer Success Manager. In fact, my top three customer success leaders that I hired at Omniture came from very diverse professional backgrounds. One was a senior director of online merchandising at a major clothing retailer, another was a product manager at Amazon, and the third was a success sales professional with IBM."

---

66   Blake, Dave. 2019. "Hiring For Customer Success". Blog. *ClientSuccess*. Accessed January 3.

"My number one hiring criteria is leadership. You can teach many skills and you can even teach leadership, but natural leaders will have the initiative to figure it out faster, and help others along the way. I look for those people who excel in their current role and show thought leadership outside their role."

Cory Martin, who has worked in the startup space for Zenreach and Zenefits, takes it a step further beyond leadership to include strong collaboration skills.[67]

"When hiring, make sure that you're hiring a builder and not a worker."

"There are a lot of great professionals out there. There are not nearly as many great 'builders' that want to build something. Ask questions during hiring to see how they think and more theoretical/planning questions, because this person will likely end up in leadership team at some point."

"Focusing on hiring the guy with 10 years of customer success (and only customer success) is great, but a diverse background will be more beneficial to a startup. You need Jacks-of-All-Trades, and Masters of One when you are a lean team. They need to master the customer success role, but need to be able to dip into other silos and help with cross-collaboration."

As Nils, Dave, and Cory have shared, even with the right business conditions and executive buy-in, starting a customer

---

67 Martin, Cory. 2017. "What Is The Best Way To Start A Customer Success Program In A SaaS Startup?". *Quora*.

success function is still tough. Finding the right person to set the right tone for your customer success team is a formidable task.

Why is this so tough? Because the customer success industry is so young.

In 2015, over 77% of customer success teams surveyed were less than three years old.[68] Now in 2018, 60% of organizations in the past two years formalized a customer success program and they had often relied on external consultants to help define their strategy and recruiting.[69] Because of the infancy of the field, it is difficult and almost impossible to find a seasoned customer success expert (especially within budget and timeline!).

Many companies often rely on external consultants, but more often than not, those who start customer success functions come from a variety of different roles and skill sets.

A Totango study revealed 43% of executives who work in customer success come from sales or account management while only 24% previously worked in success.[70] The remaining 33% of experts have different backgrounds, from marketing, engineering, consulting or finance.

Throughout my time in customer success, I found that because the industry is so young, it didn't matter so much

68 Crandell, "2015 State Of The Customer Success Profession".
69 Mura, "The Status Quo Of Customer Success In SaaS: Stats, Facts, Data, And Japanese Restaurants".
70 Totango. 2015. "2015 Customer Success Salary & State Of The Profession Report". Totango.

what your background was but rather the qualities you bring to the table – like grit, curiosity, empathy. Moreover, because each company caters to a different audience and each product is different, having previous industry experience at the beginning of the customer success journey is not as powerful a lever as it would be for starting other departments.

My background is in business and communications. In reality, I am a jack-of-all trades. Prior to being in customer success, I ran a referral program, did "customer support" at the municipal government level, and had already played key roles in the data, sales, marketing, and operations teams at the company.

While starting customer success was a challenge, it was something that was right up my alley. I wanted our customers to succeed. I wanted our students to see their hard work pay off both on their report cards and in their confidence and love for learning.

There isn't a right answer as to who should start your customer success program, but you do need someone who is motivated, gritty, a good communicator, and someone whom you trust. After all, they are on the front lines, making sure your customers are satisfied and achieving success with your product.

There are three typical ways a customer success function can evolve (either naturally or planned):

1. **From support**: Someone previously in support can better sympathize with customers when issues arise. They have

a deep understanding of customer pain points and wants to build customer value from the ground up.

2. **From sales**: Someone previously in sales intimately understands customer expectations and needs and is motivated to match the customer's enthusiasm for the product.

3. **From business or product**: Someone from a business or product background understands how to identify high level issues and tackle them systematically.

Each of these paths brings a different expertise and weakness to the customer success role. Whether the person you bring on to lead customer success represents one of the three or from somewhere else, what is important is that your customer success leader is capable and empowered to do the job that they've been hired to do.

PATH TO CUSTOMER SUCCESS: CUSTOMER SUPPORT

Within two years, Baremetrics quadrupled their customer base.[71] Josh Pigford, Founder of Baremetrics, found that because of that rapid growth they were in a bind, which made them not only start a support team, but also then turn that support team into a customer success team.

---

71 Pigford, Josh. 2017. "How To Transition From Customer "Support" To Customer "Success"". Blog. *Founders Journey*.

"The life of a startup is often reactive rather than proactive. We scale infrastructure only when the current setup is bursting at the seams. We react to running out of money at the absolute last minute (or sometimes many minutes after the last minute). And we often heed the advice of Basecamp and hire less and hire later."

"It took an out of control support load and a crazy long response time for our founder to realize it was time to hire a dedicated support person."

"In hindsight though, the job I was hired for was not what I wound up doing. I was hired to be a ticket monkey, with a little sticker mailing and tweeting on the side. And for the first six months or so, that's what I did."

"Support was hat number one, but it turned out Baremetrics needed some other things even more. We needed to focus on the entirety of the customer journey. Big companies have a team of folks focused on each step along the way, but smaller startups like Baremetrics don't have that luxury. We had to help leads understand the product, educate new customers, keep people engaged, and help guide the future direction of the product. None of that was in the job description."

"Much like a full-stack developer who can handle everything from HTML to database queries, I needed to become a full-stack customer journey person."

"For a founder looking to find their own fullstack customer journey person, the task can seem daunting. You're basically looking for one person who can wear ten differ-ent hats."

"The trick is to not to look for technical expertise nec-essarily. That can be taught. Heck, if I can go from nearly failing high school math 10+ years ago to knowing all the things about SaaS metrics, most anyone will be able to understand the ins and outs of your product with time. You're after someone with strong written and verbal com-munication skills and a desire (and proven ability) to learn new things."

As in Josh's experience at Baremetrics, a customer success leader or a team can evolve from customer support.

Customer support specialists already deal day to day with customers, so they fully understand how frustrating and prevalent certain issues can be. They've been in the weeds of the product with customers and can intimately understand what customers value and what discourages them. Because of this, not only can they come in with tac-tical suggestions on how to improve the customer experi-ence, but also better advocate for the customer within the company. Furthermore, every customer support specialist is trained in being empathetic and professional – things that a customer success team needs in spades to succeed!

Some say that customer support is a natural precursor to customer success. After all, customer support is the reac-tive version of customer success and often sits within cus-tomer success.

However, some also believe growing a customer success team out of customer support can be dangerous. Training a team to become more strategic isn't easy, especially if their last role was reactive and depended more on a playbook and set guidelines.

"Where the people come from for a customer success team depends on what your team's driver is," said Jim Jones, VP of Customer Success at ISI Telemanagement Solutions.

"A lot of times it comes out of support because they do the most interaction with a customer in small companies after the initial sale. Through this channel, you could get caught up in the dual roles of trying to elevate the conversation to spur on adoption all while answering support tickets."

"I've seen a lot more companies come at it from 'We're going to start with a few people out of support and see how this goes.'"

This was true for Uberflip, a marketing platform that helps engage audiences along their user journey. Sam Brennand, former VP of Customer Success at Uberflip, spoke about how Uberflip transformed their customer support team into customer success.[72]

"Uberflip had a customer support team right from the founding of the company in 2008, and from the start, our support team has been wowing customers with their dedication and passion. It's always fun for me to look back at

---

72 Augustin, Mathilde. 2016. "Inside Customer Success: Uberflip". Blog. *Amity*.

customer reviews from those early years as all of them mention how amazingly reactive and supportive our customer support team was – and still is."

"In 2012, our Co-Founders realized it was time to transform the customer support team into a true customer success team. We wanted to transform our team from one with a reactive approach to customer service into a one with a proactive approach to making our customers successful."

"That's when I joined the team. At the time it was only three of us: myself and two tech support reps. Almost immediately, we started to scale the team to enable us to be more proactive to ensure we were able to drive adoption, retention, and expansion: onboarding, coaching, renewals, upsell, support, and services."

However, Sam's career path to customer success at Uberflip wasn't linear. What was consistent was his commitment to helping others' succeed.

"Honestly, I kind of stumbled into the role! My first roles out of school were in consulting for a small company in the city called Venture Accelerator Partners. I worked with startups and small and medium size businesses that needed part-time help with marketing and sales. It's fun for me to look back on that experience now. At the time, my role was to help organization's build marketing strategies, help them to execute those strategies, and to ensure their success."

"We were doing customer success without really thinking about it or calling it "customer success." I did that for a few years and as part of my role I happened to meet one of Uberflip's Co-Founders, Randy, at a marketing event in the city. I chatted with him for around 20 minutes about what Uberflip was doing, added him on LinkedIn, followed him on Twitter, and over the next 6 to 12 months, I was regularly in touch with him. Over time I was able to build a relationship with Randy to the point that in 2014, just as he was looking to build out the customer success team, he happened to give me a call."

Carrie Weitzel, Head of Customer Success at LearnUpon, speaks about how she helped to build their customer success team out of a strong customer support culture.[73] Though most learning management systems (LMSs) at the time didn't have customer success teams, Brenden Noud and Des Anderson, LearnUpon's CEO and CTO respectively, were interested in better supporting their customers and helping their customers to succeed; so they looked to invest in a customer success team and reached out to Carrie.

"I was working in a customer success role for another software company when I spoke to LearnUpon. The difference I found here was that there was already a huge focus on customer support. Customer success was a natural development at the time I joined. The team was already really proactive in the way they dealt with customers."

---

73 "Why Our Customers Love Customer Success". 2018. Blog. *Inside LearnUpon*.

"Belief in customer success was driven by LearnUpon's leaders – Brendan and Des. They've always focused on how we best serve our customers. That fit my own belief that customer is king. We shared this passionate sense that, at the end of the day, if customers aren't satisfied, we don't have a company."

"At LearnUpon, customer success means following up on requests, checking a status, and coming up with a work-around in the meantime. Sometimes that means using features that are already in the LMS. Other times, we pass requests to the development team. When a customer requests something, it's not always available immediately, so the team helps you to achieve what you need anyway."

"That's how customer success differs from support. Support is focused on 'Here's the answer to your question.' Success is more like 'Here's the answer to your question – but have you thought about doing it this other way? Or this might work better for you, based on your workflow and what I understand about your company.'"

Shreesha Ramdas, CEO and Co-Founder of Strikedeck and an advisor to countless startups, however cautions against building customer success teams out of support.

"It's a common mistake to rename the customer support group as customer success. It's a different mindset – customer success is about how to help customers get on to the right path."

"Furthermore, people think that they can start a customer success group and have them also do support."

In fact, approximately 40% of Customer Success Managers are also involved in support, whether that is responding to tickets or eliminating confusion and addressing concerns directly with the customers.[74]

Shreesha suggests how you could make this transition work. "If you do that, which is fine, I recommend that you have different people focus on support and over time as support cases go down, you can make the team become more proactive."

Nevertheless, given the helper nature of those who are in support, it is of no surprise many companies look to build their first customer success teams out of customer support. While it is an easier transition, be cautious of its execution to make sure that the customer success team is proactively helping customers.

PATH TO CUSTOMER SUCCESS: SALES

Typeform is a survey company based out of Barcelona with over 2 million users. With that many customers, it was imperative that they create a customer-centric team. David Apple, Typeform's VP of Customer Success, recounts how

---

74 Mura, "The Status Quo Of Customer Success In SaaS: Stats, Facts, Data, And Japanese Restaurants".

their company's investment in retention created the customer success function within the company.[75]

"Before joining Typeform, I was VP of Sales for another startup and I originally joined Typeform to be in charge of sales. Acquiring new customers was never really our biggest challenge; our challenge was retaining our customers, especially since a lot of them use Typeform for short campaigns and then leave once those are over."

"Because it is a lot more expensive to acquire new customers than it is to retain existing ones, our CEOs decided that we needed to invest in a customer success department at Typeform, and they asked me if I would be interested in running that team. So I was just at the right place at the right time!"

"When we started, the structure was rather flat. I was the Head of Customer Success, and we had a team of five people doing everything together. It eventually became a size which I was not able to manage on my own. At this point, I started to feel the need to create more structure and to have other managers." They then grew out the support team and built out the customer experience team under customer success, which included customer education, sales, and account management.

"Like many teams, we started by focusing on giving great support. Giving great support also involved education

---

75 Augustin, Mathilde. 2016. "Inside Customer Success: Typeform". Blog. *Amity*.

because we created a Help Center to allow our customers to self-serve better."

"After a while, we started trying to understand where our customers' pain points were to better serve them. As part of that effort we launched our NPS program, and we started to put together what is now called 'Customer Voice' where we gather all the feedback from all the different sources and aggregate it to identify trends. As we started to understand our customers better, we focused more of our attention on proactive engagement to improve retention. All of this now falls under customer experience."

"We introduced Account Management when we introduced a higher price plan. Customer experience is focused on one-to-many engagement with all of our lower value customers, and Account Management focuses on providing one-to-one engagement with our higher value customers."

Finding your customer success team or first hire from sales isn't uncommon. After all, they just finished selling to them and have already begun building a strong rapport with customers.

There is a strong case here, even outside of how intertwined customer success and sales is.

First, salespeople are natural negotiators. They love to highlight all of the potential value a customer can derive from a product. For example, is the customer having an issue with a particular part of the product? Have they heard how this other part of the product can address that issue for them and more?

Second, those from sales are keen on understanding and investigating pain points, product expectations, and needs. As your product becomes more complex, those on the sales team can quickly adapt the new product complexities to their customers' needs – which they already know like the back of their hand.

Cory Martin who we introduced earlier in this chapter, and who has worked as an Account Executive at Lead Forensics, SPOTIO, and GARALI Business Solutions, agrees there are lots of similarities between customer success and sales.[76]

"Skill sets for customer success, account management and sales are not all that different in general, but really become different in application. Those skills are transferable in a majority of the cases."

"Someone with customer success and outbound sales experience will have a much easier time building the processes and hand-offs from sales to customer success, as well as understand the needs of the sales function to increase efficiency in the customer success silo. This 'diverse' experience is extremely important in my humble opinion when dealing with startups and lean companies."

---

76 Martin, "What Is The Best Way To Start A Customer Success Program In A SaaS Startup?".

However, the drawback here is they can, at times, over-sell and misalign expectations in order to please a client. Furthermore, people have also said those who go from sales to customer success do so because they no longer want to hit quotas and therefore want something "easier" but still deal with customers.

Typically, as we saw in David's experience, when customer success comes out of sales, it is a salesperson who is super customer centric, sees that retention is an issue, and wants to get dirty and solve the problem themselves.

Peter Armaly, Transformation Advisor at Oracle Marketing Cloud, is also one of those people.[77]

"I've been in the software vending business since about 1998 when I joined BMC Software. I was a pre-sales consultant and focused on helping sales land customers. Around 2007, I decided to move into the post-sales world because I wanted to get closer to the product, to the value proposition, and to the customer challenges that can be addressed through software."

"Soon after I was asked to build a new service and hire a new team for a fee-based offering called Technical Client Services. We worked with customers to understand their business goals, why they bought our products, and the struggles that they faced, and then built action plans that we executed over the course of a year. Our mission was to own and manage the customer's post-sales attempts and efforts

---

77 Augustin, "10 Leaders Share Their Customer Success Career Paths".

to achieve success with our company's solutions. That was my first formal exposure to customer success."

However, sometimes the "A-ha" moment comes from when the sales team realized they had more on their plate than expected.

Slack, a team collaboration hub service boasting over 8 million daily active users, saw a need within the user base that warranted a separate investment – an investment in a customer success team.[78]

Rav Dhaliwal, Head of Customer Success EMEA at Slack and previously an Account Manager at IBM, recounts the early days of the customer success team at Slack.[79]

"I've been fortunate enough to be at the inception of Slack's customer success team. I actually joined in the third week of its existence."

"We were around 10 million weekly active users and we have a very sticky product people spend around over 2 hours a day 2.25 hours a day on average working in Slack. So, you're probably wondering with this sort of level of adoption and continuing adoption and this level of stickiness – why on earth does Slack need a customer success team?

"Back in the summer of 2015, Slack had been around about just over a year and we had passed a really major milestone of

---

78 Lynley, Matthew. 2018. "Slack Hits 8 Million Daily Active Users With 3 Million Paid Users". *Techcrunch*, 2018.

79 Kosmowski, Christina, and Rav Dhaliwal. 2017. "We Are The Champions: Inside The Customer Success Org Of Slack, The Newest Billion Dollar Unicorn". Presentation, London, 2017.

1 million daily active users. At that time in the organization, we had account managers whose role was to answer sort of all inbound sales queries to close deals with customers teach them a lot of best practices get them launched to get them on board do some training."

"This worked fantastically well; it was a very simple mechanism. But the challenge that we found is as we started to move into more complex customers – so beyond the early adopters – , our account managers started to run into a challenge with adoption."

"The challenge here was there were these two personas – let's call them Justin and Bob. Justin is an engineer in a big company. He's super cool and very tech savvy. So, before you know it, he swiped his credit card and got all three hundred of his colleagues to use Slack. His team is using Slack to do their work now and Justin's company comes onto this and says, 'this looks like a really good thing for us to do. There's a lot of strategic advantages for us to start rolling out Slack to a wider pool and having the whole company use it.'"

"This brings us to Bob. This is where the challenge is. Bob works in Accounting and has never heard of Slack. We found that the difference between Justin and Bob was that Justin had a very strong awareness of what Slack is and has a very good desire to use it, whereas Bob wasn't in that position. Justin wanted to use Slack and Bob had been told to use it."

"And so what we realized was – as an organization – that we needed to help the Bobs of the world. After all, the bigger the companies you deal with the more people there are like Bob. We needed to help Bob change the way that he worked and that obviously involved needing a role and a function to support that. That role was customer success."

"But that's just one aspect of why we recognize the need to have a customer success team to help those Bobs of the world change the way they work. We needed a customer success team because we have to help those people who had been told to use Slack because they needed to change the way they work. That change can be very hard."

"We have a phrase where we say that 'change is inevitable, but the pain is optional.' We wanted to help people through that pain. We also wanted to make sure everyone, regardless of the type of individual, uses Slack in the most mature and sophisticated way because for us that means more product stickiness. This is obviously what we all want for our companies, but most importantly it drives the most business value for customers."

Salespeople have a unique insight into the pain points of customers. This means that particularly when retention becomes an issue, they may be best suited to jump in and help customers post-sale and start the customer success function.

PATH TO CUSTOMER SUCCESS: BUSINESS AND PRODUCT

Bradley Liou, Director of Customer Success at Densify, who was working as a consultant, joined the Densify team in August 2016.[80] Over the past two and a half years, he built and grew the customer success team completely from scratch.

"I started my career at SAP as product support, and then went on to be a consultant. Since I was in the post-sale world my whole life, I realized that it's hard for clients to get value out of the product. A lot of the time things are reactive. You're just listening to the complaints, and reacting to the client's request."

"My first customer success role was Nulogy – it used to be called Technical Account Manager. That was the time when I really learned about product adoption, mitigating the churn risk by being proactively working with the client and making sure they realize the value out of the software they get. So that got me into the CSM world, and later on I became the first CSM hired by SAP Canada. I worked closely with the product team as well as developing the processes and coaching the new hires."

"I then joined Densify to build the customer success organization from scratch. My career had always been in the post sales world, so it is a natural evolution of career development."

Consultants, like Bradley and others with business backgrounds, are great at solving problems and breaking both the problem and the solution down into easy to understand frameworks. Not only are they strong at identifying

---

80 Sutarno, Gabriella. 2018. "Inside Customer Success: Densify". Blog. *Amity.*

high-level problems, but they are also adept at attacking issues systematically and communicating with stakeholders in a clear and digestible way.

However, the downside of having consultants, business development, or product managers transition into the customer success space is they may not know the customer as intimately as a sales or support team. This means it may take slightly longer for them to fully ramp up in this area.

Tim Raftis, Head of Customer Success at Affinity, used his previous product experience to his advantage to address customer problems and start the customer success function at his company. Affinity is a relationship intelligence platform that helps people better strategically manage relationships and opportunities through integrations.

"I was a product manager for three years before Affinity and was brought on as the second business hire to basically 'do business,' which means essentially everything on the client facing and revenue side."

"For the first six months or so, we had zero revenue, zero customers. So the focus was all about getting our first customer."

"So we didn't really know exactly what our product was when I joined, it was more about like, 'Hey, we're building technology that is going to help people manage their relationships better and we have some ideas and how to do this.'"

"At the beginning, I was refining some of the product side just because that was the muscle that was most fresh. We totally redid onboarding and totally redid our dashboard."

"And then in parallel to that process, I was also just doing a lot of sales – like knocking on doors and hustling because there was no brand to speak of! Once we got some customers, I owned essentially their success and making sure that they are successful with Affinity."

"So in a product-focused way, we started by asking questions like 'well what are the retention goals and how do we set it?' After all, for a SaaS company, you know you're going to be doing well if the company has strong retention. If we don't have retention, then we don't have a business."

"From there, we looked at the product and started figuring out things like what features are most sticky, what features were out of place, and how do we build a more cohesive workflow and platform around our customers' problems that is going to give us success."

"Then, as the team grew, I've basically rose to become the leader of the customer success organization. We're now at five people including me and we're growing and hiring as we speak!"

By focusing on customer needs from a product and business perspective, Tim was able to help create a product people love and a customer success team, which helps to empower their clients even more.

Ellie Wilkinson, Senior Digital Marketing Manager at Highspot and former Manager of Customer Success at Moz, was one of the first three customer success team members at Moz.[81] She also used her previous job's skill sets to elevate the customer success role.

"Before becoming a Mozzer, I was an SEO Specialist providing consulting services for car dealership clients. Before being an SEO Specialist, I was actually a journalist. I got a lot of experience with writing, communicating, and talking to people! I've always had a passion for teaching, as well, and I was then able to bring that experience to Moz."

"My career overall has been focused on communication and teaching, and I use a lot of those skills now in customer success to help educate our customers, connect with them, learn about their goals, and show them how they can use our tools to succeed with their marketing goals."

Three months after joining Moz, Ellie rose to become the Customer Success lead. She grew the team from 3 people to 13 and drove adoption, growth, and expansion for $33 million/year of product.

Stories like Bradley's, Tim's, Ellie's, and mine show that those who may not have come from sales or support, but have a business background can also thrive in the customer success role.

---

81   Augustin, "10 Leaders Share Their Customer Success Career Paths".

***

"It doesn't matter what background they may come from. It could be someone in sales that's ready, that loves the customer relationship and wants to move that direction. Or it could be somebody in product who just has a passion for seeing customers leverage technology. The main thing is that they have the ability to develop deeper relationships with customers and align an organization around that relationship," said Dave Blake, the founder and CEO of ClientSuccess who we met earlier in the chapter.[82]

You can find your customer hero currently in support, sales, business, or from some other department. Regardless of where you find them, remember to value their strengths and skills over their resume. Someone who is motivated, communicates clearly, has grit, and is passionate about seeing your customers' success can be a star player in your company's growth strategy.

KEY TAKEAWAYS

Your first customer success hire and team can come from a number of backgrounds:

1. **From customer support**: These people sympathize and have a deep understanding of customer pain points and want to build customer value from the ground up.

---

82 Blake, Dave. 2015. "5 Hurdles To Clear For Effective Customer Success Management". Blog. *OpenView*.

However, these people risk being too reactive, instead of proactive, when interacting with customers.

2. **From sales**: Those who come from sales intimately understand customer expectations and needs and are motivated to match the customer's enthusiasm for the product. However, at times, inner tendencies of maximizing revenue or wanting to give the customer exactly what they are asking for may not align with the customer success strategy of advising what is best for the customer.

3. **From business or product**: Customer success leads and members who come from a business or product background can be extremely sharp and are able to identify high-level issues and tackle them systematically. They can use their previous strengths and skill sets to complement the customer success role as well. However, because they have not interacted directly with the customer as often, they may need more time to ramp up and get to know customers.

Ultimately, what is most important are the strengths and skills your customer success team brings to the table and whether you can see that person making both your company and your customers successful.

PART III

THE LAY OF
THE LAND

So, now you have an idea of how to create your customer success team at your company. Let's learn how you build your team and how to create a culture that empowers your customer success team to thrive. Afterward, let's get the "lay of the land" and explore the four main phases of a customer's journey with regard to customer success – onboarding, engagement, renewals, and advocacy. Bringing these four phases together will be the Customer Feedback chapter where we better understand how feedback is the glue that can make customer success – and subsequently your customers and your company – thrive.

CULTURE

The real competitive advantage in any business is one word only, which is "people".

– Kamil Toume, Business Leadership Thought Leader

Katie Rogers, VP of Customer Success at Salesloft, was her company's very first Customer Success Manager, and she has seen her company grow 20x each year for two years in a row.[83]

At the beginning, she was the "customer success superwoman" – handling all of her company's accounts while running customer support and optimizing process workflows. However, she soon realized that she could no longer do it on her own; she needed to build a team.

---

83   Calendly. 2016. "Salesloft's Katie Rogers On Scaling Customer Success To Support 2000% Growth". Blog. *Calendly.*

"It took time to realize that we weren't moving fast enough with me heading every project. We had to look at our metrics, and figure out which skills we were missing that would help us hit those metrics faster."

She wanted to find someone who could complement her strengths. To meet the demands of her company's rapid growth, she needed to hire someone who could help her hit the goals with which she struggled. This was when she hired Constance-Marie James, a former tutoring business owner, to run customer training.

"Constance is a training expert," said Katie. "I learn from her every day, and she's made such a huge impact here. That wouldn't have been the case if I'd brought on another Katie Rogers. We needed someone who could really own customer training."

As she hired more and more people, she wanted to keep her team's culture positive to motivate her people through the ups and downs of being in customer success.

"When we're all making client calls together, as soon as I hear something I like, I'll send praise to that team member," she said. "And whether it's Slack or email, it's important to share that praise with the entire team. When you do that, everyone knows how high the bar's been set, and who set it. It's a shared moment of happiness, and it's also a chance for others to reflect on their own work."

"Walking into the office after a trip and hearing praise fly back and forth between people, you just smile. That's when you know the culture is real, and it's something people want to stick around for."

In addition, she emphasized the importance of customer success's role within the company and how by empowering her team members, she can see her team grow and shine!

"Companies that give customer success the same authority as other departments will see more loyal team members and greater client LTV."

At Salesloft, Katie focused on hiring people who could deliver what her customers needed by creating a great culture which kept people motivated, and by cultivating an environment that empowers her team members to grow their careers.

Before even diving into what the layout of your customer success strategy should be, focus on your customer success team and the culture you want to create. After all, customer success is a relationship-focused role. That starts with creating a good culture and work ethic for your team to reach their goals.

Like Katie, I was a team of one for a long time. However, when our customer base began to grow, I started the hiring search for my "Constance."

Throughout the search, I had one thing in mind: find someone with whom you can create a great customer success culture. I knew I could teach them other skills, but there were three that I couldn't train. So, I wanted to find someone who had these four attributes:

1. *Empathy*

2. *Strong communication skills*

3. *Hustle*

4. *A potential to thrive within our customer success team*

My new hire needed empathy because our User Complexity was very high. Our parents were – and still are – extremely sensitive about their children's education (as they should be!) and I needed someone who could be there not only to help the customer where they are, but also sense other hesitations and creatively think about how we can help them.

My new hire needed strong communication skills because customer success needs to provide clear guidance to everyone with whom we communicate, from parents to the sales team to the product team, all while balancing the emotions behind and priorities of each stakeholder and customer.

My new hire needed to have hustle because after all, we are a startup; we quickly evolve so our processes must evolve with them. I needed someone who could efficiently grind through the work but also think strategically of how we could move forward.

Furthermore, though I never explicitly mentioned it to anyone at the time, I was also looking for someone that I could see thriving at our office and building a more personal and trusted advisor relationship with our customers.

I interviewed dozens of people, but it was tough to find people who fit those four criteria. A few of them had the perfect resume, but when I met them in person, they lacked the grit needed for the job. Others were off the charts in terms of hustle and empathy, but it would take a solid five minutes for them to get a point across. Finding someone to be your first or second hire on your team is never easy, but it was an important leadership lesson for me to focus on culture right from the beginning.

To create a strong culture for the customer success function, tackle the following 3 steps:

1. **Hire talented individuals**: Culture starts with the people; find and hire the right people for your customer success team that can help your customers succeed and your company thrive. Once hired, be sure to train them well so that they themselves are set up for success.

2. **Create a stellar team culture that is conducive to customer success's success**: Customer success can be a tiring job, create a culture that not only motivates your team, but also empowers them to take more ownership and champion the customer throughout the company.

3. **Recognize and retain top talent**: Good customer success hires can be hard to keep, especially in the early days; the knowledge that they have from working with some of your first customers can really help your team and company grow; create a culture where they can advance their career in your company.

By following these steps, you can create an all-star customer success team that can execute and elevate your customer success strategy long-term.

HIRING TALENTED INDIVIDUALS

"Once you've identified where the problems or focus areas are in your customer journey it's time to start thinking about what skills and competencies you need to solve them," says Phil O'Doherty, Senior Manager of Customer Success at HubSpot.[84]

"The unfortunate reality of this phase is you can't have everything. In many cases you will have to be willing to compromise on certain areas."

First, Phil recommends that you understand what your company's priorities are and then determine the type of hire you need to match those priorities.

"My advice is to think about three to four key skills quadrants you need and decide early what parts you can compromise or take risks on. For example, if your company develops project management software for enterprises – your Customer Success Managers might need technical skills, previous project management experience, client facing skills or evidence of driving customer success, and sales or account management exposure."

---

84 O'Doherty, Phil. 2015. "How To Hire For Customer Success Teams". Blog. *Keep | Grow.*

"You would either need to be very lucky or extremely well-funded to find someone amazing at all those things. In that case it becomes a decision on which areas you need to import and which areas you can train and develop on the job."

"In our previous example it could be that project management can be learned during training and we can compromise slightly on technical skills but they need to hit the ground running with sales and customer skills."

A 2018 McKinsey report also found taking the time to hire the right people is the foundation for a good customer success team.[85]

"A talented staff is the backbone of any strong customer success effort, but software vendors will find stiff competition when looking for skilled employees. Strong customer success leaders are in short supply, especially with companies across industries ramping up hiring."

"Complicating the matter, many organizations are unsure what customer success skills their employees need, since these vary widely by product or market context. To ensure that they hire and retain the right talent, companies must take a more thoughtful approach to talent grounded in a strong understanding of their ideal CSM profile."

It is important, especially early on, to make sure you are getting A+ players on your customer success team. To do so,

---

85   Atkins, Charles, Shobhit Gupta, and Paul Roche. 2018. "Introducing Customer Success 2.0: The New Growth Engine". McKinsey & Company.

first understand what your company needs in a customer success hire. What qualities are you looking for? What skill sets does your team currently lack? What goals do you want this next hire to achieve?

Because customer success is such a new industry, it is hard to pinpoint where to find a good customer success person – whether new hire or not, and perhaps more interestingly, what makes a good customer success hire.

I spoke with Shreesha Ramdas, CEO and Co-Founder of Strikedeck.

"There are four main attributes to a good CSM: 1. Project management skills, 2. communication skills, 3. An understanding of the business domain, and 4. Selling skills. It is hard to find a person with all four as a strength when hiring a CSM. However, someone with three is good; two is less so, but still good."

I asked him to dive a bit more into each of those four attributes and how they translate to the role.

"Project management skills is perhaps the most important. It's about being good at expectation setting, and expectation setting is critical when you are a CSM. You must ensure that you are meeting deadlines and expectations and communicating early with updates and when problems arise."

"As a CSM, having good communication skills is about being good at maintaining relationships. The third attribute, having a good understanding of the business domain is also important because you want to become a trusted advisor to your clients. You want your customers to look up to you for advice and to trust that you have the competency to solve their issues."

"Last but not least, selling is also an important skill even if your team doesn't deal with renewals, a good CSM needs to sell the vision of the company and sell how the product can impact the customer's business and bring value. Just like a CEO who has to sell the company's vision to employees and sell the vision to investors, CSMs do something similar. Prospects sometimes forget the vision after a while, so the CSM has to remind them of why they bought the product. Also, sometimes the business environment changes, so the CSM needs to help the customer adapt to that as well."

I also spoke with Maranda Dziekonski, VP of Customer Success at Pared and former VP of Customer Operations at HelloSign, about some of her best hiring decisions and what she looks for in her own customer success team.

"This is something that I'm really passionate about. When I hired Andrew Hall at HelloSign, I knew that he was going to be a great addition to the team. There were many things that made him awesome, but what really stuck out to me was he knew how to turn a reactive moment into something proactive. His intellectual curiosity was very high. He knew what questions to ask to get to the root cause and was an amazing project manager. He also had the ever so important soft skills such as empathy for the customer experience. As well, we can't forget had the ability to really balance the customer demands with the business needs."

"So when I'm hiring somebody, on top of everything that I mentioned about Andrew, I look for someone that is hungry and scrappy, especially if it's early on in building out the team. I do believe that I can teach someone how to use Excel and I can teach someone how to use a product/software. But there are some pretty tangible skills I can't teach."

"For example, if they can't figure out something, how do they react? I need folks that have that curiosity and want to dig deeper and really understand why something's behaving the way it's behaving, and then they go and go and go until they have solved it. Sometimes that means that they're bothering multiple people in the organization to where people are saying, 'Oh just go away already,' but it's being the advocate for the customer internally and externally to the point where they get things resolved."

"Another thing is the GSD factor – the 'gets sh*t done' factor."

"There are individuals who like to come into a set work day – you know, 'Here is your manual. Welcome aboard. This is what's going to make you successful.' And that's okay. There's nothing wrong with that. But early on, a customer success person in a startup should know that they're not going to get that manual handed to them. They're going to help create that manual and that should excite them. They are going to come to work and every day is probably going to be different."

"It is human nature to react when something's on fire. But I'm also looking for individuals who pause and look at the bigger picture. They should look at the entire customer base for trends and then create a plan to move forward.

"For example, if you have one customer that is always on fire, instead of reacting, pause and think, 'We have other customers that are very similar (business size, problems that they are solving for with this product) and they're not on fire. They're actually successful with their use case. Why are they successful and why is this customer struggling?' Dig in, learn, teach. Help your customers evolve."

Jason Lemkin, founder of SaaStr, also shares how finding the right new hire also comes from intuition.[86]

"Don't hire someone you don't intuitively believe in, no matter what her experience. They need to make you comfortable in the interview process with your product and processes. If they don't make you comfortable, they won't make the customers comfortable, either."

However, there are a number of hiring mistakes people can make when it comes to finding the right fit for customer success. Shreesha of Strikedeck starts us off:

"When it comes to hiring mistakes, I see people hire support people as CSMs but don't help them to evolve them into

---

86 Lemkin, Jason. 2017. "What Is The Best Way To Start A Customer Success Program In A SaaS Startup?". *Quora.*

a CSMs. For example, not giving them the proper training to help them help customers get onto the success path. Those in support may have the empathy needed and the product knowledge, but they may not have the communication skills to build those relationships."

"At the end, it's also about the training. With good training, a CSM can help convey the potential of the product to the customer. Looking at the four attributes of a good CSM that I mentioned before and see where an incoming CSM is weaker among the four attributes. If they are weak at project management skills, give them playbooks to better manage their time and to learn those skills. If it's understanding the business domain, this is something that the business and management can easily help with. I also believe that CSMs should also be using the product themselves whenever possible."

Training is an extremely important part of the equation that customer success teams often overlook. The 2018 Coastal Cloud Report found that "there is significant underinvestment in the training and professional development of customer success teams. Companies that invest more have better retention."[87]

Lukas Martinak, VP of Customer Success at Kentico Software, shares how thorough training and mentoring plays a big role in training their incoming CSMs.[88]

---

87   Coastal Cloud. 2018. "2018 Customer Success Industry Report."
88   Martinak, Lukas. 2018. AMA with Lukas Martinak of Kentico Interview by Lauren Olerich. In person. Slack.

"There are many ways to help scale CSM enablement and to improve ramp times for new CSMs! First, when you hire a new CSM, I believe it's important for them to meet the team in person because it enables future communication. Let them watch recordings of sessions with customers conducted by senior CSMs."

"Secondly, assign them a buddy who could help with anything, such as day-to-day tasks, meeting preparations, product knowledge, etc. Regarding buddies, we don't have any specific rules like having a buddy for a month – for us, you have a buddy "forever" – it just fades away as the new person will need them less and less."

"Lastly, let them bring some value to customers as soon as possible (even if this is just a small part of the CSM work), so that they see the first results of their work and want to get more."

The culture starts with the people! Think critically about what type of people, their qualities and their skill sets, you want to hire and how they can best add value to your customer success team. Once you've found those people, be sure to provide adequate training to nurture them and form a stellar customer success team.

CREATING A STELLAR CUSTOMER SUCCESS TEAM CULTURE

Diane Gherson is the Chief Human Resources Officer at IBM and she's seen how important team culture can augment the customer's experience.[89]

"Like a lot of other companies, we started with the belief that if people felt great about working with us, our clients would too. That wasn't a new thought, but it's certainly one we took very seriously, going back about four or five years. We've since seen it borne out."

"We've found that employee engagement explains two-thirds of our client experience scores. And if we're able to increase client satisfaction by five points on an account, we see an extra 20% in revenue, on average. So clearly, there's an impact. That's the business case for the change."

The 2018 Coastal Cloud Report also shared this same sentiment: "Culture matters. Participants at companies where the success of customers is the responsibility of the whole company achieve better net dollar retention."[90]

The proof is in the numbers as well. Companies with happy employees enjoy 81% higher customer satisfaction and 50% lower employee turnover.[91] Each standard deviation increase in turnover equaled a 40% reduction in profit.

---

89 Burrell, Lisa. 2018. "Co-Creating The Employee Experience". *Harvard Business Review*, 2018.

90 Coastal Cloud, "2018 Customer Success Industry Report."

91 Freshour, Eric. 2018. "Human Powered: Empowering Employees To Deliver Great Experiences In A Digital Age". Presentation, San Francisco, 2018.

Undoubtedly, it is important to create a progressive culture that empowers them to serve your customers well. While customers can challenge even the best customer success people, having a strong support culture for the customer success team will help CSMs feel supported and comfortable to reach out for help when they need it.

Justine Burns, Director of Customer Success at Jobber, explains how culture is important to their function and how it defines their team.[92]

"There's a strong feeling of belonging and an understanding that what they do is truly helping our customers succeed as business owners. This shows in the way team members work together as part of a team – it's heartwarming and motivating."

"At Jobber, we really care about culture. Our hiring managers have to submit all applicants to culture interviews before hiring them. For customer success, this is essential inasmuch as I'm hiring people who love people, it's what I care about and it's 100% something that matters as the team grows."

Brian Hall also shared how important the collaborative spirit is for culture. Brian is President of Carema Consulting with over 20 years of core leadership team experience building and leading scalable customer-facing teams at B2B companies.

---

92 Augustin, Mathilde. 2018. "Inside Customer Success: Jobber". Blog. *Amity*.

"The biggest rule of thumb that I have when it comes to mitigating a situation where you need to build customer loyalty and delight and the account is at risk – is 'never lose alone.' This applies to every CSM. The moment that you suspect that an account that is at risk, rush over and solicit other people's help to strategically attack that situation. The beauty of a company is that you have multiple people that you lean on and triage the situation."

"Sometimes you'll get individuals who say that they don't want to reach out because they think 'I don't want to give bad news' and 'I want to be a hero!' The truth is – it's not about the individual but it's about galvanizing the team to save this client."

"To create the culture to promote this sort of 'never lose alone' behavior, constantly reiterate that – whether it's through coaching, reiterating it at department meetings, or recognizing those CSMs that have taken the strategy to heart."

"The most common push back that you would get is 'people will be mad at me' or 'I feel like I'm asking too many questions' – but believe me, if you don't share in that experience with others and seek their advice and counsel, the questions that you will get from the CEO will be ten times worse."

Culture needs to extend beyond the customer success team as well. By creating a collaborative culture both within and outside the team, customer success – and subsequently customers – can truly thrive.

"In my experience, the most successful customer success leaders are able to focus and communicate, not only with their customers but also with their teams," said Krysta Gahagen, Customer Success Manager at Sparkcentral.[93]

"They grow and invest in their colleagues and the customer success field similar to how they help and nurture their customers. Their leadership pushes everyone forward, not just themselves."

Lincoln Murphy, Founder of Sixteen Ventures, also agrees.[94]

"Customer success needs to be part of the DNA. This comes back to organizational culture, which is driven at the executive level."

"If there isn't alignment from the executive level, two things happen: 1) Your customers will leave. They will feel like they aren't being listened to, and they will stop feeding back their ideas and will start to look for another solution that helps them reach their desired outcome. 2) Your customer success team will leave. When you are a customer advocate in your organization and nothing is done with the feedback, it's the most frustrating thing in the world. Leaders must ensure there is alignment between their teams. When customers leave and your team members leave, you're in big trouble."

93 McLaren, "14 Quotes On Succeeding In Customer Success Leadership".
94 McClafferty, Alex. 2015. "Customer Success: The Best Kept Secret Of Hyper-Growth Startups". *Forbes*, 2015.

Creating a team culture that promotes collaboration and purpose both within and outside of customer success is a great asset not only for your company, but also your customers.

RECOGNIZING AND RETAINING TOP TALENT

"Especially for early stage companies, you must remember that your people are your most important asset, that every new hire is precious, and that there's currently a war for talent," says Brian Hall of Carema Consulting.[95]

Because the industry is so young, top talent that have already proven themselves in the customer success world is hard to snag, but also sometimes hard to keep. In fact, LinkedIn announced that being a Customer Success Manager was the third most promising career in 2018 with strong job openings, 91% year-over-year job growth, and a very high likelihood of promotion or advancement.[96]

Kristen Hayer, Founder and CEO of The Success League, shares how tough it can be when turnover is high.[97]

"The average tenure of a Customer Success Manager is only 1.65 years. That's just a little over a year and a half, and in a field where it often takes six months for a new team member to get up to speed on their solution and customers,

---

95 VentureSCALE. 2018. "EIR Spotlight: Brian Hall". Blog. *VentureS-CALE.*

96 Bowley, Rachel. 2018. "LinkedIn Data Reveals The Most Promising Jobs And In-Demand Skills Of 2018". Blog. *LinkedIn Official Blog.*

97 Hayer, Kristen. 2018. "5 Ways To Get Your Best CSMs To Stick Around". Blog. *The Success League.*

that's a very short period of time. If you think about it, if it takes six months to ramp up and three months to find another job, that only leaves about nine months of productive work."

"Considering how much it costs to hire new CSMs, engaging employees should be an important focus of every customer success leader."

To retain top talent, first understand what your team motivations are and then figure out what you can do to help them achieve those goals.

As reported by Lisa Abbott, VP of Marketing at Wootric, Eddie Nguyen, VP of Customer Success at brightwheel, said that it starts with understanding your team members' motivations.[98]

"Hire who is right for the company and find out how committed they are regarding staying with the company. What are their goals? Can you help them succeed?"

"Then understand their currency. Some people are motivated by money, some want recognition, others want more trust to work on tougher projects. Find out what they like so you can give it when they perform well. Additionally, when you ask for feedback, you should take steps to appreciate the input, and take action to make changes needed. No one will leave feedback if it isn't acted upon."

---

98 Abbott, Lisa. 2017. "How SaaS Companies Hire & Scale Customer Success: Perspectives From Leaders At Jobscience & Brightwheel". Blog. *Wootric*.

John Kelly, Managing Director at CustomerLink, shares how he approaches retention at his company.[99]

"The best way to approach your talent retention strategy is to be crystal clear about the role, competencies, and personal characteristics that are required. This will significantly increase chances of retention and success."

"To avoid fatigue and burnout associated with customer problem solving, and to keep CSM development on track, there are a few career development tactics that you can consider. For example, rotate CSMs across the customer lifecycle – onboarding, adoption, and renewal, or develop team members from one-to-many customer management to one-to-one customer management, or give CSMs additional leadership roles within the team."

Junan Pang, Director of Customer Success at Optimizely, also motivates his team by telling them where they fit in the bigger picture and how they and the team will evolve going forward.[100]

"To help motivate my team, I help them understand where we were going as an organization as well as where they are going individually."

"For us at Optimizely, we don't think of CSMs as just project managers or just coordinators, but more trusted

99 Kelly, John. 2019. "Hiring, Developing, And Retaining Your Customer Success Team". Blog. *Natero*. Accessed January 5.
100 Chiu, Edward. 2018. *What You Need To Know When Building A Strategic Customer Success Team*. Video.

advisors. That term is thrown around a lot in the industry, but for us it means that our CSMs are being our customer's shepherd through the journey as the customer grows with experimentation."

"So, especially as we move into the next phase of growth for our company and our customers, the most motivating thing for my team will be to help them understand the history and evolution of their role so that they can get behind it."

Katie Rogers of Salesloft also champions empowering her own team members to be in charge of their careers.[101] For example, Aly Merritt, who was Katie's first customer success hire, transitioned from customer success to product after two years.

"Aly knew she wanted to work on product but when she came on board, we didn't have a product team yet. So, while she grew as a CSM, I had her go out and research the most important skills and responsibilities of a product manager. She built those skills on the side, so when leadership announced they were looking for product managers, I was able to raise my hand and vouch for Aly."

As reported by the Calendy team on their blog, Katie also shares some of her tips for encouraging this sort of culture within a customer success team.

"Over the years, I've come up with some best practices to help my team members transition to new teams. First, share

101 Calendly, "Salesloft's Katie Rogers On Scaling Customer Success To Support 2000% Growth".

with team members what growth options are available *now*, and what skills those options require. If those don't appeal to a team member eager to move up, encourage them to be transparent about what they *do* want."

"Put the onus on them to figure out the responsibilities and skills of their desired role. Once they've identified those, help them create a development plan. Around the nine month mark, connect people who want to transition with their peers who've already done so, to give them perspective on the culture and workload of different departments."

"Lastly, encourage people to seek out skill development, not higher titles. In a fast-changing company, being great at the work will be more rewarding (and make an employee more valuable) than taking a title that could become irrelevant."

Even if you've hired the right people and created a great culture, people still may leave due to the competitive job landscape. To retain top talent, better understand their goals and motivations and help them see a career with your company and work on what they are passionate about.

***

Todd Eby, founder of SuccessHacker, once said, "Culture eats strategy for lunch. Yes, you need to build a kick-ass customer success strategy to be successful.[102] Just don't forget the people that power it. Make sure that you put in place the culture and foundations necessary to support and drive your strategy. Get this wrong and it will make for tough going – unhappy employees will never generate happy customers."

To have a good customer success function, you have to start with a great customer success team. By finding, training and maintaining a team culture that can really hustle and focus on the customer, your team can drive great value for your company and your customers.

KEY TAKEAWAYS

Culture is the foundation of a high-performing customer success team. To cultivate a good culture, there are three main components:

1. **Hire and train high performing individuals**: Especially in the early days, it is important you have an all-star team to set the cadence and tone with your first customers. Training is also important to keep everyone up to speed and constantly improving in their roles.
2. **Create a positive and self-reinforcing culture**: Being in customer success is about collaboration, so create an environment where your team can thrive off each other and in turn, help your customers thrive.

---

102 Harvey, Kate. 2016. "16 Ways To Master Customer Success From Industry Leaders". Blog. *Chargify.*

3. **Retain top talent**: Keeping those individuals who can connect with your customers and setting them up for success will be crucial to your team's growth. Focus on how they want to grow so that you can keep their institutional knowledge within the company.

By creating a good customer success culture, you set yourself and your customers up for success!

ONBOARDING

—

"The better you onboard a customer and implement the new relationship, the longer you'll see benefits in return. The customer who's successfully onboarded will come back with fewer issues because they got the info they needed early on, not halfway through."

— Karin Ronde, Manager of Customer Success, UberEats

In 2011, Huddle noticed that Sharepoint, their largest legacy competitor in the enterprise content collaboration space, was failing to onboard their customers properly, causing 86% of Sharepoint users to go back to email for document collaboration instead of using Sharepoint.[103] Furthermore,

---

103 Huddle. 2011. "Huddle Announces Industry-First, 100 Per Cent Adoption Guarantee."

Huddle found that SharePoint's average user adoption was 32% within the first three months. Huddle's was 90% – three times more than SharePoint's.

What was Huddle's secret sauce? Relentless, radical onboarding.

"Adoption is key to the success of a new technology deployment. However, with the rise of the consumerization of IT and high expectations from the user community, it's not easily achievable for most," said Alastair Mitchell, CEO of Huddle.

So, Huddle decided to announce an industry first: 100% adoption guarantee. Within 90 days, 100% of the customer's initial user groups would be trained and active on Huddle – or they would receive a full refund.

To achieve this, Huddle focused on deploying their product in a small team for a few months as a pilot. Based on the customer's organization's needs and how the trial went, the Huddle team will assist to develop a plan to help more of their customer's teams adopt Huddle. Then, if the customer ever needed a refresher or further support, one would have to look no further than Huddle's self-serve site where you can choose from "Getting started user guides" which detailed step by step how to get started to "Best Practices" webinars and videos.

A year after this adoption guarantee was launched, nearly 90% of enterprises say Huddle is easy to use and user adoption is high at their companies.[104]

"There is no reason why enterprise has to have software that sucks," Alastair, Huddle's CEO, said. "You should have easy to use, secure software that everyone loves using and everyone will use."[105]

Lincoln Murphy, Founder of Sixteen Ventures, conjectures, "Huddle likely looked at the data and determined that if they get customers engaged fully within the first 90 days they're likely to stay on for the full estimated lifetime in our plan of maybe 3 to 5 years. Huddle probably saw in their data that customers who aren't fully engaged after 90 days don't stay customers very long… perhaps not even long-enough to pay back what it cost to acquire them in the first place."[106]

***

Talk to anyone in the customer success industry, and they'll say that onboarding is perhaps the most crucial part of the customer's journey. It is where the customer starts

---

104 MarketWired. 2012. "Huddle On Track For Future IPO, Leading Enterprise Content Collaboration Market."

105 Forrest, Conner. 2015. "Huddle Brings Clarity Back To Enterprise Content Collaboration". *Techrepublic*, 2015.

106 Murphy, Lincoln. 2019. "SaaS Customer Retention Is The Key To Long-Term Profitability". Blog. *Customer Success-Driven Growth.* Accessed January 5.

their journey with your company, where they get their first impressions of the company, and where they take their first steps to becoming (hopefully) an avid user of your product.

Research shows a poor onboarding experience can doom customers from the start:

- An estimated 40% to 60% of free trial users who only use your product once will never come back.[107]
- Quettra research showed that mobile apps lose 75% of your new users on average within the first week, whereas top apps only lose 32%.[108]
- A 2017 Local Analytics study showed that out of 2.5 million apps, one in four users will abandon your app after only having one session.[109]
- 23% of people leave a service due to bad onboarding.[110]
- According to the Conpass study, 96.7% of consumers surveyed churned because they could not see the value during the first interaction.[111] Of this number, 73.3% leave within 5 minutes.[112]

107 McKenzie, Patrick. 2012. "Designing First Run Experiences To Delight Users". Blog. *Inside Intercom.*

108 Chen, Andrew. 2019. "New Data Shows Losing 80% Of Mobile Users Is Normal, And Why The Best Apps Do Better". Blog. *@Andrewchen.* Accessed January 5.

109 O'Connell, Caitlin. 2017. "24% Of Users Abandon An App After One Use". Blog. *Localytics.*

110 "The Three Leading Causes Of Customer Churn". 2015. Blog. *Retently.*

111 Azevedo, Aline. 2018. "Cliente Insatisfeito: Como Prever Um Churn + Bônus". Blog. *Tracksale Satisfação De Clientes.*

112 Nayak, Arnab. 2019. "7 Types Of SaaS Customer Churn You May Not Be Aware Of!". Blog. *CustomerSuccessBox.* Accessed January 5.

- Jason Krigfeld, Chief Experience Officer at Lua also adds, "Within the first 48 hours, onboarding is the most important because churn is highest during that time."[113]

However, research also shows a great onboarding experience can set your customer up for success.

- With a "true onboarding experience," such as beginner tutorial screens, only 9% of users abandoned the app after one use.[114]
- KickOffLabs found that improvements in a user's first 5 minutes can drive 50% increase in lifetime value.[115]

Indubitably, onboarding is a crucial phase of the customer journey.

When I started my customer success journey, we were working with schools to share our homework help mobile app with their students. We purposefully made the onboarding process very simple. After teachers told their students about our service, all the students had to do was download the app and enter in the code associated with your school. It was a two-step process – how hard could it be?

113 Brandall, Benjamin. 2018. "14 Top SaaS Companies Reveal Their Customer Success Process". Blog. *Process.St*.
114 O'Connell, Caitlin. 2017. "24% Of Users Abandon An App After One Use". Blog. *Localytics*.
115 Agrawal, Pulkit. 2019. "How The Aha Moment Unlocks Successful User Onboarding". Blog. *Chameleon*. Accessed January 5.

After onboarding one school, we found that the answer was that it was too hard. We needed a much better solution.

First, we realized if you gave someone something and didn't tell them what it was, they won't use it. We didn't provide teachers who were onboarding students with materials for them to refer to or a forum for them to learn about our service and ask questions. We needed a better way to educate the student on how we could benefit them and educate the teacher to help encourage best practices and help troubleshoot as necessary.

Second, we realized that what we had thought was a two step process was actually more like a ten step process, which had multiple points of failure. For example, to download the app from the App Store, you needed to know your iTunes password, which most students didn't know or were lazy to enter. Other students would delete their activation texts by accident, which meant they couldn't go to the next step (unless they knew to hit the back button on the app and try again). If a teacher or a student failed along any point of the ten step process, they would get discouraged and sometimes even stop the onboarding process altogether.

Lastly, we realized once the students were all set up with our product – no one – not the teacher, principal, or administrator – knew what to do or expect next. Everyone was left hanging in the air, confused, and a bit overwhelmed from the lack of guidance.

To combat this, we distributed pamphlets, hosted webinars, and sometimes even went in person to present at school events and staff meetings. This way, teachers and principals could better understand the value of the service we provided and were therefore not only more likely to onboard their students, but also to evangelize the service!

We also redesigned our onboarding process so every student was directed to one website portal. From there, we could track exactly where students dropped off if they did and reach out to get them back on track. Lastly, we built a dashboard where teachers and administrators could get visibility into exactly what was going on with their contract, view an onboarding checklist, and learn ways to get their students engaged so they could get the most value possible.

From these efforts, we saw those classrooms which successfully onboarded students notice huge benefits within their students' confidence and mindsets around learning. We would then ask those teachers and principals about their onboarding experiences and share their tips with our customers who were just starting out so that they can better onboard their students.

***

There are so many components to onboarding – from first product experience, to a proper sales hand-off, to providing a sustainable support structure for the customer. There's the customer support side, the customer experience side, and so many other perspectives to approach onboarding. It can be overwhelming, but let's take it step by step.

There are seven primary objectives during this onboarding phase: three objectives for the customer, and four objectives for the customer success team.

For the customer, onboarding is when they:

1. **Learn how to use the product**: Educate and familiarize the end user with the product so that they can get started.

2. **Drive early adoption**: Show them out how get value from the product.

3. **Realize the long-term potential**: Help your customers learn what long-term value your product provides!

For the customer success team, onboarding is what you work on:

1. **Seamless sales hand-off**: Make a great first impression during the sales hand-off to show your customer how valued they are.

2. **Efficiency**: Because there aren't enough hours in the day to show each customer everything that they need to know, be efficient to maximize impact per effort. For example, you could provide a one-to-many onboarding or self-serve options.

3. **Segmentation**: Each customer is different, and therefore may warrant a different onboarding experience. For

example, a customer with a thousand employees should be catered to differently compared to an office of just ten employees. Segment your customers so that you can provide the best experience possible that matches their needs!

4. **Expectation management**: Build on the customer's momentum, curiosity, and manage expectations early on to set both your customer and yourself up for success.

However, figuring out the best onboarding process for your company is not easy. There are technical restraints and company bandwidth issues that must be considered. Also, you do not want to overwhelm the customer with information. All of this must be balanced against building a scalable onboarding experience. It takes an incredible amount of fine-tuning and trial and error to get it under control, but it is worth every ounce of effort.

CUSTOMER ONBOARDING OBJECTIVE: EDUCATING THE CUSTOMER

"The onboarding period is, for a business, perhaps the most critical time in a SaaS customer's life," says Alex Turnbull, CEO and Founder of Groove.[116]

"When a customer signs up for Groove, they get a series of onboarding prompts in their Groove inbox." These prompts

---

116 Turnbull, Alex. 2015. "How We Measure And Optimize Customer Success Metrics In Our SaaS Startup". Blog. *Groove HQ.*

include interactive actions, such as how to share a private note or how to get started on their Apps menu, where customers would learn how to use the Groove platform.

"Free users who complete the prompts within 24 hours are almost 80% more likely to convert to paid customers than those who don't. That's a *massive* drop-off, and we use the 24-hour mark as a benchmark for early customer success."

By having an accessible and user-friendly way to learn about how to use Groove, they are able help their new users adopt their product in an on-demand fashion.

According to the 2018 Coastal Cloud Report, "the number one customer journey challenge, as mentioned by 37% of participants, is lack of product adoption."[117] Product adoption is exactly what this objective – educating the customer – combats.

The objective behind educating the customer is to make sure they know what value your company can bring and how you will do so. Most customers will not know how to use your product from the get go regardless of how intuitive it is. People are excited to get their hands dirty so they don't always have time to read through a dry, hundred page technical document. Therefore, make it easy for stakeholders and end users alike to learn and digest information.

There are multiple ways to educate your customer. You will need to figure out what will work best for your customers' schedule, bandwidth, and learning style. Keeping in mind

---

117 Coastal Cloud, "2018 Customer Success Industry Report."

your Product Complexity and User Complexity scores, here are some questions to ask yourself while thinking about what would work best for your customers:

- How tech-savvy is your customer?
- Does your customer need to teach other people how to use the product? Do they need to involve other people to implement or use your product?
- How busy are they? What is their attention span like in regard to interacting with a product like yours?
- How do they prefer to receive and absorb information? Webinars? In-person meetings?
- What parts of your product are "must-knows" and how complex are they?

When you are beginning to compile all these things it may seem overwhelming, but take it step by step. Putting something out there is better than doing nothing. Furthermore, the reality is you will always create more material as your product evolves and disseminate the material to your customers as you prepare them. As those are released, you will hear feedback on what is still confusing them or what else they would like to see.

Companies nowadays are also catching on to the importance of customer education and of scaling customer education. Research from Brandon Hall shows that 54% of companies are investing in some sort of customer training program, and a survey from Training Industry found that

93% of companies reported they saw increased customer satisfaction – and 88% reported increased customer retention as a result of customer training.[118][119]

Jennifer Walker, Director of Customer Success at Motivis Learning, described her need to onboard a person who would then train the remaining faculty members and end users at the institutions with which she works. Jennifer is not able to be in the room with the end user, so she's figured out a creative solution to this challenge.

"We do walkthroughs when we onboard and throughout the implementation, we've been training them and training them and training them."

"After training, we created a 'train the trainer' module. We have this one customer and his job was to onboard the new faculty members. And for this module, I said, 'You know what would be great? If you would do a demo of how you're training your faculty members. This way I can hear it from your mouth and you can walk me through the solution.' And from there, I can interpret – are you spot on? are you framing it differently than I would? and address it accordingly."

Jennifer's innovative solution not only helps her customer increase adoption, but also helps her team become more efficient.

---

118 "How To Train Your Customers". 2012. Blog. *Chief Learning Officer.*
119 Expertus. 2008. "Research By Expertus And Training Industry, Inc. Delves Into Motivation For Customer Training."

Lukas Martinak manages the customer success department at Kentico Software where he works with over a thousand partners to power 25,000 websites in over 100 countries.[120] To help empower their customers to self-serve their queries, Lukas talks about how he built out a customer education platform.

"We've built e-learning courses for both technical and business people that replaced the instructor-led training webinars. It is much more convenient for customers to let their people go through the e-learning when they have time and at their own pace. However, when you provide them with access to e-learning and say, 'you can use it as you need', we found it quite hard to get all of them to finish the course – that's the part we haven't figured out yet and we are experimenting with some reminders and gamification."

"With Kentico Cloud, we implemented the interactive guides as a part of the product itself. The built-in training guides a user through the most important scenarios and they can use it anytime they want. I'd say it's even more convenient than the e-learning, however it has some limits as well."

"We also have technical writers and content developers writing documentation, tutorials, and knowledge base articles for users. And I shouldn't forget to mention community forums, Stack Overflow, etc., where the people in the community help each other with some help of our team."

---

120 Martinak, AMA with Lukas Martinak of Kentico.

However, sometimes you want to go one step beyond just on-demand help. Jo Massie, Head of Customer Success at Slido, shares how she started other customer education initiatives to better help their users where they are.[121]

"To help our customers learn how to use Slido, we have three methods. One, we've tried to push as many of our training sessions as possible into group training webinars. Two, we just launched our in-app video academy which quickly shares how to use our key features. And three, we run Master classes in the cities with the highest concentration of customers. These generally focus on a particular persona or use case and we share guidance on how to best apply our features in their job to be done."

"Furthermore, we assigned an Onboarding Specialist to our customers who weren't receiving high-touch support. This specialist is the one who looks after new licenses in their first 90 days to ensure that they are able to implement and make the necessary changes in their organization. We know how critical this period is and know that if they hit a certain threshold in this time that we will probably retain them throughout the year."

Customer education is a mission critical objective in the onboarding phase, but there is no right way to do it. Reflect on your company's Product Complexity and User Complexity

---

121 Massie, Jo. 2018. AMA with Jo Massie of Slido Interview by Lauren Olerich. In person. Slack.

to best understand how you can meet your customers where they are and how you can best guide them to success.

CUSTOMER ONBOARDING OBJECTIVE: DYNAMIC EARLY ADOPTION

Adam Joseph, Founder of CSM Insight, previously ran customer success at a couple of large software businesses for over a decade.[122] He's seen the power of understanding early on how your customer defines success and how you can help them find that success early on.

"What is critical is during the pre-sales process, ensure that your sales team (or pre-Sales Engineers) ask what success looks like from the customer's perspective as an actual metric – both in the short term (i.e. when you can consider the implementation stage to be complete) and the long term (i.e. the factors that will decide to renew or grow)."

"Too often, 'success' is subjective, 'we want to sell more by using your product.' We need to establish exactly how the customer is going to judge ROI. By doing that you will have a great handle on whether the requirements are being met (and hopefully exceeded)."

During the early days of a customer's journey, there is an "excitement multiplier" that will magnify the initiatives you run for your customers. By getting them engaged as soon

---

122 Joseph, Adam, and Michelle Garnham. 2018. AMA with Michelle Garnham of infinity co and Adam Joseph of CSM Insight Interview by Lauren Olerich. In person. Slack.

as possible, not only are you setting them up for success, but your customer can also see derived value early.

"If a customer doesn't understand the context of your app, can't immediately see its benefits, or has a bad initial experience, you've likely squandered your only chance from the get-go," warned Lesley Park, former Marketing Consultant at Framed.[123]

Seeing these early wins with your product will then act as an incentive to continue engagement. Use this excitement to your advantage to show the customer exactly how much potential and benefit your product has to offer and what's to come. Driving early adoption also helps to identify key end users who could help not only prove value to the stakeholders, but also provide testimonials and contract negotiations later on.

"Your first users should feel that signing up with you was one of the best choices they ever made," said Paul Graham, Co-Founder and Partner at Y Combinator.[124]

"And you in turn should be racking your brains to think of new ways to delight them."

The objective behind dynamic early adoption is to figure out how their organization can derive the most value possible and to hit the ground running.

---

123 Price, Shayla. 2019. "Customer Onboarding: Your Secret Sauce To Reducing SaaS Churn". Blog. *Neil Patel*. Accessed January 5.
124 Graham, Paul. 2013. "Do Things That Don't Scale". Blog. *Paul Graham*.

To achieve this goal, follow these three steps:

1. *Define what "success" is from the customer's point of view*
2. *Determine the onboarding strategy that sets them up for success*
3. *Create product stickiness to establish quick value wins*

You should already have a general idea from sales and marketing of what would generally define success for your customer. However, figuring out exactly how your customer measures success and what metrics they are holding you accountable to is where customer success comes in. With this information, customer success can subsequently help make sure that customers are finding said success.

Simply put, customers want you to help them address their pain point. During this onboarding phase, we want to make sure that not only is the customer set up for success, but also that they are seeing value and success – or at least the potential for success – early on.

"The goal of your onboarding process should be to help your users hit their "A-ha" moment – the moment when use of your product clicks for them," says Peter Schroeder, Head of Marketing at Northpass.[125] "Facebook, for example, considers that moment reached when a user has added at least seven friends within the first 10 days."

---

125 Schroeder, Peter. 2019. "Six Steps To An Effective Customer Onboarding Program". Blog. *Northpass*. Accessed January 5.

Intercom, a live chat messaging company, actually takes this a step forward with a concept that they call "Day Zero."[126] Nate Munger, Senior Customer Advocate at Intercom, explains more.

"We're strong proponents of the idea that successful onboarding is about finding the common ground where both you and your customer get value."

"Every new customer has the *potential* to be successful with your product. But no matter how well-designed your product and how smooth your onboarding, new customers still have to do some groundwork before they can start to unlock full value from it."

"When our customers complete that initial work and are able to start getting the full benefit of Intercom, we call it "Day Zero." Your product has a Day Zero too. Maybe it's reached when customers have invited five teammates to collaborate. Or integrated your product with one of their core systems."

"There could be multiple tasks your customer must complete to be fully set up for success, but the concept applies across the board: Day Zero is the moment when a customer has completed the necessary tasks so they can start to realize the full value of your product for the job they are hiring it to do."

---

126 Munger, Nate. 2016. "Day Zero: A New Way To Define Customer Success". Blog. *Inside Intercom.*

"Achieving Day Zero doesn't mean customers *are* realizing value, it means they're *able* to begin realizing the full value. A customer could achieve Day Zero without going on to successfully use your product, but if they *don't* reach Day Zero real success will be difficult, if not impossible."

To determine your own Day Zero, David recommends starting by brainstorming and backing up proposals with data before going out to test the hypothesis on your customers.

"We began by choosing just 12 new customers and focused on getting them to Day Zero. In parallel with those experiments we also began to informally educate our Account Executives about Day Zero, encouraging them to introduce the importance of custom data early on in their conversations with potential customers."

"To help them do that we built a very basic custom data planning tool to share with customers. It was invaluable in helping non-technical customers identify the custom attributes they needed and helping them share these with their engineering team."

"With the parameters of our experiment set, we spent an entire quarter focusing on it. What we found confirmed customers who got to Day Zero saw more success, and they saw it sooner. For customers who had reached Day Zero, onboarding didn't involve theoretical discussions about potential value they could achieve if they added custom data. Instead, the Success Manager could train them in the practical implementation of their use case. This was the result we had hoped for. It allowed us to move forward with formalizing our new processes and launching systems to manage and track the way we onboarded customers."

Lastly, creating product stickiness during the onboarding phase helps improve long-term user engagement with your product. There are two typical ways to create product stickiness at this stage. The first is to encourage users to generate their own value inside your product, and the second is to encourage habit-forming behavior.

Ed Shelley, Director of Product at ChartMogul, shares how he views these two methods as ways to onboard users and to empower them to quickly see value in your product.[127]

"Encouraging users to generate value inside your product is common on large platforms, where the user generates, stores, and works with their own data. It could be in the form of custom reports, complex workflows, automation, or generation of data. If that 'thing' the customer generates is proprietary to your product, leaving means throwing away what may be hours of invested time and resources."

"Just like those carefully curated Spotify playlists we can't let go of, the more times users invest in value creation inside your product, the stronger the stickiness."

"Another technique to leverage is enforcing customer habits. As your customer, I've spent the past nine months of my life routinely running a report and checking key metrics

---

127 Shelley, Ed. 2018. "Lock-In Vs. Stickiness In SaaS: Retaining Customers The Right Way". Blog. *ChartMogul.*

in your platform with my morning coffee. The notification I receive in my inbox when the report is ready gives me a pleasant feeling, and it's going to take a lot for me to abandon this habit."

During the onboarding phase, use customer excitement as a springboard to driving early adoption. Figure out how your customers define success and set them up for it. Engage them early and quickly show them how your product can give them quick wins while creating habits out of your service.

CUSTOMER ONBOARDING OBJECTIVE: LONG-TERM VALUE AFFIRMATION

"You can provide a perfect customer onboarding experience with seamless setup and great training; the customer can absolutely *love* your product or service; there can be a 100% adoption rate and you can still lose the customer. It happens across industries all the time. Why?" asks Vikki Pope, VP of Client Success at MapAnything.[128]

"It happens because decision makers and key stakeholders are unable to see the benefits of using the products or services in which they've invested. When they can't see the value, they can't justify spending money on it."

"You need to establish clear goals, objectives, and strategies/tactics to establish value and communicate it to your clients."

---

128 Pope, Vikki. 2016. "Three Steps To Building An Effective Client Success Plan". Blog. *Gainsight*.

"At MapAnything, our customers' goals vary: increase sales, boost field sales or service productivity, improve marketing campaigns, cut transportation costs, and more. Our Client Success Managers understand their customers' goals and all activities – installation & configuration, training, check ins, etc. – are framed around those goals."

"To achieve these goals, we help our customers set measurable objectives with decision-makers and key stakeholders, such as 'increase sales meetings by 25%' or 'increase selling time and decrease drive time.' ... This is important for the evaluation process when the client decides whether or not to continue using your product or service."

"After that, we train all of the end users. We do this through custom training sessions for individual companies and through [a] weekly training course through MapAnything University. We ensure that all end users know how to use and understand the benefits of the primary product features that will help them meet their objectives."

"For example, to help them increase their sales meetings by 25% and increase selling time and decrease drive time, we'll teach them how to build and optimize daily routes, find nearby customers to add to routes, and self-source leads. These strategies drive the change that helps the company meet its goals and objectives."

The objective behind value affirmation is to show the customer you are setting them up for success to reach their goal. The customer journey may have just started, but you as their customer success point person will be there to guide them along the way and make sure that they have everything that they need to succeed. By showing them a glimpse into what the future holds, customer success can also begin to become that trusted advisor in the customer's eyes.

Tabitha Jean Naylor, the founder of Successful Startup 101, stresses the importance of setting your customers – and subsequently, yourself – up for success.[129]

"It's really important that you establish the parameters for success. What does that mean? It simply means that you communicate with your client or customer what services you are going to provide, how you will provide them, and when you will provide them."

"By clearly defining your goals, it's much easier to achieve success, and by the way, if your goals aren't in sync with your client's goals that will become apparent at the onboarding process, giving you time to get on the same page."

Demonstrating long-term value to a customer can exist in many forms. This will depend on your company's Product Complexity and User Complexity; however, some examples include a personalized, goal-oriented call, tiered training academies, and developing success plans jointly with the customer.

---

129 Smartsheet. 2019. "The Advanced Guide To Customer Onboarding". Blog. *Smartsheet*. Accessed January 5.

Kia Puhm, Founder and CEO of K!A CX Consulting, shares how she recommends building an effective customer success plan to create alignment and accountability.[130]

"The customer success plan is the map with the directions that provide details about the different steps, activities, and milestones along the way so the customer can track their progress."

"While customers have good intentions when it comes to using a product, their time and energy can be divided between different priorities. It can be easy for a customer to postpone learning and using your product, or veer off course, especially if they aren't being held accountable or there is not a plan that ensures their success."[131]

"A customer success plan plays a key role because it allows customer success teams to keep customers motivated, focused, and moving forward to reach their goals."

"The best customer success plans tie the context of the overall product vision to the tactics that must be executed in order to realize the value proposition. They articulate that vision through the effective use of visuals so that they are easy to understand and simple to follow."

"In addition to containing the larger, strategic, context for the product, customer success plans should incorporate the

---

130 Puhm, Kia. 2017. "Customer Success Plans Unplugged: How To Use Them To Drive Adoption And Expansion Part I". Blog. *KIA CX Consulting*.

131 Puhm, Kia. 2017. "Customer Success Plan: Motivation And Focus For Adoption And Expansion". Blog. *KIA CX Consulting*.

key components of scope, time and the notion of progress, to make them an effective tool in the customer success or account manager's toolbox."

"They visually display the entire map from point A to B, contain the high-level steps to get there, the time estimates for each segment of the journey, and they indicate where one currently is along the path to the final destination."

Bradley Liou, Director of Customer Success at Densify, shares how they view this part of the onboarding process as the most impactful and how they use it to drive goal-oriented objectives with their customers to start thinking about where the customer wants to be down the line.[132]

"I think the most powerful part is we really focus on success planning and creating a concrete 90-day plan, a quarterly plan, for our customer. The process is done during the onboarding stage, and then every three months we would revisit and build it. We engage with the customer biweekly and check on the status."

"The 90-day plan is really focused on the customer's outcome, not just the product itself."

"The most powerful part is something we call a maturity model, which tells the customer by using our software, what are the six different value domains you will receive and what are the different levels of maturity you can achieve. We have six value domains and five maturity levels."

---

132 Sutarno, "Inside Customer Success: Densify".

"Think of it as a matrix with thirty boxes in it. We map all our customers to each of the boxes and we talk with their executives saying, which step do you want, do you want to go to level 3 this year, do you want to go to level 2 because of the internal process. Based on that, we create action items. I think that is our most powerful part in our engagement model."

By showing your customer the long-term value you can provide them early on, you can maintain a sense of excitement and keep them engaged (and accountable!) in the long term.

***

Onboarding is not only a crucial phase to get the customer started on the right foot, but it is also the time where customer success can deliver a great first impression, learn more about the customer to become more efficient, and set clear expectations with the customer.

INTERNAL ONBOARDING OBJECTIVE: SEAMLESS SALES HANDOFF

"It's essential that all teams across your organization work together to ensure the customer is successful. Customer success should make up the DNA of your company culture, no matter the department. Customer success begins to be measured the minute the deal is signed. Your sales and customer success teams must ensure your new customers receive the promised value and results." says Burke Alder, Customer Success Strategist at ClientSuccess.[133]

"No matter how seamless the sales process may have looked, there are almost always some 'gotchas' to watch out for during the knowledge transfer process."

"It's important for your Customer Success Manager to know if anyone in the organization was against the selection of your service (perhaps they favored a competitor, had a bad relationship with your organization in the past, or just didn't like your offering). Beyond any negative relationships, the knowledge transfer should also expose any red flags that happened during the sales process that could reappear: lack of responsiveness, stakeholders going dark, inaccurate information, missed deadlines, etc. If any of these things happened during the sales process, there's a strong likelihood that they will happen again during the handoff/implementation process."

"A successful knowledge transfer builds trust. This is when partnerships are established with transparency and an eagerness for customer success. To maximize the knowledge transfer, both parties need to foster a trusted work environment. As an organization, it's in your best interest to take the lead in creating this environment."

---

133 Alder, Burke. 2019. "Fives Steps To Establish A Successful Knowledge Transfer Between Sales And Customer Success". Blog. *ClientSuccess*. Accessed January 5.

Before the customer success team can jump in and start onboarding the new customer, it is important that there is a seamless sales handoff. This is the moment the sales team has hyped the customer up for – the delivery of the service they feel would be a valuable addition to them, so first impressions matter.

This means – does your customer success team (which includes everyone who will interact with the customer post-sales) have everything it needs to set customers up for success? When a customer calls, can the customer success team bring up the account in question quickly and efficiently and be able to have actionable next steps to help the customer? If a customer has any special circumstances, how does sales communicate that to the customer success team?

The objective of a sales handoff is for the customer success team to be set up for success and to create the best first experience as a customer moves from one department to another.

Whether you have five customer success people staffed on an account or one, you want to set your customers up for success by providing a good first customer experience, or you risk increasing churn right at the start. This is catching things such as what sales or marketing promised the customer doesn't align with what they will experience later on, or if customer success is asking a new customer all of the exact same questions the sales people had asked already.

Rebecca Mass, Senior Customer Success Manager at Bizzabo understands the importance of a strong handoff. Her company provides an all-in-one event software that empowers marketers to run impactful events. At the beginning, there was sometimes misalignment between the original goals shared during the sales process, and what the Customer Success Manager learned on an initial kick-off call.

"Our handoffs early on were less structured, and it took some time for us to find the right framework to ensure a proper handoff from sales to customer success. We eventually established a process and alignment to make sure the right questions are asked during the sales process to make sure we are all aligned on maximizing lifetime value for our customers."

"It is important for the account executive to gather as much information as possible during the sales process so that the Customer Success Manager is armed with as much knowledge about the new customer's expected business outcomes. Clients spent a lot of time sharing their goals, needs, and business objectives during the buying process, and the last thing we want is to have them feel like they are repeating themselves when they get introduced to a Customer Success Manager post sales."

"What it came down to was a top down approach to align not only sales and customer success, but our entire organization. We've hired people who have the same kind of mentality and culture, and who want to maximize value for our customers. We've also dedicated a lot of time and resources into internal trainings to make sure both sales and customer success have the product knowledge needed to be able to provide the best recommendations for our clients."

"I appreciate the fact that as an organization we are all aligned on partnering with customers that we believe can be successful with us for the long term. Our customer success team also collaborates closely with account executives during the pre-sale process. It's so nice to be a part of a company that truly believes that customers' success is everyone's job."

In addition to a good sales handoff, customer success needs to work with sales to address bad fit customers. These are the customers where it will be much harder if not impossible for them to find success with your product. For example, if you offer a dog walking service, a bad fit customer would be one that owns a cat and not a dog.

These bad fit customers will drain time and resources away from customer success and may also hurt the brand as these are customers who had trusted your company to deliver on something which wasn't going to happen.

"So there's a couple things that you can do with your sales team to prevent bad fit customers from coming in. 1) Make sure that you guys agree on customer personas and 2) make sure that there's accountability in there for the sales team to where they're signing the right folks," said Maranda Dziekonski, VP of Customer Success at Pared.

"Customer success and sales have to be a close knit team because it benefits everybody in the organization and the customer. If you guys aren't close knit and linking arms, you're definitely going to be duking it out all the time; it's going to feel like it's a constant battle where you would keep getting these customers that aren't getting the product that they were sold on, aren't adopting the product, or who knows – there's so many possible reasons. It's so, so important that sales and customer success are very aligned."

"To get this conversation started, I would propose to have a white boarding session with sales. First, talk about what the customer personas are, then talk about the customers and what are the attributes of a great fit customer. See where you guys overlap, see where you're missing attributes, and see how you can create alignment. That's always a good starting point as long as you have a great relationship with the leader of sales."

"Also, bring some examples to the discussion. For example, 'Customer one, two, three, and four are very successful. However, customers five, six, seven are floundering and I really want to just kind of noodle with you on what I'm seeing so we can work together to try to not repeat these.'"

"When you're early on, it's tough because sales wants to close all deals that they can get across their table because they have goals to meet. Part of what I've done to solve that in my organizations is to make sure that we have the appropriate claw backs. So – and it depends on the time, but say in the first 30, 60, 90 days – if a customer churns, then we take the money back from the salesperson and that really incentivizes them to make sure that they are signing the right customers, not just signing a customer-defined customer."

Having a good sales handoff process is crucial to making sure your customer is properly set up for success.

INTERNAL ONBOARDING OBJECTIVE: EFFICIENT ONBOARDING PRACTICES

Back when he had just joined Higher Logic back in 2017 as their Chief Customer Officer, Jamey Jeff saw how even for a complex product, which needed a lot of handholding, being opportunistic and creative was key.

"At the beginning, everyone was getting the same onboarding experience. We were overcomplicating it for some customers. So we said – let's not show them all ten thousand features, and instead only show them the ten key features that they need to know to get started."

"Furthermore, in the past, we had an onboarding call for every customer. This took each implementation manager roughly one hour per call. With twenty accounts per implementation manager, this meant that each member of the implementation team was spending over twenty hours a week on onboarding calls – including preparation and follow up beyond the call itself – which was incredibly time consuming."

"To streamline the process, we decided to host an onboarding webinar once a week for all new SMB customers. The change was great because customers could hear the questions other new users had *and* it saved nineteen hours a week for the implementation manager."

As much as we would like to provide a five-star experience to each of our customers, the reality is we need to make sure our onboarding processes are scalable which requires not only some creativity but also some product automation as well.

By creating more efficient onboarding processes, your customer success team will save significant amounts of time and be empowered to become better holistic Customer Success Managers instead of just "onboarding advisors."

To achieve this, review your own onboarding process and see where there could be inefficiencies or misalignment. For example, are there repetitive actions or tasks that could be batched? Are there places where customers always get confused, yet there is no documentation available?

Once you've found areas of improvement, think creatively on how to address these inefficiencies. Common ideas include webinars instead of 1:1s as Jamey did, training people to train others, and creating a self-serve knowledge portal.

Jennifer Walker of Motivis Learning realized while having a good onboarding call with her account's point of contact was helpful, the company also needed to implement an in-app walkthrough and support solution. This solution would be a joint project between product, engineering, and customer support to be successful.

"A while ago, and it's taken us some time to put this in place, we started advocating for an in-app help solution. You can develop these flows for what shows up and what order for what scenarios for what a person does, it can be segmented. We ended up deciding to build our own and develop our own to call attention to new features."

"When it comes to support, we implemented an in-app help center with content from Zendesk that flies out within the application so that people can have contextualized help that is unique to who that person is, student, instructor or whatever and on the page that they're on. So it's not just all the articles at once that the customer has to search through, it's *contextualized* help."

"Using analytics you can figure out what articles people are using and if no one looking at articles, why not? So we'll just hopefully continue to learn from that and then iterate on our design of what in-app help looks like. But I do think in this day and age that everyone's reading emails and not everyone's looking at the user guide. Even if you send a 65 page comprehensive PDF of how to use your product, it's hard to maintain. No one's reading it and it's frustrating to go through."

"It's hard to figure out if you're going too far with it or not because you don't want articles that you can't maintain. For a team of one, if you're wanting the idea of creating really robust articles with tons of links is a really inspiring idea, but depending on how many product releases you have, it can get really hard. You got screenshots and links and all sorts of content where it's noticeable if it's out of date. How does one person keep up with that? You have to act smart; what are the top 20 articles and then maintain those really, really well."

Ryan DeForest, Head of User Success at Gong.io, also implemented a self-serve model at his company to make processes more efficient.[134] However, he included a data layer over the onboarding experience to better understand his users' experiences to the minute.

"When I started at Gong.io, I reported directly to my COO and our knowledge base consisted of three downloadable Google Docs. So my early project was to develop an early support model and I took it from just a simple 'make sure that SLAs are up to par' and added a bunch of data to make it more usable."

"So I track not only what their problem was, but I also track how many articles a customer looked at during the week, which articles they were searching before they submitted the support ticket. I can also track, based on an onboarding call with the CSM, whether a user is having problems getting started or if a setup is taking longer than 10 minutes during the first call, and I get notified whenever that happens."

Harvard Business Review noted once you have the data on where customers are getting stuck, you could also more

134 UserIQ. 2018. "User Adoption Expedition: Camp San Francisco". Presentation, San Francisco, 2018.

proactively address them.[135] For example, they found while most support calls can be resolved on first-contact, 22% of repeat calls involve downstream issues related to the problem which prompted the original call, even if the original issue was addressed well on the first call.

Harvard Business Review then cited Bell Canada as a successful example of this. "Bell Canada met this challenge by mining its customer interaction data to understand the relationships among various customer issues. Using what it learned about 'event clusters,' Bell began training its reps not only to resolve the customer's primary issue but also to anticipate and address common downstream issues. For instance, a high percentage of customers who ordered a particular feature called back for instructions on using it. The company's service reps now give a quick tutorial to customers about key aspects of the feature before hanging up. This sort of forward resolution enabled Bell to reduce its 'calls per event' by 16% and its customer churn by 6%."

"For complex downstream issues that would take excessive time to address in the initial call, the company sends follow-up emails – for example, explaining how to interpret the first billing statement. Bell Canada is currently weaving this issue-prediction approach into the call-routing experience for the customer."

---

135 Dixon, Matthew, Karen Freeman, and Nicholas Toman. 2010. "Stop Trying To Delight Your Customers". *Harvard Business Review*, 2010.

Onboarding processes can be time consuming and overwhelming at times. Take the time now to find inefficiencies and quick wins to save you and your customer a lot of time in the long-run.

INTERNAL ONBOARDING OBJECTIVE: CUSTOMER SEGMENTATION

Being efficient by itself isn't enough or may not be the right solution for every type of account. Jamey Jeff, Managing Director of Customer Success Solutions at Coastal Cloud, says that it's about segmenting your accounts based on sophistication when it comes to onboarding.

"Customers start using your product with varying levels of experience. Some are novices and don't know much about your product; they will need more handholding during the onboarding process. On the other hand, some are already experts; these are the users who perhaps have been a customer of yours before at their previous companies – they might know more about the product than you do!" Experts often just want you to get out of their way when it comes to onboarding."

"Clearly, these two types of customer personas will need different experiences."

"For example, say you're selling cars. There are some customers who will flip through the entire owner's manual before even getting into the car. Then, there are others that want to just start the car and turn on the radio and go. These two types of customers should have different car buying experiences. By swapping their experiences, you will starve those in group one and overwhelm those in group two."

"By segmenting your customers, you can invest your time more wisely. Most companies just look at deal value or customer size when segmenting. This is important to ensure you're profitably servicing your customers, but sophistication is just as important. Large enterprise customers can be novices, and SMB customers can be experts. They both are going to need different onboarding experiences. Know what they need and when they no longer need you to be there."

The objective of segmentation is to create the most appropriate experience possible for your customer. It is important the organization understands the customer's needs and caters to the customer at their level, especially at scale. By grouping your customers into similar characteristics, you can better address their concerns and help set everyone in the group up for success.

According to the 2016 TSIA Customer Success Baseline Survey, the top three ways to segment customers is by:

1. Account Size (81%)
2. Geography (58%)
3. Customer's Line of Business (37%)[136]

---

136 Nanus and Pickens,"Building A Business Case For Customer Success".

Growth potential, product offering, and high/low touch were trailing behind at 33%, 29% and 22% respectively. However, it seems like there is a recent shift toward the latter three categories.

Nevertheless, you should segment your customers based on how you and your team see fit. As we saw in Jamey's example, it doesn't necessarily have to be on a traditional line and it could be subjective.

Allison Pickens, COO of Gainsight, shares how Gainsight segments their customers.[137]

"We segment our customers based on customer size, so number of employees. We also name them after planets, so Mars is for the small businesses, Venus is for mid-sized businesses, and Jupiter is enterprise."

"The reason we went with customer size as opposed to deal size or any other traditional metric is because we wanted to base it off of something simple, automated, and public information."

"Even if the deal size is small, but the company size is large, we treat them the same as other Jupiter customers because they have the potential for future growth. Furthermore, after determining their size, we then treat them accordingly. For example, a kickoff for a Jupiter customer is going to be very different from a kickoff for a company that is 50 people in a WeWork in San Francisco."

---

137 Pickens and DeWahl, "#Techtalks: All About The Customer".

Brian Kaminski, Chief Customer Officer at Conversica, discusses how they came up with their segments through an exercise of adoption curves.[138]

"For us, we focus a lot on our different types of customers. What are their various needs? What is the trajectory they should be on?"

"We then visualize that as a trajectory curve and if a customer falls behind or falls off the curve, that's when we start to intervene more aggressively. Fundamentally, we're setting the expectation before they buy from us that this is how the adoption curves are supposed to look. So our CSMs are really focused on understanding how to get the customer on the curve and our adoption team is really focused on keeping them on track even post-implementation."

"We originally had one curve and all of our enterprise customers were way off that curve. So, we needed to build out a separate curve. After all, in a lot of cases, their things are a lot more stable that it seems.

"Over time, we realized that there are a couple different curves. Now, we find that there are customers that for one reason fall in between some of those curves and that tends to sort of throw us off a little bit because it looks like maybe we should be intervening or maybe they're having a bad experience. But when you actually dig in, you're finding out that actually it's just something's different with their organizations."

---

138 UserIQ, "User Adoption Expedition: Camp San Francisco".

"Using these curves, we focus our adoption on keeping customers on the curve through interdepartmental efforts with operations (to drive automation in scale) and support (to understand what inquiries customers are asking)."

"We recently started looking at, – as we focus more on not just the company but on users, – segmenting the users within our database. For example, the executive level user is going to have a very different usage pattern than a usual manager or leader and we're starting to look at different usage patterns and different users and making sure that they are staying on track."

Segmentation, particularly during onboarding, is a powerful tool to drive better customer experiences and better customer success strategies to set customers up for success in the long-run.

INTERNAL ONBOARDING OBJECTIVE: EXPECTATION MANAGEMENT

"Managing expectations is the hardest thing and it has to be done from the onset of the relationship," says Ebonie Gibbs, Customer Success and Marketing Manager at EVERFI, who works within the EdTech industry with high-profile sports and entertainment partners.

"You have to have a strong understanding of the contract contents so you can determine the best way to meet expectations without going against what you are legally bound to."

"Furthermore, you need to understand each organization's unique priorities, the account's priorities, and if possible – the 'trickle down' priorities that come from the decision makers on your accounts! So for example, if a partner of mine wants to have twenty-five events over the life of the contract, and wants to stick to a particular list of schools with students within their target age group, I need to know that upfront so that I can develop an execution plan that ensures we meet those expectations. It is imperative to understand that if they have a wish list, we need to work with them to understand how that may overlap with the current plans and priorities."

Managing expectations, while maintaining excitement and momentum, is crucial to a customer's onboarding journey. Oversell, and your team, customer success and otherwise, will have a much harder time working with them in the coming months. Undersell, and your team may not be able to even keep the contract for over a contract cycle. So, be realistic and transparent with what you can offer your customer and what you can do to make sure they can be successful with your product.

By managing expectations, not only are you setting your customer up with a practical understanding of what is going to happen, but you are also setting your company up for success by having a clear alignment of what would be delivered.

"Learning to set expectations earlier is key," said Tiffany Cosgrove, Director of Customer Success at Calendly.[139]

"When an account requires more handholding comes on board, lay out for them what the implementation process looks like: 'Typically, people do A, B, and C within X period of time.'"

From there, the team at Calendly suggests that you make sure that your team is empowered to set the right expectations on the frameworks to expect and when to be passed along to other departments. This is particularly important when dealing with lower-tiered customers who often get forgotten when customer success teams scale.

Another thing Jennifer Walker of Motivis Learning makes sure is solidified at the onboarding call are the expectations around ongoing support throughout the contract.

"During onboarding phase, I have a customer success meeting with my point of contact and we go through responsibilities on their side and determine all major milestones in the project. It helps them clarify their mind about who they need to be involving throughout the way."

"We also have a conversation around support and I'll ask 'when your people have a problem, who do they go to?' and clarify the process as necessary for them. Part of the onboarding process is to help them think through what their onboarding support looks like."

---

139 "How 3 High-Growth Companies Think About Scaling Customer Success". 2016. Blog. *Calendly*.

"Having that conversation around support as part of implementation has served us well, and people are happy to talk that through with you. But you can't expect necessarily that they'll have a full team of train the trainers system, or training opportunities three times a month."

As exciting as the onboarding phase is, it is important to make sure customers have realistic expectations of what to expect from your company so that both you and your company are set up for success.

***

Onboarding is perhaps the most important part of the customer journey. Ultimately, it's all about setting the stage up for success. For the customer, it's understanding how to derive the maximum value possible out of your product and setting reasonable objectives to hit the customers' goals. For the customer success team, it's about creating the best first impression of the customer experience for the customer and adjusting appropriately to where they need to be met.

Creating an amazing onboarding process takes time and experimentation, but as long as you have your customers top of mind, just start.

KEY TAKEAWAYS

There are seven main objectives during the onboarding phase for both the customer and for the customer success team.

For the customer, their objectives are:

1. **To educate themselves about how to use the product**: Reflecting on your Product Complexity and User Complexity scores, think about how your customers can best learn how to use the product and start their customer journey on the right foot

2. **To determine what defines success and see early returns on investment**: Feed off or your customer's momentum and give them a taste of what success looks like with your product! Here, you want to determine how your customer defines success, execute on an onboarding strategy that sets them up for success, and then create product stickiness to help them realize quick value from their investments.

3. **To affirm the long-term value that your product can provide the customer**: Show your customer the potential benefits that they can reap from a long-term partnership with your company. To do this, you can set up a success plan or determine milestones to help guide them in the right directly.

For the customer success team, their objectives are:

1. **To orchestrate a seamless sales handoff**: Make a solid first impression to the customer by listening to what the customer has already told the sales team and also give feedback back to the sales team if you find that a customer is a bad fit

2. **To be creatively efficient in managing your time**: Whether it's by providing in-app tool tips or figuring out a one to many model for onboarding your customers, by saving time your customer success team can dedicate more time to creating a better overall customer experience.

3. **To better understand your customers so that you can meet them where they are**: By understanding the types of customers you have, you can then segment their onboarding experiences (and customer journeys in general) and better cater to their needs and expectations.

4. **To build on the customer's excitement and manage their expectations**: Keeping customer expectations realistic – not overselling or underselling the product – will help set your customers up for long-term success.

With a comprehensive and efficient onboarding process, your customers will be better set up for success long-term.

ENGAGEMENT

"The path to retaining users is to continually demonstrate the value of your product to them. While this is especially important for new users, it's equally as important to continue demonstrating value to older users, to make sure they continue coming back as well."

– *Craig Morrison, Founder of Kwilia and UsabilityHour*

Kayla Murphy, Co-Founder of Trustfuel, works with early stage customer success teams and recommends focusing on one thing at a time.[140]

"Start with one focus and build processes to go with it. Institute QBRs (Quarterly Business Reviews) or regular

---

140 DeMeré, Nichole. 2017. "How To Start A Customer Success Program From Scratch". Blog. *Wootric.*

check-ins. Start tracking your usage data and figuring out which metrics give you the best picture of customer health."

"Just start."

"Many of the teams I work with felt a great deal of analysis paralysis at the beginning of their customer success journey. They were worried about annoying customers, tracking the wrong metrics, or focusing so much on unhealthy accounts that morale dies. You have to start somewhere and no one knows more about your customers right now than you. Start being proactive and consistently evaluate your processes."

In the onboarding phase, customer success's focus is to make sure the customer is set up for success – that they have all of the tools that they need to really make the most out of the product. The next phase, engagement, is all about empowering (and at times reeducating and reminding) the customer to really maximize the value and understand what is going on.

Overall, in the world of customer success, there is so much focus given to the first month of the customer's journey (e.g. onboarding) and the last months of the customer's journey (e.g. renewals and upsells). However, what about the middle? Yes, there are re-engagement campaigns, product release emails, QBRs, and periodic check-ins – but why is there such a wide gap in knowledge when it comes to this part of the customer's journey?

One might argue customer success is such a new industry that we, as an industry, have "80-20'd" the situation

– spending 80% of the time on the most important 20% – and focused only on what would deliver the most return with the least amount of effort. One might argue mapping out the customer journey, maintaining check-ins and QBRs, is all you really need for the middle.

However, I think this part of the customer journey has a lot more room to grow.

When I first started customer success, I had the hardest time figuring out a good strategy to keep users engaged. Not only were there few best practices out there about this, but this phase was also very product and user specific. Engaging a B2B customer, for example, will be very different from engaging a B2C customer.

I remember after we had onboarded one of our very first schools onto our product, I was pumped. I had a roster of students I could monitor and I saw that they were having sessions. This was great! Onboarding went well. At this point, I thought, "I can start thinking about how we can make the next onboarding better. What trends from the sessions can we glean so we can give our leadership team a report on how things are going at this school?"

However, I hadn't really given much thought to how we could provide any insight to the schools themselves on how their students were doing. First off, we didn't have the systems for it and second, we didn't really know what they wanted or expected.

After a month or so, we had a teacher come up to us and ask how his class is doing. He's been hearing anecdotally from his students they are using it, but was curious as to who was using the service and if there were any insights for him as their teacher he could act on.

We presented him a summary of what his students have been doing on our platform over the past few months. He scanned the roster, paused for a bit, and pointed to one of the names. [I've changed her name here to protect her privacy.]

"Wait – Maria had an hour session yesterday? You mean the Maria that sits in the back of the classroom and never raises her hand?" he exclaimed.

Apparently, she had been doing better on her homework and the teacher didn't fully understand why since she never came to him with questions. He was eager to share this news with his fellow teachers.

That math teacher's response made me realize there is something here. We can generate so much more excitement and drive more value for customers even after onboarding.

We started getting a better sense of what teachers and administrators were interested in seeing. We first started with executive summaries. That evolved into presentation decks on student usage. Then there was a shortened email version. Then we added full-blown reports with complete analysis.

Our teachers were so excited by learning about what their students were up to on our service that they would ask for even more data and ask for reports more frequently. As the only person behind the scenes compiling the data and reports, I was swamped. With so few customers, how we were supposed to scale if I was already spending so much time building one-off reports? Yes, they were similar, but they were still very time-consuming.

I wanted to create something that teachers and administrators could check and interact with in real time to see how their students were doing on our service. Inspired by the classroom websites I saw many of our teachers had for their students, I designed and built a "dashboard" website where a school could go in and look at transcripts of sessions their students had and high level statistics.

It was an instant hit. Teachers and administrators alike would go in on their own time and play around with the data filters to learn more about the students benefiting from our service and see which students could probably use the service more. However, what I was also excited about was that by creating these dashboards, the number of requests I received for custom reports went down significantly. Coupled with a loose QBR process, we found that this was one of the best ways to engage with our customers to drive value long-term and for them to realize that value as well.

* * *

Engagement ultimately comes down to demonstrating value and maintaining channels of communication.

For the customer, this phase is about:

1. **Demonstrating current value**: Help your customer understand the value they are deriving from your product, whether that is through data or anecdotes.

2. **Showing how to derive more value**: Educate your customer on how they can maximize the value that they receive, whether that is presenting a more efficient way of using your product or demonstrating how your product can be used for other use cases that they may not have thought of yet.

For the customer success team, you want to:

1. **Maintain a pulse on the customer**: Simply put, track how your customers are doing! Look out for red flags that may jeopardize the contract and help guide customers back on track.

2. **Develop a trusted advisor relationship with your customer**: Show your customer that you are there to help them achieve their long-term goals. After all, a customer's success is a success for customer success!

By providing the appropriate communications, you can set yourself up for success come renewals (and beyond).

DEMONSTRATING CURRENT VALUE

"It's funny just running through my list of software companies I have worked for or worked with. I can't think of anybody really that does that 'middle part' well,'" says Jim Jones, VP of Customer Success at ISI Telemanagement Solutions.

"But there is a lot of stuff that you can do in the middle. I worked with a company in Chicago called SAVO [since acquired by Seismic] that is in the sales enablement space. One of the things we did there was six-month engagement strategy, where we would conduct a sales enablement program review. For every one of the touch points within the program, we'd create a playbook to make sure our customers were on the right track."

"From what I've seen at the companies I've ever walked in to lead customer success, the processes around what happens after onboarding is all a bit nebulous. For example, I've noticed two things in particular for QBRs. Number one, everyone does it differently. And number two, there is a good chunk of the customers where the CSMs will say, 'Well, the customer says "don't call me", so I don't bother to think to call them.' My perspective is that we still need to check in and to tell them what we're providing for them."

"We got into a model where even if the customer didn't want to do the QBR on the phone, we would still prepare the deck and send it to them because part of the point of the QBR was to show them, the customer, that we were achieving their goals and their business objectives. It's important to push that across!"

"The important thing to remember here is – *you should always be moving the ball down field preparing for the best conversation possible come renewals.*"

This is why showing your customers the value you constantly provide is important – you want to show you care about them and their success! John Gattorna, a visiting professor at Macquarie Graduate School of Management, found a staggering 68% of customers leave as a result of perceived indifference.[141]

By touching base and demonstrating what you are already providing to your customers, not only can you get a good verbal and qualitative pulse check from your customers, but it's also a great way to strategize about what they could do next to maximize the value that they receive from your product.

"The metric I've watched most closely is how much the customer has realized their Cloud Cost Saving after using our software," said Bradley Liou, Director of Customer Success at Densify.[142]

"Since the outcome is easy to measure, we can actually present a report of how much our customers have saved in the cloud-based on Densify's machine learning recommendation. When customers have achieved their business outcome and they have good experience, it tells us that we are making our customer successful."

---

141 "CSAT Stat Of The Month". 2019. Blog. *CustomerThermometer*. Accessed January 6.
142 Sutarno, "Inside Customer Success: Densify".

When it comes to engagement, quarterly business reviews (QBRs) are a common, but powerful tool for you and your customer.

QBRs are a wonderful structured touch point where you and your customer review together how things are going, flag any strategic concerns, and get a deeper understanding about how to deliver more value to the customer going forward. This is where you would start to become more of an advisor; strategizing with the customer to figure out the best next course of action and build trust to strengthen the relationship.

Allison Pickens, COO of Gainsight, speaks what she calls "the most strategic post-sale touch point."[143]

"A critical part of the CSM role is demonstrating value to the client. QBRs allow us to demonstrate to the client the value that they've been able to achieve through the platform, and align on ways to drive more value."

Lincoln Murphy, Founder of Sixteen Ventures, adds, "What your client's executive team thinks of your product or service carries a lot of weight, and QBRs are the perfect time to show exactly how big of an impact you've had on their business."[144]

143 Pickens, Allison. 2019. "The Essential Guide To Quarterly Business Reviews". Blog. *Gainsight*. Accessed January 6.
144 Murphy, Lincoln. 2018. "The Power Of The Quarterly Business Review – QBR". Blog. *Gainsight*.

"A QBR should be a strategic event, not a tactical one. The kinds of topics that are appropriate for a QBR might include: Return on Investment (ROI) in your product, Additional use cases they're exploring or you've noticed, Phase 2 (or 3 or 4) of the implementation, and Major roadblocks or obstacles to success (and how to get back on track)."

"The selfish goal of a QBR from your perspective is to move the customer in the direction you desire. If you are a company that has renewal events (i.e. not monthly auto-renews, but generally annual or bi-annual contracts that need to be manually reviewed, often requiring a new contract with new signatures to be executed), successful QBRs should lead to the renewal being a non-event."

"All-in-all, the QBR is a tremendous opportunity to strengthen your relationship with your customer. If done well, it can be equal parts aspiration and inspiration. Most customers truly want to be great customers. They would love to have the highest health score (aspiration) and are excited to be part of the innovation you are bringing to the marketplace (inspiration)."

However, sometimes you can't always provide QBRs for everyone.

When Jamey Jeff was Chief Customer Officer at Track-Maven back in 2014, they conducted QBRs for every customer. However, preparing QBRs, scheduling meetings, and leading meetings with the customers was time consuming, and his team didn't feel that the QBRs were always valuable. Determined to make sure the team was delivering valuable customer insights, and was efficient in doing so, Jamey scheduled a meeting with all of the CSMs on his team and asked them to bring a print out of their portfolios to the meeting.

The CSMs gathered in the office conference room, portfolios in hand. Jamey asked a simple question – "If we were to eliminate QBRs, what would happen?" Some mentioned their customers would care a lot, whereas others say that their customers probably wouldn't even notice. However, what was clear was QBRs were taking a lot of time for everyone to complete.

"I then asked my CSMs to go through their portfolio and assign a score of 1 next to the customer if they believed the customer wouldn't even notice that the QBR didn't happen, a score of 2 if the customer would want to want an explanation, but would be OK with not holding the QBR, or a score of 3 if the customer would churn if we didn't continue their QBRs."

"It was such a simple exercise. We tallied the results afterwards and found that 75% of all customers in the portfolios had a score of 1."

"We realized that we had spent all of this time on QBRs that we felt weren't valuable to the vast majority of our customers. The result shed a light on a clear problem and was able to help us focus the team and our efforts much better," said Jamey.

"You have to make sure that you are doing what is most valuable for your customers and really challenge yourself to see where you get too caught up in the inertia of 'the way we've always done things'. It was clear that for a majority of our customers, we had been too focused on sticking to our process at the expense of delivering something useful."

Because your customer purchased your product to solve a pain point, show them you are doing so and don't be shy about it. By sharing how much value your customers are already deriving post onboarding – whether through a QBR or another means – they can get a better understanding of what to do next and how to continue the momentum.

SHOWING HOW TO DERIVE EVEN MORE VALUE

"I almost lost a customer when our customer champion left for another job," recounts Rachel English, Director of Insights for Customer Success at Zuora.[145]

"In this particular case, I found out because I had set our customer analytics system to alert me when the usage volume within any account suddenly dropped off, and also when one of our 'Power Users' switched to a less active persona. Both alerts were triggered, so I knew something was amiss within the account."

---

145 DeMeré, Nichole. 2016. ""I Almost Lost A Customer When Our Champion Left": A Customer Success Story From Zuora". Blog. *Wootric.*

She reached out to the account by phone to speak with the executive buyer and the new customer champion for the account.

"Through in-depth conversations with these key people, I was able to: 1) Share metrics that clearly depicted the growing value they were receiving from utilizing our solution; 2) Give them visibility into which of their users were actively achieving that value, and which might need to be reengaged; 3) Confirm that the new hire did plan to become a Power User and our new champion; and 4) Schedule a customized training session to help educate and engage all of their users."

By sharing with her customer how they can continue to derive more value even with their customer champion and power user gone, Rachel was able to save the account and put them back on a good path toward success.

Once you've determined and demonstrated the value you've already brought to the customer, continue that momentum and show them how they can derive even more value.

The onboarding phase oftentimes contains a lot of information dumping and therefore, there is bound to be something that falls through the cracks.

So, use this opportunity to:

- *reintroduce those missed opportunities for value*
- *share best practices on how to more efficiently use your product*

- *introduce advance use cases for your customer to take advantage of*

By showing your customer how you can do more, you may not only earn their trust, but also help set up your company for success and expansion come renewals times.

Jim Jones of ISI Telemanagement Solutions, shares an exercise he uses with his clients to figure out how to create more value for their clients.

"We're doing an exercise right now that we call white spacing."

"Start with a graph. On the x-axis, you've got a bunch of use cases for your product that your customer cares about. For example, my company right now sells to telecommunication companies, so people that have large call centers like Hawaiian Airlines, United Airlines, and credit card companies. So, these telecom companies are concerned about things like the talk time for their call center agents, compliance and all that. So on this x-axis, you would put the use case of having some sort of call recording ability to track unauthorized calls or making sure that calls are compliant. On the y-axis, you've got the features of your product."

"From there, you can then map out how each of your products can address each of those use cases. Once you have this map, you can then bring it to the customer to help increase business value for them."

"I know from past experience that when you take this white spacing exercise out and show it to customers, they're going to go, 'Wow, I didn't even know you could do that in your product!' It shows them more value and then it makes your product stickier within the enterprise. To me, that's a big part of the role of the CSM and that's a big part of what has to happen in that 10 months between the onboarding and the renewal."

Sujan Patel, Co-Founder of Mailshake and Managing Director at Ramp Ventures, noticed early on at Mailshake how he could keep engaging with his customers – just ask![146]

"I noticed a funny thing. Just offering to help while proactively engaging customers can actually improve retention and customer happiness."

"Now, notice that I didn't actually say 'solve their problems.' Simply offering to help can be enough. Don't wait until you have some huge disaster. Go out and get in front of your customers. That way, if they have a problem, they aren't going to churn when they know how to find you and get help."

"With Mailshake, we put a little button at the very top of the product that said, 'Need help with keyword research? Get in touch.' Maybe two people in three months clicked it, so we offered it in the first email we send out instead. Then, we tested it in the fifth email and in a bunch of different places inside the app. All of them had mixed results, but if you

---

146 Patel, Sujan. 2018. "7 Lessons From 90 Days In Customer Success". Blog. *Sujan Patel.*

combined all of them together, we were able to get 40% or so of our customers to engage, and raise their hand saying, 'Hey, I actually do need help.' Knowing that let us optimize it even more."

"Don't just give up saying, 'Oh, my customers won't engage.' They will. You just haven't tried hard enough."

Keep the momentum from the onboarding phase going by keeping the learning going. Demonstrate to your customers how your product can provide even more benefits to your customers beyond what they have already experienced.

***

As much as the engagement phase is about solidifying current and potential value for the customer, this phase is also a great opportunity for the customer success team to set themselves up for success by keeping a finger on the customer's pulse and providing appropriate communication channels to build that trusted advisor relationship.

MAINTAINING A PULSE ON CUSTOMERS

"There is an incredible amount to learn from customers outside of that 1:1 opportunity that you have a responsibility to know," says Jeff Cann, Senior Director of Client Experience at Sysomos.[147]

---

147 McLaren, "14 Quotes On Succeeding In Customer Success Leadership".

"Product usage behaviors, areas of your application customers may have challenges with, NPS, the frequency of support requests. All of this information is critical to understanding the health and success of your customers and you owe it to them to be diligent with how you not only learn from it but act on it."

As Jeff said, understanding the health of our customers is vital to operationalizing engagement metrics. By doing so, you can get a better pulse on your customers and address them accordingly to make sure that they are on the right track.

After onboarding, the guardrails come down; customers may falter a bit. They may forget certain product features, use them inefficiently, or completely fail to remember the pain point that instigated the purchase of your product.

Manny Medina, the CEO of Outreach, shares how to make sure your customers are always on track.[148] [149]

"Success in the subscription economy means further embedding yourself in the life of the customer and figuring what they are trying to get done with your product. You are not second-guessing customers; instead you are putting them through a path of continuous improvement – sometimes even if they don't realize they need one."

148 Medina, Manny. 2015. "Uncomfortably-Close Customer Success". Blog. *Outreach.*
149 Brandall, Benjamin. 2015. "Why Is Customer Success Important? A Guide For SaaS Companies". Blog. *Process.St.*

"In our case, if we don't see 20%+ reply rates on emails sent to at least 250 prospects by week two of a user's life with us, we descend on that user like a worried mother and we get involved. We look for signs of potential bad user experiences or technical glitches. If none are obvious, we contact the customer to walk us through her copy, her user profile, her sales process, testing strategy, etc. We brainstorm with them and come up with a solution."

"Sounds like too much? You bet it is. And we like it that way."

"Just as the practice of intrusive college advising – proactively intervening at the first indication of academic difficulty – works to increase retention in some populations of college freshmen, uncomfortably close customer success leads to a greater proportion of successful customers, customers who achieved what they set out to do with us. And often more."

While Manny may be exaggerating a bit, the sentiment is spot on. You want to keep a close eye on customers to understand their usage behaviors and steer them back on track if they are off course. If the customer has a great experience, highlight that and encourage the behavior around that. If the customer had a poor experience, you want to have flags available to address the situation promptly. After all, research has shown that it takes more than 11 exceptionally good experiences to overcome 1 poor one.[150]

---

150 "75 Customer Service Facts, Quotes & Statistics". 2019. Blog. *Helpscout*. Accessed January 6.

Justin Wiesenfeld, Customer Success Guru at Piktochart, shares how they track "engagement moments" and use that as a springboard to leading them to success.[151]

"By keeping a finger on customer pulse, we've been able to understand their "engagement moments" or milestones."

"By the way, 'engagement,' in our opinion, is when our users become invested and are truly getting value out of using Piktochart. Whether they are creating their first infographic or sharing their 100th poster, it means they'll be nurtured every step of the way to becoming Pikto-pros."

Perhaps the most common way to measure engagement is the customer health score. This is a composite score consisting of the metrics that are important to your customer's success. For example, this may include adoption metrics like number of users created, or product usage metrics, like daily active users, or relationship metrics like how good the Customer Success Manager feels about this account or has the account showed any signs of wanting to leave.

George Szundi, Head of Marketing at Natero, a data-driven customer success platform, summarizes this well: "An ideal health score captures the attributes that best reflect a successful customer. These health scores help CSMs gauge the status of their accounts and prioritize customer outreach. They can also be used as one of several

---

151 Wiesenfeld, Justin. 2019. "Why We Choose To Make Customer Success Our Priority". Blog. *Piktochart*. Accessed January 6.

ways to measure the performance of the customer success team."[152]

This score will be different at every company and for every product; however it can be a powerful tool for the customer success team during the engagement phase.

At TrustRadius, Patrick Hansen, VP of Customer Success, breaks down their Customer Health Score.[153]

"One thing we've put in place over the past roughly 6 months that is working very well for us is a very, very simple "health pulse" for every single subscription we manage. We don't have a fancy solution like Gainsight to help us with this and we haven't tried to come up with some complex scoring system baked into our CRM (Salesforce)."

"We have a simple scale that consists of: 1) Green – Client is doing the right things and has affirmed that they have us in budget and intend to renew, 2) Yellow – Client is doing the right things, but has not yet affirmed that they have us in budget and intend to renew, 3) Orange – Client is not doing the right things, but has not yet told us they intend to cancel, and 4) Red – Client has told us they intend to cancel."

"This is to get ahead of cancellations so that they are very rarely a surprise."

152 Szundi, George. 2019. "Designing Customer Health Scores". Blog. *Natero*. Accessed January 6.
153 Hansen, Patrick, and Grishma Govani. 2018. AMA with Patrick Hansen and Grishma Govani of TrustRadius Interview by Lauren Olerich. In person. Slack.

"Our CSMs actively maintain this scale for every client and I review this health pulse weekly in portfolio reviews, with the scrutiny increasing two quarters out from the renewal."

"The real judgement call here is between Yellow and Orange – basically, "is the client doing the right things." We use Pendo and our own infrastructure to monitor adoption, in addition to QBRs to stay aligned to client goals. All that makes it very clear very quickly (without having to automate just yet) whether a client is Yellow or Orange."

"I use the scale to forecast gross retention and it's been eerily accurate."

Jamie Domenici, Global Senior VP of Customer Adoption, Marketing, and Business Development at Salesforce, explains how she has operationalized the engagement phase to create an early warning system.[154]

"At Salesforce, we really try to provide proactive support. We want to identify at the customer's going to have a problem before they have a problem so that we can help solve it."

"But that is really hard to do, so we created the Early Warning System or EWS. This is basically an algorithm that has multiple features, such as how often are users logging into the system ("true login"), feature usage and utilization, and volume of support cases. We take all of this information and bubble that up into a score."

---

154 UserIQ, "User Adoption Expedition: Camp San Francisco".

"We have customers of different sizes, of different industries, of different regions and all have different needs, but you also have a lot of similarities. So we look at all of our customers and we've cluster them together to identify who is doing good – by our definition of good – and which customers need to be more like them."

"For the Early Warning System, each customer will get a score, and if the score goes red, then we're warned and we will proactively reach out to the customer or use a recommendation engine to suggest what they should be doing."

"What this allowed for us is proactive support so that we can avoid as many problems as possible."

Maintaining a pulse on the customer is tough, but imperative. While the process behind this will differ at every company, while creating yours refer back to your Product Complexity and User Complexity scores. What is important is first understanding what behaviors are most important to your company and your customers' success. Once you figure that out, then you can operationalize those behaviors.

DEVELOPING THE TRUSTED ADVISOR RELATIONSHIP

"Honestly, I think that the best thing that your can do is to listen to the customers – both in regards to what they're telling you but also in regards to how they're behaving with your platform." says Jo Massie, Head of Customer Success at Slido.[155]

"Then, particularly for the smaller customers, to try to operationalize that, my number one thing I try to encourage everyone in our team to ask is 'What needs to happen for me to not need to have that conversation again?' We aren't the quickest at fixing this always yet (we're a bootstrapped startup after all) but as long as we're thinking about it, it's the starting point."

To maintain engagement with even their smallest accounts, Jo reaches out to them through multiple high-touch, and one-to-many channels such as roadshows and video calls.

"We try to ensure that our team can get time to do customer roadshow trips at least twice a year. It's actually quite handy because when you tell a customer that you are only in their city for a couple of days, it can be a great way to engage previously apathetic or non-responsive people!"

"We also rely heavily on using Zoom and try to do video calls whenever bandwidth allows – even if the customer doesn't turn on their video, we like them to be able to see and put a face to us."

A key part about the engagement phase for the customer success team is further developing that trusted advisor relationship – for small and large accounts alike! By developing

---

155   Massie, AMA with Jo Massie of Slido.

this sort of relationship, your deeper understanding of the customer will both better serve them and set up your company for long-term success in both the renewal and advocacy phases.

To do this, just as in developing any relationship, you must first understand the context you are building the relationship on, and at times, navigate through tough conversations and guide them in a manner that is genuine and professional.

First, to establish clear and transparent communication, set yourself up for success. Jack Gerli, Client Success Manager at Delighted, makes sure his customer always know what is going on and his team is aware of key customer events.

"We focus on moving as far up the value chain as possible – establishing a presence as early as possible in to the customer journey."

"We do this because we know that there is a domino effect – the earlier that I can insert my team into the customer's journey, the more control I have over the how product is viewed and used, and the more I can be informed."

"We've increased revenue by ten times in a couple of years and a lot of that is driven through realizing opportunities within accounts that the customers don't realize. You become a consultant for them, empowered by understanding their pain points and usage.

"To accomplish this, we're diligent on how much we automate and how we feed ourselves data. We're thinking about in six months, what do the key metrics and KPIs look like for a healthy account? And how do we get there?"

"You have to have that conversation with your future self. Everything that you're doing now is going to affect future you, so you should set yourself up for success today."

Another large component of customer success is about developing trust between your company and the customer.

As the liaison to the customer, we get the privilege of delivering the good news and working with customers to get the most value possible out of our product. However, sometimes this means we have to deliver bad news – a discontinuation of a product, a missed product deadline, or a reprioritization of a feature, which the customer was really looking forward to.

Mike Griffin, VP of Customer Success at LivePerson, discussed how to navigate these sorts of conversations.

"Every day that you wake up, think about the value that you are bringing to the client. Escalation calls can be a lot of back and forth when you deliver the news that was promised but isn't going to be delivered on time."

"Here you have to understand where the customer is coming from. The executive on the other end is going to express their dissatisfaction. They are doing their job and you are doing your job."

These sorts of conversations are important. We want to make sure our customers feel heard and have an outlet to express their frustration. This is also a great opportunity for us as a customer success team to further understand pain points and come up with creative solutions to temporarily relieve the situation or to even avoid the pain altogether.

"Before you even go into this call," Mike continues, "work internally first to understand what you can do for your client. Think through what solutions we can offer and what other ways that we can use to address this situation. This will make the call with the client more productive than just being sorry."

"You also have to put yourself in their mindset. They have a secondary pain point of "why are you just telling me this bad news now?' and provide answers and solutions to help them work through the situation."

"As customer success, we want to help them build their business and build value at their company so that they can take the credit. Therefore, you have to build that honest relationship. To tell them no or that something isn't going to happen, you have to tell them as clearly as you can. For most software companies, these conversations are about framing things in the context that they aren't buying a customized solution, so you have to understand what resources that you have as well as the resources that they have."

"Also remind them that while I may be bringing bad news today, but better news came out yesterday and more good news is coming down the road map. By being forthright, timely, and honest, you can create that trusted relationship with the customer."

However, sometimes on these escalation calls, Mike says that it can be helpful to bring in more internal stakeholders to understand the customer's point of view.

"There are two things to know when bringing non-client facing roles onto these calls – A) be mindful of what you put in front of the client. Do not promise anything that you can't deliver on! And, B) have a prep call with your non-client facing coworkers, first, before going on the call. It may sound silly to do role playing prior to the call, but for those who aren't normally in front of customers, this will help."

"Having them on these calls will help let them feel the pain around these conversations. It's not about treating them like children, but they need to stand by what they are building."

"After all, organizations that fail are those where client management or customer success doesn't have a say at the table. You have to have those internal conversations beforehand to confirm what is going to be delivered."

Allison Pickens, COO of Gainsight, understands how hard having these sorts of conversations can be for lots of customer success teams.[156] [157]

"Customer success and customer experience people tend to be of the helper type – we always want to help and please

156 Pickens and DeWahl, "#Techtalks: All About The Customer".
157 Pickens, Allison. 2018. "The Be Brave Campaign". Blog. *LinkedIn*.

people! This makes it hard for us to tell clients no, which is why at Gainsight we launched the Be Brave campaign where we showcase the heroes in our community who have overcome difficult challenges."

"You have to be brave in customer success. Sometimes that means you are sticking up for what you believe is the right thing for your client to do and sharing that perspective with your client. When you believe the client is going down the wrong path, it's saying something to the effect of "I've worked with hundreds of other customers that are similar to you and this is how they've done it to achieve success. I will fully support you, but this is my obligation to you to share this information with you."

Becoming that trusted advisor is a critical part of the engagement phase. Do it well to set yourself up for success long-term.

***

The engagement phase is going to look different for every company depending on your Product Complexity and User Complexity scores. However, one thing remains the same: continually show the customer the value you are and that you can bring to them. Build systems around that objective so you can create that trusted relationship and set yourself up for success for the next phases.

KEY TAKEAWAYS

The engagement phase is all about demonstrating value (both past and future) and building systems that continually demonstrate value and to address any early warning signs.

For the customer,

1. **Share the impact that your product has already provided**: Keep your customers in the loop of the achievements that your product has enabled!

2. **Educate them about how to derive more value**: The learning never has to stop! Demonstrate to your customers how they can get even more value out of your product, whether that is re-educating them on something they might have missed or showing them a new feature they hadn't used yet.

For the customer success team,

1. **Maintain a pulse on the customer**: Operationalize your engagement metrics so you can more efficiently track how every single one of your accounts is doing.

2. **Become your customer's trusted advisor**: Show your customer you are not only there for them, but are constantly looking out for their best interests.

By completing these objectives, you will be setting both your customer success team and customers up for long-term success.

RENEWALS

—

"Today, getting tons of new users isn't hard. What's hard is keeping them."

– Hiten Shah, Co-Founder of Crazy Egg

"We started with the end in mind," said Ari Klein, Head of Customer Success at DocSend.[158]

"The first thing we did was automate the creation of renewal opportunities so they would, at the very least, be on our radar. We instituted a "contract end date" field in our CRM that is a mandatory requirement for sales reps to complete before a deal is moved to the "closed-won" stage. The renewal opportunity's projected close date is the "contract

---

158 Klein, Ari. 2019. "A Push System For Customer Success". Blog. *Natero.* Accessed January 6.

end date" plus one day and automatically drives a set of tasks through the life of the customer's contract."

When DocSend started out and was growing fast, they created a tracking process so they were always on top of renewals.

"When you're managing a large – and increasing – portfolio of customers who all joined at different times and are at different stages in their lifecycle, it becomes exceedingly complex to stay proactive without a smart system in place."

"Specifically, we built an internal "push system" to nudge us about the important – and not just urgent – activities we should be thinking about with each customer. Each notification/task includes a high-level goal (onboarding, adoption, expansion, engagement, or renewal) and a few example tactics and strategies."

Throughout the customer journey, they mapped out regular check-ins, scheduled "Best Practice Reviews," and "Product Engagement Checks." With 60 days left until contract renewal, they began the renewal conversation. During this conversation, they would have four goals, as explained by Ari.

"First, refresh your memory on current contract, and create account renewal plan. Next, get in touch with decision maker to avoid an "11th hour" upsell or renewal conversation. Next, identify strategic initiatives, any upsell or expansion (size or duration/commitment) opportunity, and discuss appropriate DocSend plan. And lastly, communicate any price changes (e.g. expiring promotional pricing)."

Then when the day came, the customer success team would tie up any loose ends and execute the renewal agreement.

"Truth be told, we probably did things ad hoc for longer than I would have liked, but that's the reality of an early-stage, resource-constrained startup. We didn't arrive at our current process until nearly a year after our product launch, when a few renewals "snuck up" on us."

"You never want to be surprised or have to backpedal into a renewal conversation."

"Even though the most important thing after a launch is to land new customers, my one piece of advice is to set some time aside to look ahead and instrument yourself so you're not caught off guard when it's renewal time."

***

Like DocSend, many companies initially invest in customer success to boost renewal rates with the philosophy that with better service throughout the customer's journey, the more likely they are to renew. While correct, the renewals phase isn't just an "oh it renewed, let's move on" situation, it is a *phase.*

In the onboarding phase, the customer learned about the value of your product and worked with you to be set up for success. In the engagement phase, the customer got a better understanding of the value already being derived from the product, and how they could derive even more value. During these two phases, both the customer success and broader company teams can look at usage metrics to determine success.

The renewal phase of the customer journey is a culmination of those efforts where you now reiterate the value derived by the customer and help them think strategically about how your team and your company can provide more value as each company matures. This phase contains a key "moment of truth" as this is when your customer will confirm whether they've committed for another term. As this is the first official point where money is on the line for the customer success team, leadership will also be paying close attention to this.

Undoubtedly, this is a phase that gets a lot of attention particularly from internal stakeholders, and the statistics back it up:

- Renewals and upsells can account for 70% to 95% of revenue for SaaS companies[159]
- 66% of customer success organization charters stated reducing churn as one of their top three objectives, and 57% of charters also cited increasing renewals as a priority.[160]

---

159 Bernazzani, Sophia. 2018. "Why Customer Success Matters". Blog. *HubSpot*.
160 "Tech Customer Success Programs Focus On Increasing Product Usage, Cutting Churn". 2018. Blog. *Marketing Charts*.

- Customer success executives are most commonly measured by their performance on renewals (68%) and churn rate (55%).[161]

Renewal conversations are always some of the toughest. In 2015, Preact found, "maintaining and increasing sales with customers under contract was one of companies' biggest challenges with only 30% of companies saying they're growing revenue from current users.[162] Half said they were losing 10% or more in top line renewals annually."

During these conversations both sides are on alert, particularly if the customer didn't fully realize the value they wanted (due to miscommunication, misaligned expectations of their own needs, or something else).

Tomasz Tunguz, Partner at Redpoint Ventures, observes, "Renewal conversations occur with much greater frequency than with perpetual software sales. Startups that manage customer renewals better than their peers grow faster and require less capital."[163]

Not surprisingly, at the beginning of my customer success journey, I had found renewals daunting. I was up for the challenge, but I was scared to start the renewal conversation. *What do I say?*

---

161 Ibid.
162 Preact and Service Excellence Partners, "2015 Customer Success Priorities Survey".
163 Tunguz, Tomasz. 2014. "Why Customer Success? Why Now?". Blog. *Tomasz Tunguz.*

What if they don't want to renew?

She said she wanted to wait until her kids' grades come out, but her renewal is due before then; how do I navigate this conversation?

I quickly learned in customer success that – to rephrase a common saying – churn happens.

However, for every renewal opportunity, it was another opportunity to receive feedback, realign expectations, and set my parents and students up for success next term. Better yet, you could expand the account or put them on a better-suited plan.

For example, did they have another sibling who could benefit from the service? Did they feel like they were getting the help and support they needed from our product and customer success team? Can I help shed some light on upcoming feature releases they may be interested in or suggest a new method of using the service so they can get even more out of the product?

What made renewals at my company slightly different was every semester there could be no more need for the product (e.g. the child graduated!) or there could be a new use case for the product (e.g. their child doesn't learn well from this year's math teacher). This meant that during this phase, realigning expectations for the upcoming semester and showing the parent how their child could continue to use our service even with a new learning environment was imperative.

My confidence grew as I had more and more of these discussions with our customers. I started providing more content upfront, such as providing testimonials, preemptively answering any questions they may have, and creating a more user-friendly cadence for handling renewals. For example, if summer break was coming up, their child may not have homework assigned; so I would prepare them for their renewal by helping them figure out ways to keep their children's math skills sharp over the summer so the child is ready for the next school year.

Some of these discussions were delightful; parents would tell me stories about how their child was using our product and that their investment was paying off. "Jen – it's so great to hear from you! Of course, we'll be renewing. His progress report came in the other day and it was the highest math grade that we've ever seen." Typically, out of excitement and glee, they'd send me screenshots of their kids' report cards or the score on a recent math quiz.

Of course, sometimes the family decided to no longer stay with us and we would part as friends. For those who decided to leave regardless of what plan they were on, we made sure to write out a "churn story" and share it with the company on a regular basis. These stories are meant to read as narratives so anyone who read them could get a better sense of that family's experience with us; these proved to be a valuable source of feedback for our company.

Overall, I learned what was most powerful in this phase was creating a trusted advisor relationship with our customers and setting them up for success long-term. It was to show them that we cared about them and their family's success, and didn't see them as recurring revenue.

To be clear, customer success doesn't always own renewals and some argue that – like most other phases – it is owned by the company as a whole. However, customer success plays a key part in developing that trusted relationship between the customer and the company, setting up expectations and maximizing value derived throughout the customer's journey – all of which are absolutely critical components of the renewals phase.

"If no one owns renewals, they will not get the attention they deserve," said Greg Poirier, President of CloudKettle.[164]

"That being said, most salespeople who are really good at closing business, are really bad at managing the renewal process. The skill set required to keep an existing customer happy is different from the skill set that's required to close net new business. Of course, there are some exceptions to this rule. However, you can't design a scalable process around those outliers."

"Each customer should be passed from sales to customer success after the sale is closed … Companies, especially fast-growing SaaS companies, tend to focus on new business

164 Poirier, Greg. 2018. "The 5 Steps For A Successful SaaS B2B Renewal". Blog. *CloudKettle*.

– winning new logos, increasing market share, creating momentum. However, as unsexy as they are, renewals and upselling will ensure future growth and success."

"The worst thing you can do is call a customer and let them know a renewal is due next month when they haven't heard from you since they bought the product. Map out a process outlining when customers will be contacted and what will be covered."

The most common practice here is to create a separate role within customer success specifically to handle renewals.

Allison Pickens, COO of Gainsight, recalls how they created this role within their organization.[165]

"We found that once we reached a certain size, it didn't make sense for CSMs to own renewals and upsell."

"First, skill set – selling requires a different skill set from the primary responsibility of CSMs: advising the customer about their strategy for deriving value from the product. Second – the advisor role – CSMs sometimes feel that having to discuss pricing with customers compromises their ability to serve as the trusted advisor to the customer."

Therefore, they hired their first Renewals and Expansion (R&E) manager to help the customer success team.

"Our Renewals and Expansion Manager is accountable for the renewal and upsell; he has a quota for each. That allows

---

165 Pickens, Allison. 2018. "Renewals & Expansions: A Primer". Blog. *Gainsight.*

the CSM to focus on helping the customer derive value from the product."

"He is accountable for all activities directly related to the renewal and upsell, but the CSM does continue to play a role. The R&E Manager learns from the CSM the history of the customer relationship, and he'll inform the CSM of the renewal status on weekly calls leading up to the renewal. In general, the two parties are kept "Informed" of each other's activities."

"As a result ... we simply achieved greater specialization within the customer success team."

According to the 2015 TSIA Expand Selling Practices and Metrics Survey, customer success is expanding its responsibilities in expansion.[166] 24% of CSMs' primary responsibility is expansion, compared to the 61% of sales representatives whose primary responsibility is expansion. Going forward, this number is set to hit 30% for CSMs and the percentage of sales representatives expected to focus on expansion will drop to 37%.

There are three key aspects to the renewal phase:

1. **Understanding value derived**: Review how the past subscription period went, from metrics to concerns addressed to any other positive externalities.

2. **Understanding future value**: Understand what the future term looks like, flagging any new or upcoming

---

166 Nanus and Pickens,"Building A Business Case For Customer Success".

developments, and confirm the potential that your company can bring to your customer over the next subscription period.

3. **Thinking long-term and building the advisor relationship**: Join your customer to strategically think long-term and become that trusted advisor for the customer.

By going through these three things with your customer, you can help them either renew, expand, or move on and set them up for success – even if it isn't with your company.

UNDERSTANDING VALUE DERIVED

"Initial purchase decisions are based on hope. Renewal decisions are based on experience," said Jason Whitehead, CEO of Tri Tuns.[167]

"When your customer makes their initial purchase decision, they are buying your software based on their hopes and expectations that in the near future they will realize tangible business benefits from its use. All of the evidence they consider – marketing information, product demos, references from previous customers, reviews on social media – all contribute to their expectations for the future."

"This is very different from how customers make renewal decisions. The decision to renew is based on customers' actual experience working directly with your product in their

---

167 Whitehead, Jason. 2014. "Customer Success Management And The Critical Path To SaaS Renewals". Blog. *OpenView*.

organization. If the customer's experience is positive and the value they have received from using your software matched their expectations, customers renew quickly and easily. If it doesn't, well, you know what happens."

"Poor user adoption and the lack of perceived value by customers is the greatest challenge faced by SaaS vendors. Quite simply, a customer that is not using your software and not realizing measurable business value from their IT investment will not be your customer for long."

Whenever money is involved, there is a double take within the customer's mind – do I need this? Does my team need this? Is it worth the amount I am paying? As customer success, our job is to remind them, proactively, about the value they are receiving in a tasteful manner.

There are two main ways to look at this. First, there is the data – as the idiom goes, the numbers never lie. By showing stakeholders and champions the data of what your company has provided, they can better understand the impact (and also feel good, hopefully, about finding your product!).

Brooke Goodbary, a customer success consultant currently at dataxu, formerly at Intercom and Thunder, shares how data can be a powerful aid for demonstrating value to your customers.[168]

"Customer trust is built on delivering on promises. Customer success teams need to deliver on the promises

---

168 Goodbary, Brooke. 2015. "6 Strategies For Building Customer Trust". Blog. *Medium.*

and expectations of their product to deliver value to customers. Which means no 'just checking-in' emails – you should be adding value during every interaction."

"Opportunities to tie the value of your product to hard numbers is the most compelling way to demonstrate value: an advertising analytics product increased conversion rates by 10% which resulted in an additional $120,000 ARR; a HR product increased employee retention by 5% decreased staffing and recruiting costs by $50,000; and so on. Being able to make a case for how your product is producing value allows customer success teams to build customer trust."

Second is looking at qualitative impact. Did you help reduce stress for a stakeholder? Did you help provide and maintain a system of theirs, which means they no longer have to worry about it? These things are harder to quantify but much more emotional and they should be aware of that because it is a huge value add!

Demonstrating value consistently throughout the customer journey can be incredibly persuasive. So, by the time you get to this phase, your customer would already have an idea of approximately how much value they have derived.

As David Benjamin, President of Blackbaud's International Markets Group, says, "Legacy organizations only engage with customers once they've signed them up, and at the point of renewal; modern organizations have regular touch points, starting that engagement particularly with your customer success teams as early in the sales cycle as possible."[169]

To do this successfully, best practice is to make sure your team is correctly setting the stage and being transparent with your customer from day one.

"Renewal time doesn't just pop up out of nowhere. It's part of the customer life cycle, and we know about it from the moment we sign the contract. Long before we ask our customers to renew, we have been setting the stage for this event," says Haresh Gangwani, CEO and Co-Founder at Bolstra.[170]

"While these things may not be immediate prerequisites, they are the key events that have already gone into readying customers for renewal. We should be regarding each of them as *seeds that are planted along the way to ensure success with the customer*, and, subsequently, feed the renewal process."

"While we hope that most renewals happen almost organically because our customers are deriving continuous (and improving) value from our solution, we know that customer success teams exist because that isn't always the case. Having a game plan for securing renewals is a key part of doing customer success, and the plan should (literally) begin during the sales process."

---

169 Benjamin, David. 2017. "Customer Success: It's Not About Changing Your Product, It's About Changing". Presentation, London, 2017.

170 Gangwani, Haresh. 2017. "A 3-Step Guide To Making Renewals Happen". Blog. *Bolstra*.

By focusing on the value already derived, renewals will be able to come more easily. Adam Kuznia, Chief Customer Officer at DataCamp, tells us more about why focusing on value during this process is key – if not, the key.[171]

"We should be focused on value. Customers don't renew because you've been focusing on renewal. They renew because they are extracting value."

"If the customer is truly seeing value – the account will actually renew itself. If we focus enough on value, the customer should be asking us to renew to ensure they don't have a lapse in service. Take it a step further and our customers should be asking us to expand if the value is there."

"It's easy to say that. But how do we put that idea at the center of the way we operate – just like we put the customer at the center of the way our companies operate? For me – it's two simple questions I ask with every customer engagement: Where are you finding the most value? Where do you think we need to focus on driving more value?"

"Let's unpack the first one – where are you finding the most value? There are a few reasons I ask this question: First, to understand what narrative we should be telling as we present each QBR and to clearly communicate the value that we are driving across multiple layers of the customer's organization. If not clearly communicated, it can easily be forgotten about. Second, to solve for the greater good. It

---

171 Kuznia, Adam. 2017. "Stop Focusing On Renewals". Blog. *OUT-COMES: The Customer Success Community.*

allows me to bring this value-centric story to the rest of my customer base and take the learnings from one customer and let them permeate through the rest of the business. And lastly – if retention is in jeopardy, it allows me to go back and re-communicate the value the customer has been seeing all along. We'll have eleven months of value-driving examples to walk through."

"And the second one – where do you think we need to focus driving more value? I ask this because it helps us focus. As the breadth of platforms evolve at an alarmingly rapid rate, it's important that we don't get distracted by all of the bells and whistles our product teams are building. I'm not saying we shouldn't be considering those and trying to deliver value on those fronts – but rather focus our energy where it can have the most impact. The customer can help us understand exactly where we can have the most impact for them. And you should ask them directly."

"Ask your customers those two questions as part of your formal QBR agenda – or just ask them next time you talk to them. They will actually help you retain and grow your business because they are also focused on value, not the renewal."

By making sure your customer understands the value they have received from your product, you can make your renewals process much smoother and transparent.

UNDERSTANDING FUTURE VALUE

"The new subscription model is a true test of the value a business provides," says Jonas Stanford, Director of Customer Success at Unbounce.[172]

"The longer customers see value in a service, the longer they'll remain a customer. So, company success and customer success are now inherently linked together."

"Once you know what final outcome they need, you lead them to that outcome – you become a trusted adviser who protects them. And they have reason to remain your client for a lifetime."

For a company to keep customers for a lifetime, customers must first understand why they should stay for a lifetime. By telling them more about what your future partnership holds, whether through expansions or otherwise, you can help your customers reach their long-term goals.

Helping customers understand future value comes down to two things:

1. Understanding how to get better value out of the product and whether they have any unexplored use cases for the product
2. Understanding what upcoming projects and features in the roadmap could be highly valuable to them.

---

172 Johnson, Eric. 2019. "Customer Success". Blog. *Typeform*. Accessed January 6.

First, particularly for those customers who may not have maximized their value the first time around, use this opportunity to educate and excite them about new ways they can use your product. For example, did they not use the "filter" function of the dashboard, but they used the "export report" function multiple times? Teach them about filters and use that as an opportunity to show future value to stakeholders quickly. Do they love the service, but never refer any of their friends? Tell them about your referral program!

Second, and most exciting for customers, is the understanding of future developments or add-ons to your product that could help get them more value. This is especially exciting for those customers who asked for or inspired those features! Giving them a glimpse (and timeline – again, remember to manage expectations!) of what is to come may also deter them from shopping around with other competitors.

To do this successfully, show your products' future potential for your customer upfront in the conversation.

"Before you prepare the proposal for another year of services, you'll want an idea of how you can really improve things for next year," said Matt Doyle, VP and Co-Founder of Excel Builders.[173]

"Develop an idea of how something can be done better. That way, when you ask your clients to sign up again,

173 Doyle, Matt. 2018. "4 Steps To Take Before Asking A Client To Renew". *Inc*, 2018.

they're getting something fresh and exciting like the first time they signed up."

"When you talk to your client about signing up again, keep them interested by making sure they understand all the ways that their services will get even better next year."

"In my experience, these pitches are the easiest to deliver of any you will ever give because they are based on a keen awareness of the client and their actual needs. Clients usually love to see that you've been thinking about their needs seriously, which can improve your chances of getting the response you hope for."

So far, what we've covered is pre-renewal. However, say you have already confirmed the renewal – amazing! Nevertheless, the work doesn't stop there. Use this opportunity to learn more about the customer and realign growth expectations.

"Once you do lock in a renewal, this is a valuable opportunity to evaluate what you did right – and maybe more important, what you can improve on!" says Jacob Rouser, Marketing Manager at CodeScience who specializes in marketing strategies for B2B organizations, SaaS companies, and startups.[174]

"Speak with customers about why they renewed and what they feel like should be improved. Salesforce states that renewals are an opportunity to 1) identify potential for

174 Rouser, Jacob. 2018. "Building A Customer Success Framework: How To Delight Customers And Drive Renewals". Blog. *Codescience*.

growth: are there add-ons or other products your customer needs? 2) improve payment terms: is there an arrangement that gives you more stability and makes sense for your customer? and 3) adjust pricing to reflect market rate, product innovation, or recoup discounts. Identify issues with accounts before they become problems."

Furthermore, and perhaps most importantly, use this renewal discussion to set your customers up for success for the next subscription period.

"The renewal event is an opportunity that allows them to re-engage with their customers in a full review of the success of their relationship to-date and define the objectives for next contractual year," says Daniel Farkas, VP of Customer Success and Renewals at Box.[175]

"Renewal is an event in which most customers will want to engage, even those that remained silent most of the contractual year."

"To help introduce continuity to our ongoing sales and customer success efforts, we created the renewals management team which helps to renew on time, maximize the renewal amount, and (most importantly) set the customer for success in the next contractual period."

The renewals phase is an amazing opportunity to elicit more excitement for your product and for what's to come. Even after your renewal is complete, be sure to continue the

---

175 Farkas, Daniel. 2018. "A Practical Guide To Renewals, Upsells And Customer Success". Blog. *Heresy.*

conversation with your customer and set them up for success for the next period and periods to come.

THINKING LONG-TERM STRATEGICALLY AND BUILDING THE ADVISOR RELATIONSHIP

"You must understand and appreciate exactly what your clients need when they do business with you – even if they are unable to articulate that exact result themselves," said Jay Abraham, Founder and CEO of the Abraham Group and growth guru who has helped to increase the bottom lines of over 10,000 clients creating $21.7 billion in growth.[176] [177]

"Once you know what final outcome they need, you lead them to that outcome – you become a trusted adviser who protects them. And they have reason to remain your client for a lifetime."

Similar to helping your customers understand the future value you can provide, the customer success team needs to develop a trusted advisor relationship with them to better understand their long-term needs and prepare them (and your own company) accordingly. By looking beyond the subscription periods and focusing on the customer relationship and the potential that it can achieve, customer success

---

176 Markidan, Len. 2015. "10 Customer Retention Strategies To Implement Today". Blog. *Groove HQ*.

177 Abraham, Jay. 2018. A Q&A with Jay Abraham: Strategies from Creating $21.7 Billion in Growth Interview by Adam Siddiq. Radio. The Soulfully Optimized Life.

teams can develop a strong bond and make sure that you are always on the same page as your customers mature alongside your organization.

"Renewals and growth conversations should be a natural extension of your efforts to help your customers achieve their strategic goals," says Robert Asscherick, Head of Customer Success at CircleCI.[178]

"Understanding your customers' interdepartmental and divisional dependencies exposes organic white space conversations. After all, renewal discussions should not be transactional so start early, discuss your customer's growth expectations, long-term initiatives, next year's plans, etc."

"Always be asking who, how, why, when can we be helping you more, knowing the external factors is mission critical – leadership changes, mergers or acquisitions, funding, product releases, expansion – the more you know, the better your team will protect and grow your revenue."

Trust is incredibly important for customer success teams to build.

"Research has shown that the level of trust that a customer has tracks very closely with their level of loyalty. When those levels of trust are high, renewing tends to be a no-brainer,"

---

178 Samuels, David, Robert Asscherick, and Sean Cox. 2014. "How To Prep For And Drive Renewals". Presentation, LinkedIn, 2014.

says Ed Powers, VP of Customer Success, simPRO Software Group.[179][180]

"People do business with people who they know, like, and trust and researchers call this affective commitment. On the other hand, when trust is low, researches call this calculative commitment so rather than just renew automatically, they'd say wait a minute, let's look at who else is in the market and compare. And there are some other studies that also show that there's a bit of a halo effect, so when levels of trust are high, customers seem to be a lot more forgiving."

"Psychologists tell us that trust really boils down into three fundamental factors: ability, benevolence, and integrity. Ability is competence, predictability, consistency, knowing what to expect. Benevolence is caring, goodwill, empathy, commitment to shared values, shared goals. Integrity – things like fairness, objectivity, honesty, open communication. These are the fundamental elements of trust."

"To build trust, showing the customer that you can be trusted is really important. In writing, they always say don't tell, you want to show people. And that's exactly the same thing in our relationships with our customers is that we have to show them, we can't just assume that they will see that."

---

179 Powers, Ed. 2017. "The Customer Success Trust Framework". Presentation, Webinar, 2017.
180 Powers, Ed. 2014. "Why Trust Matters For Customer Success". Blog. *Service Excellence Partners.*

"So how do you build trust? The key is to not leave things to chance. Systematically drive up the customer's trust in us."

"To do this, I like to refer to the five critical moments in the customer experience. We may interact hundreds of times with customers, but turns out that there are five types of interactions that are really impactful – connection: build relationships through commonality, power: increase mastery, autonomy, and voice, proof: show that you keep your promises, 'wow': surprise and delight, and 'truth': show character when the chips are down."

"Customer success teams that skillfully manage five critical moments in the customer experience create conditions for strong, trusting relationships to form. Lower churn and greater revenue from upselling and referrals result."

Ryan van Biljon, VP of Sales and Services at Samanage, spoke about how he values and drives customer trust within his team.[181]

"Having someone dedicated to building the relationship and long-term partnership with the customer means this person is closest to the customer and knows best how they do business. It's a much more meaningful way to grow an account than having a traditional sales team member check in each quarter looking for more money."

"At Samanage, ... a major contributor to the success of this approach is our customer success team. The key is to

---

181   van Biljon, Ryan. 2018. "How Customer Success Creates Product Stickiness For SaaS Companies". *Forbes*, 2018.

establish frequent, ongoing touch points with your customer. Have your customer success team set up a regular cadence of reviews so you keep a steady pulse on the customer's progress, needs, and opportunities to evolve their business goals."

Once you form that long-term partnership with your customer, learn about their goals and then break them down into meaningful and actionable items, as Brooke Goodbary of dataxu, explains.[182]

"Demonstrate your skills and capabilities by working towards shared goals with your customers."

"These goals can be broken down into next steps – smaller tasks that allow you to make progress towards that larger goal. This keeps you and your point of contact on track and creates accountability around who is supposed to be working on what, towards what aim. Collaborating with customers creates real connections with your points of contact."

"Coming full circle, hear everything a customer says and let them talk about the things that are important to them. You will want to make sure you get the answers to some basic need-to-know questions, but it's also important to ask open-ended questions that they can respond to as they like."

"Over time, you will be able to ask increasingly thoughtful questions that demonstrate you have a good grasp of their business and the challenges they face. Not well versed in the most important trends in their industry or the internal

---

182 Goodbary, "6 Strategies For Building Customer Trust".

politics of their multinational business? Asking great questions will leverage your customer's knowledge and help make you an expert. You'll be surprised by what you can learn just by asking the right questions."

Jason Whitehead of TriTuns takes it a step further and says to think and prepare for the next twenty years.[183]

"You may have won the deal but already lost the renewal."

"Selling for the '20-year renewal' requires you shift your sales discussion from the features, functionality and potential benefits of your system to instead focus on how your customer success capabilities will ensure customers are successful in adopting the system. From that flows the clear business value from the use of your software, and based on that, customers will be thrilled to continue renewing for the next twenty years."

"Most technology project plans focus on the path to go-live and a little bit beyond. But when you map out the critical path to ROI and renewals, you quickly see that accelerated and sustained, effective user adoption is what leads to renewals."

"So, what are actions and deliverables required over time to make sure you get the levels of user adoption you need to deliver 20 years' worth of renewable value to your customer? Not sure? Chances are, your customers don't know either, which is why you need to help them figure it out. When

---

183 Whitehead, Jason. 2017. "User Adoption & The 20-Year Renewal". Blog. *Amity.*

you walk your prospect through a 20-year renewal time-frame, what will become clear is that after the system is live what becomes most important is having a sustained effort to maximize adoption. Help your customer discover that over 20 years there will be changes to their internal structure, staff composition, products/services, operating environment, and overall organizational performance. The key to a 20-year renewal is helping them develop the capability to accelerate and sustain effective internal user adoption over the course of 20 years of ongoing organizational change and uncertainty."

By becoming a trusted advisor throughout the renewals process, you can help your customer plan for the long term and set them up for success with your product, thus further solidifying future renewals in the process.

CHURN

"Disappointment equals expectations minus reality, and disappointment is a leading contributor to customer churn. So, if you are setting unattainable expectations before they start using your product or service, it will be very hard to deliver a great customer experience and build advocacy," said Jonas Stanford of Unbounce.[184]

An account churns when they decide to end ties with your company. While you may still part as friends, the experience can really sting, especially the first few that leave.

---

184 Johnson, "Customer Success".

After all, if an account churns, not only do you lose all of the future potential revenue you could have captured from that account, but you could have also lost other business because, well, people talk. This is why it is so important to mitigate risks and manage expectations early in the customer success journey!

Tomasz Tunguz of Redpoint Ventures showed through his research that if a SaaS business is losing 2% to 3% of its customer base each month, they need to grow by at least 27% to 47% each year just to maintain the same revenue.[185] [186] Furthermore, while enterprises should be aiming for between 6% and 10% churn, the SMB market creeps up to between 31% and 58% annual churn. For mid-market SaaS companies, a figure between 11% and 22% is desirable.[187] Without a strong customer retention strategy to build this loyalty, the average business will lose 20% of its customers every year. In some industries, like B2B SaaS, this customer churn can be as high as 80%

As George Szundi, Product Marketing Manager at Natero, says: "Once you've identified a potential churn situation, engage while there's time to make a difference. A week before

185 Tunguz, Tomasz. 2015. "The Innovator's Dilemma For SaaS Startups". Blog. *Tomasz Tunguz*.

186 Simek, Elyse. 2018. "6 Surefire Strategies To Increase Customer Retention". Blog. *Userlane*.

187 Ismail, Kaya. 2018. "Enterprise SaaS Churn Rates: What's Acceptable?". *CMSWire*, 2018.

renewal is not the time to discover an account is in trouble – by then there is little you can do to help."[188]

Even though there is so much effort put into churn, the customer success industry is only starting to learn about churn trends and is still trying to figure out how best to tackle it as the statistics show:

- Frederick Reichheld of Bain & Company (the inventor of the net promoter score) shows increasing customer retention rates by 5% increases profits by 25% to 95%.[189] [190]

- According to the Preact 2015 CSM Priorities Survey, 14% of customer success teams don't know their annual account churn rate.[191]
- Over 30% of SaaS companies have over 10% churn, which can kill a business in the long term.[192]
- A SaaS Capital study found that a "1% difference in churn can have a 12% impact on company valuation in 5 years".[193]

---

188 Johnson, "Customer Success".
189 Reichheld, "Prescription For Cutting Costs: Loyal Relationships".
190 Gallo, Amy. 2014. "The Value Of Keeping The Right Customers". *Harvard Business Review*, 2014.
191 Preact and Service Excellence Partners, "2015 Customer Success Priorities Survey".
192 Murphy, Lincoln. 2019. "SaaS Churn Rate: What's Acceptable?". Blog. *Customer Success-Driven Growth*. Accessed January 6.
193 Virgillito, Dan. 2015. "10 Actionable Ways To Reduce SaaS Churn Rate". Blog. *Elegant Themes*.

- Research by Pacific Crest, which surveyed 336 SaaS companies, revealed that the annual median SaaS churn rate for companies earning more than $2.5 million in revenue, was around 6%.[194] [195]

- A 2015 Bain & Company report found that a customer is 4 times more likely to buy from a competitor after churning if the root problem was service related.[196]

- 85% of consumers churn because of poor service that could have been prevented and over half of Americans have scrapped a planned purchase or transaction because of bad service.[197] [198]

- 67% of customer churn could be avoided if the business resolved the customer's issue during their first interaction.[199]

- 11% of customer churn could be avoided if the business simply reached out to the customer.[200]

194 Skok, David. 2015. "2014 Pacific Crest SaaS Survey – Part 2". *forEntrepreneurs.*

195 Ismail,"Enterprise SaaS Churn Rates: What's Acceptable?"..

196 Seebacher, Noreen. 2016. "CMSWire's Top 10 Customer Experience & Marketing Stories Of 2016". *CMSWire,* 2016.

197 Kolsky, Esteban. 2015. "CX For Executives". Presentation, Las Vegas, 2015.

198 American Express. 2017. "#Wellactually, Americans Say Customer Service Is Better Than Ever."

199 Kolsky, "CX For Executives".

200 Ibid.

- 50% of customers naturally churn every 5 years. However, only 1 out of 26 unhappy customers complain; the rest simply churn.[201]

While there are a number of ways to combat churn, which depend on your Product Complexity and User Complexity, it boils down to two main things:

1. *Craft a strategy:* Determine how you can and will respond to each churn and what your option space looks like; for example, what is the limit of negotiation your customer success team can engage in before moving on? Or what types of refunds are allowed given a poor experience? As Ingmar Zahorsky, Director of Customer Success at ChartMogul, said, "Having a defined strategy for dealing with churn is paramount for a subscription business to maximize customer happiness and to attain predictable revenue growth."[202]

2. *Learn from each customer that leaves:* Get to the bottom of why they have decided to end the partnership, if there was anything in particular they were looking for, and if they had any feedback or suggestions for your company. As Emily Smith, SaaS Growth Specialist at CoBloom, said, "Talk to lost opportunities – customers who churned or never converted after a free trial. This will

---

201 Ibid.
202 Johnson, "Customer Success".

help you identify your customers' success factors, their top priorities. If you don't understand what's important to your customers, you can't be sure if you're helping them to succeed."[203]

The second point is especially important. Without learning about why customers are leaving, customer success teams can't properly anticipate how to prevent current or future customers from leaving too.

Blake Toder, Senior Manager and Inbound Success Coach at HubSpot, shared how he learned about customer success's role in churns and how he as a customer success team member could deliver the most impact when it came to fighting churn.[204]

"When I was hired a few months earlier, I was expected to quickly improve retention of our newest product with a low-cost, scalable service model. I approached this new role the only way I knew: Talking to customers to improve retention one conversation at a time."

"I thought the more hours I spent talking to them, the higher retention would be. But there were too many customers. For every one I spoke to, five more seemed to appear. Retention kept going down."

203 Given, Blake. 2019. "10 Companies Mastering Customer Success". Blog. *Tenfold*. Accessed January 6.
204 Toder, Blake. 2017. "The Voice Of The Customer". Blog. *LinkedIn*.

"One day, Andy Pitre, a Product Manager at HubSpot, popped into the room. I was listening to recordings of my calls, trying to find a better way to talk to customers."

"Andy laughed, 'Churn is a team problem, and the customer success department acts as the captain," he said. "They don't single handedly carry the team.'"

"Andy described the multiple players on the company 'team': engineering, marketing, sales, and services. Each plays a role in customer retention. At a product-driven company, Andy estimated the engineering team has about 60% direct influence on retention, as product quality contributes most directly to the customer experience. Sales and marketing have 15% direct influence each by targeting good-fit customers and using the right messaging, respectively. My team, the customer service department, has 10% direct influence through consultative interactions with the customer."

"I was pretty disheartened. The department I was heading – that was created to raise customer retention – had the least control over that number?"

"Then Andy explained, the indirect influence of customer service is critical, since customer conversation insights inform the rest of the company. It's like the product team is the car's engine, and the customer success team is the gas."

"Andy's words helped me break down my job as a Customer Success Manager. I first had to fulfill my direct influence responsibilities by talking to customers and maximizing that 10% influence. My second priority was using each conversation with customers to better understand their needs – and sharing those with others. With that in mind, our team starting sending a weekly email called the 'Voice of the Customer.' This email summarized the trends we were hearing on the phone. We also included a list of the top 'blockers' to a customer's activation and expansion with our product. For teams that didn't interact directly with customers, this newsletter was their primary way to understand the customer experience."

Besides calls and an email distribution list, HubSpot also dove deep into the data to learn more about why customers churned. Harvard Business Review reports how they did it.[205]

"HubSpot, a Boston-based firm that provides 'inbound marketing' software tools to small and medium-sized businesses to attract prospective customers to their websites, is one of the more 'sophisticated churn managers.' The company's software is available to customers through the cloud so it is able to track real-time customer usage of its tools and features."

"When the economy crashed in 2008 and the company's churn rate shot up, HubSpot delved deep into its churn data to see what it could find out about which customers were more likely to leave and when. Using that analysis, the firm targeted customers they suspected might cancel and offered

---

205 Gallo, "The Value Of Keeping The Right Customers".

services, like extra training on particular features, to convince them to stay."

Jill Avery, Senior Lecturer at Harvard Business School and an author of *Harvard Business Review's Go To Market Tools*, also shares how important listening to why people churn is.[206]

"If I'm interested in keeping customers, I'm interested in understanding how many leave and the underlying reasons why they are ending their relationship with me."

"Looking at churn rates by customer segment illuminates which types of customers are at risk and which may require an intervention. It's a nice simple metric that tells us a lot about when and how to interact with customers."

"By the time you see an increase in your churn rate it is six or eight months after the point in time when you actually failed the customer. If churn is your only measure of customer happiness, then you're always six months too late to influence your future."

"The most innovative firms are using churn rate analysis as an opportunity to get ahead of losing customers rather than just accept it."

By creating a transparent and honest process around churn, the customer success team can prevent future customers from encountering similar issues and help your company improve their processes and product.

---

206 Ibid.

EXPANSIONS, CROSS-SELLS, AND UPSELLS

"SaaS companies can accelerate time to profit by upselling and upgrading current customers, but only if it follows an exceptionally low cost purchase process distinct from the new customer acquisition process," says Joel York, Chief Marketing Officer at Accellion and entrepreneur.[207]

"Two great examples of upselling and upgrades in practice are Salesforce and Xignite. Salesforce has standard user-based subscription pricing, but then breaks its subscriptions into carefully designed modules of increasing functionality. If you've ever been a Salesforce customer, then you know that 90% of the upgrade process consists of you, as the customer, repeatedly bumping into the limits of your current subscription. When you need more users, or you need the capabilities of enterprise over professional, then you go online or pick up the phone and order them. The cost to Salesforce is *minuscule* compared to the original customer acquisition cost (which includes not only customers, but all the prospects that didn't buy). Salesforce is a master of application discovery, which is the process of letting less experienced customers discover for themselves the value of more advanced product capabilities."

"Xignite is a cloud services provider of on-demand market data. Unlike monolithic end-user applications such

---

207 York, Joel. 2019. "SaaS Revenue | The Beauty Of Upselling And Upgrades". Blog. *Chaotic Flow*. Accessed January 6.

as Salesforce, Xignite's Web services can be purchased separately and mixed and matched at will. The company offers a market data catalog of more than 50 services with usage-based subscription plans, all of which can be easily purchased online. The range of potential recurring revenue from the lowest plan for a single service to the largest plan for all services gives an upsell potential for each customer of around 1000:1 or total potential upsell of 100,000%!"

The renewals phase has always been an exciting time for upselling and product expansions. Not only is it a great way to check in with the customer's needs to see if we are a still a good fit for them, but it's also a wonderful way of telling how our company could be providing more value for them if they only so chose to. This can also help increase product stickiness as well.

To align on definitions, expanding a contract typically refers to the addition of more users for the same product. For example, if I currently had 10 licenses on a platform, I could expand my contract to 100 licenses. Cross-sells refer to the additional purchase of related services. For example, if I used a service to create a website, I could be cross-sold to buy a live chat functionality for my website. Upselling is the general catch all term for expansions, cross-sells, and general subscription upgrades. For example, I could have been previously on a Basic package that had 5 features, and now I could be upsold to the Premium package which has 10 features.

According to Gareth Goh, Customer Marketing Manager at DataRobot, "upsells are the Holy Grail," and he provided some statistics from a Pacific Crest survey to back him up:

"The average CAC (customer acquisition cost) on upsells was $0.17 per dollar revenue, about 19% of the CAC for new customers ($0.92). Furthermore, the companies with the highest revenues saw upsells make up a bigger percentage of all new ACV (average contract value) than other companies and the companies that grew the fastest relied more on upsells than their slower-growing peers."[208]

A 2015 Pacific Crest survey also showed that "for companies above $40 million in revenue, the top 50% of fastest growing companies generated 37% of new ACV from upsells to existing customers. In comparison, the bottom half of companies in that revenue range, or the slowest growers, received only 27% of new ACV from upsells."[209]

With statistics like these, it is no wonder that upselling is starting to get more attention. However, this is still very much a growing area for customer success with only 20% of customer success teams currently expected to work on upselling.[210]

---

208 Goh, Gareth. 2014. "4 Tips To Perfect The Art Of The Upsell". Blog. *Insight Squared*.

209 "Customer Success: Unlocking Growth From Existing Accounts In SaaS Companies". 2019. Blog. *JMSearch*. Accessed January 6.

210 Mura, "The Status Quo Of Customer Success In SaaS: Stats, Facts, Data, And Japanese Restaurants".

Daniel Farkas of Box explains how important expansions are for customer success and business in general.[211]

"There are three outcomes of a renewal transaction. Churn (not good), expansion (great), and a flat renewal."

"If you believe a flat renewal is good for you, then you need to ask yourself why. Typically a flat renewal tells you that the customer doesn't see a reason to grow your partnership (unless they already expanded mid-term or bought everything you have to offer)."

"Every customer wants to grow their own business, and so they typically need to grow relationships with their suppliers too. And if they don't do it with you, they will do it with someone else ... so think twice. And this takes us back to the beginning. You need to optimize your efforts towards upsells. It matters a lot where your new revenue comes from. Net new logos are as important as revenue from existing customers. I, therefore, feel the answer lies in the guidance that whatever system you choose, someone absolutely needs to be incentivized to keep the growth of your install base a priority."

Ryan van Biljon of Samanage also shares how crucial – but delicate – upsell conversations can be.[212]

"As a cloud-based software company, our goal is to convince businesses that it's worth their investment to overhaul

---

211 Farkas "A Practical Guide To Renewals, Upsells And Customer Success".
212 van Biljon, Ryan. 2018. "Using 'Land And Expand' To Drive Revenue". *Forbes*, 2018.

their current solutions or practices and adopt our product throughout their entire organization. We know it will pay off for them, but from their point of view, it's a large risk. We can't expect customers to purchase and implement our products throughout their entire organization right away."

"The key is to find any opportunity, even if it's a small one (and a low risk one for your customer), and prove that you're worth the investment. That could be the start of a long relationship. As our company has evolved to focus on expansion, the relationships with customers are more important to our success than ever before."

"Nurturing these relationships is no small task – especially as we grow bigger and bigger – but our success depends on earning trust. Even though our goal is to bring our service management solution to the entire organization, we often start somewhere smaller. Like many software as a service (SaaS) products, our foot-in-the-door is usually the IT department. Once we close a deal with an IT leader, our work is only beginning. We need to dedicate our people and resources to ensure success for that IT leader, and hopefully, they will be a champion of our product for expansion."

"Ideally, here's how that looks: We land a small deal by showing specific examples of how we can address that IT leader's needs, but now is also our opportunity to make a real impression. Our implementation team is all-hands-on-deck to get them ready for launch. Our customer success team sets up regular reviews, monitoring progress and lending expertise to meet their evolving business goals. Our 24/7 support team is on standby for anything that might pop up. We'll even make onsite visits if that's what it takes to help our customers get the most from our product. We want to give them immediate value in as many tangible ways as possible. Not only are we delivering our end of the partnership – we're cultivating champions of our product. That's why 60% of our customers expand within the first 90 days. If we've done our jobs, they'll like our product, they'll like us and they'll be excited to see what we can do for the rest of their organization."

When it comes to upselling, it is easy to get caught up in figuring out a sales pitch – but keep it simple. As customer success, there are a number of great ways to approach this topic while being customer centric.

"But upselling is a tricky topic. At what point in the customer journey should we reach out, and with which offers?" said Nikhil Hasija, CEO of Azuqua.[213]

"Take advantage of natural usage milestones. You can set up alerts so that you get a notification when your customer nears their utilization limits (if that exists in your product). Let's say a customer is on a pricing plan that allows them to add only five additional users. For this scenario, your upsell pitch might go as follows: 'Congratulations! You've successfully added another user. You have 1 seat left in your plan.

213 Hasija, Nikhil. 2018. "3 Ways To Drive More Upsells That Every CSM Needs To Know". Blog. *Gainsight*.

Would you like to purchase more users or learn how to buy seats in bulk to save?' The goal here is to take advantage of natural usage milestones and give customers the promotions that are best suited for them."

"Examples of milestones include when a customer tells you they want something new, when a customer exhibits in-app behavior that indicates interest in a feature they don't already have, when the engineering team completes a feature that specific customers have requested, when a customer engages with marketing material about more advanced features, and when a customer nears utilization thresholds."

However, upselling isn't something that you should be doing to all customers. Subha Shetty, VP of Product and User Experience at Zenfolio, talked about how it took a while for her to realize, but it's not about necessarily optimizing each customer on a plan to upgrade to higher and larger plans, but rather to help them determine the best plan that would make them the happiest.[214]

"So at Zenfolio, we have month to month packages. We have monthly plans and annual plans, starter plans and advanced plans, and upgrade paths to go along with it. So, we had thought of this happy path where customers would go from starter to advanced to pro and etc."

"We spent an incredible amount of time getting people to upgrade. We tried everything that we could – from pricing

---

214 UserIQ, "User Adoption Expedition: Camp San Francisco".

promotions to exclusive features – and we noticed that people were just not upgrading at the rate that we were expecting. Our initial reaction was that we were doing something wrong. So let's play around with the features within each of the plans or undercut the pricing a bit more."

"But through understanding what the customer truly wants, we realized that our customers weren't on the path or mindset to upgrade. And that is okay!"

"Our customers had identified themselves as certain types of customers and choose the plan that had best fit their needs and be happy with that plan. So we realized that customers were not thinking of upgrading per se, but rather they were looking for their identity within a plan and start with and stay with the plan that is best for them and that they could stick with for a long period of time."

"This realization dramatically changed our customer experience. It's not about moving people up but to the plan that best fits them. We really needed to create the best experience for those customers and build plans for them and their needs."

Lincoln Murphy, Founder of Sixteen Ventures, agrees and summarizes this learning perfectly.[215]

"Our customers are always changing. They're always growing. In order for our customers to achieve that desired

215 Murphy, Lincoln. 2019. "Customer Success: Who Should Handle Upsells?". Blog. *Customer Success-Driven Growth*. Accessed January 6.

outcome, they're probably going to have to buy more from us right? They're gonna have to add capacity. They're going to have to take add-ons. They're going to have to buy services. By staying with them as they grow, that's customer success."

"Customers achieve success on their own cadence on their own time frame. That may or may not fit within this nice little contract or this nice little subscription that your company provides. If you're thinking about upsells in some way of, 'Well, I don't want to hound our customers for money,' you shouldn't be doing that. Upsells should not be shoving product and services onto our customers that really don't need it. That's not what expansion should be in a customer success driven company."

Expansions, cross-sells, and upsells are great opportunities to attend better to your customers' needs while improving customer satisfaction and dependency. Even more crucially, your role as customer success is to act as a trusted partner and determine what's best for them.

***

Renewals at many times can be considered as a momentous tell-all moment within your customer's journey, but in reality, it is a time for you and the customer to check in and get excited about the value that your customer is getting and can get from your product.

KEY TAKEAWAYS

The renewals phase is about three main things:

1. **Understanding value derived**: Recap with your customer how the past subscription period went and the value that they derived. This should be a review of what you've already been telling them throughout the engagement phase, but it is helpful to present it again for all stakeholders to be on the same page.

2. **Understanding future value**: Show and excite your customer about the potential that your company can provide them, whether that is underutilized features or undiscovered use cases for your product or an upcoming future development.

3. **Thinking long-term and building the advisor relationship**: Become that trusted advisor for the customer so that you can help them think long-term with your product. Learn about and strategize around how your partnership can mature as both your customer and your own company grow.

In this phase, also creating a thorough understanding of why and how an account can churn or expand is a great and necessary learning experience for the customer success function. Whether the account expands or churns, designing a strong renewal process can not only improve your customer experience, but also set your company and your customers up for long-term success.

ADVOCACY

"Once you create a loyal customer base, it's tough for a competitor to take that away."

– Joe Mansueto, Founder and CEO *at Morningstar, Inc.*

In October 2015, Consumer Reports found that 97% of Tesla owners are expecting that their next car would also be a Tesla.[216]

With such a high satisfaction rating, it is no surprise that Tesla had known about this and wanted to capitalize on this opportunity. In July 2015, they launched their first ever referral program.

---

216 Luckerson, Victor. 2015. "Tesla's Elon Musk Responds To Consumer Reports Model S Criticism". *Fortune*, 2015.

Elon Musk, Co-Founder, CEO, and Product Architect of Tesla, sent an email to all current Tesla owners to announce the details himself.[217]

From: "Elon Musk" <elon@teslamotors.com>

Subject: Trying something new (plus party at the Gigafactory and a Founder Series Model X)

Date: July 29, 2015 at 2:05:31 PM PDT

Word of mouth has always been a major part of how Tesla sales have grown. When I meet Tesla owners, one of the first things they often tell me is how they have convinced many others to buy the car....

... If we can amplify word of mouth, then we don't need to open as many new stores in the future. So, we are going to try an experiment. ...

From now through October 31st, if someone buys a new Model S through your link, they will get $1,000 off the purchase price and you will get a $1,000 credit in your Tesla account...

Just for fun, there will also be some things that money can't buy. If five of your friends order a Model S, you and a guest will

---

217 Gerke, Grant. 2015. "Tesla Model S In Insane Mode On German Autobahn". Blog. *Teslarati.*

receive an invitation to tour the Gigafac-
tory in Nevada – the world's biggest factory
by footprint – and attend the grand opening
party. ... At ten orders, you get the right to
purchase a Founder Series Model X, which is
not available to the public, with all options
free (value of about $25,000). The first person
to reach ten will get the entire car for free.
Elon

Within two weeks, Bjørn Nyland from Norway already referred 10 new Model S owners and was the winner of the free Model X.[218] [219]

Because this was such a success, Tesla ran another iteration also available only to current Tesla car owners; however, this time the car was a a Ludicrous enabled Model S P90D and a front row seat to the Gigafactory opening.[220]

This time, the program achieved 42x ROI.[221]

Wei from China referred 188 people in two months, which represented not only the most referrals in the world but also $16 million dollars of sales all by one person. Sylvain Juteau,

218 Nyland, Bjørn. 2015. *News Update: Tesla Referral Program And Model X*. Video.
219 Hanley, Steve. 2015. "First 'Winner' Of Tesla's Referral Program Confirmed By Musk". Blog. *Teslarati*.
220 Hanley, Steve. 2016. "Bjørn Nyland Wins Second Tesla Referral Contest". Blog. *Teslarati*.
221 Patapoutian, Talia. 2019. "Case Study: Tesla's Customer-Centric Referral Program". Blog. *Swell*. Accessed January 6.

who won the contest for the North American region with 34 referrals, reported that the total number of referrals in this round was almost 5,000 – amounting to almost half a billion dollars of sales – and represented nearly a third of all of the Model S cars Tesla delivered in Q4 of 2015.[222] [223]

At the time of this book's publication, Tesla's referral program is still going strong with its most recent program offering prizes such as the launching of a personal laser-etched photo into deep space aboard a SpaceX rocket.

***

Tesla car owners were extremely enthusiastic about sharing their love for Tesla with their friends and wanted to be part of the Tesla company journey. In fact, throughout these first referral programs, Elon would directly respond on Twitter to excited participants showing his appreciation for their enthusiasm and support.[224]

This is exactly what the advocacy phase is all about.

Advocacy is the phase where we empower our customers who love our product and not only have them share that love with their friends and the rest of the community, but also become part of our company's journey.

---

222 Hanley, "Bjørn Nyland Wins Second Tesla Referral Contest".
223 Toledano, Eyal. 2016. "How Tesla's Magnetic Referral Program Delivered Over 40X ROI In Q4 2015". Blog. *Business 2 Community*.
224 Hanley, "Bjørn Nyland Wins Second Tesla Referral Contest".

As Chad Horenfeldt, VP of Client Success at Updater, said, "Advocacy should be part of the core customer success team metrics and goals. Try and make every customer an advocate."[225]

This phase is also particularly exciting for other teams. For example, marketing can get testimonials and case studies. Sales can get referrals to sell to and references to help them sell to others. Product can get input and feedback directly from those customers who are power users and are enthusiastic.

Advocacy is something which comes in many forms – from the informal to the super structured. Listen to your customers to get the best sense of what advocacy could look like for your customers.

Early on in my customer success career, I fondly recall a time when this phase really came to life. The first time that I went to an exhibit hall to table for my company, I was still getting my pitch down. I'm not a trained salesperson, and this was one of the first times I was telling potential customers in person about our product.

It was a long day at the conference, but toward the end I was pitching to a pair of math teachers. It was going alright, and it was obvious everyone had a long day. However, one of our current customers came by and recognized their friends whom I had been pitching.

---

225 Duris, Sue. 2016. "Five Key B2B Customer Experience Trends For 2017". Blog. *M4communications, Inc.*.

"These guys are amazing – you should really consider it for your school," they chirped. "My son loves it! We bought it last year, and our students have really been enjoying it, and our math scores went up by 20 points. Anyways, got to go – talk to you later!"

As they sped off, their friends' faces lit up. Even my face lit up. It was always nice to hear directly from our customers about how we've been helping them – completely unprompted too!

These math teachers were sold. One teacher started filling out our forms to get a trial for her classroom, and the other asked me for more details on how she could get her students started.

These customers, like those teachers who came over to their friends, are some of your company's most powerful voices. Your advocates can provide some of the highest impact to your company.

David Berk, Head of Sales at Hired Inc, a job search marketplace, said, "The old adage of 'great people know great people' is at the very core of our business. We knew early on that if we could deliver a superlative experience to the most talented professionals in the tech and sales industries, they would actively promote our platform to their networks."[226]

---

226 McClafferty, Alex. 2015. "3 Startup Experts Reveal Their Customer Success Secrets". *Forbes*, 2015.

By having your current customers help you promote, you can essentially create a second fanatical sales force to help ensure your company's success.

"Satisfied customers will tell their colleagues about Rackspace, becoming promoters for our brand and an external sales force for our company. Therefore, fanatical support is essential to our business; it is what lies at the core of our company because we know it's essential to our success," Mark Roenigk, COO of Rackspace, also concurs.[227]

Nick Mehta, CEO of Gainsight, champions this model of scaling.[228]

"You can take advantage and have above-average economics by leveraging a sales force that is 10 times your size and more than 10 times less expensive-namely your clients."

"Why hire 10 reps when you can 'hire' 10,000 happy customers to sell for you? And in focused markets, everyone knows everyone. So, make a client happy and when they switch jobs, they bring you along. Screw something up and that will kill 10 new deals for you. Advocacy isn't 'nice to have,' it's essential."

However, advocacy – like the rest of customer success – isn't a solo effort. It requires the entire company to be bought in and in sync. For example, marketing needs to

---

227 "10 Quotes On The Power Of Being Customer-Focused". 2013. Blog. *OpenView*.

228 Mehta, Nick. 2018. "4 Reasons You'Ll Miss Your Number Without Customer Success". Blog. *Gainsight*.

share similar value propositions and sales representatives need to know how to take proper care of a referral when they come in.

"Smart companies have realized that customer loyalty is the most powerful sales and marketing tool that they have," said Bill Price, President at Driva Solutions.[229]

Michael LeBoeuf, Professor Emeritus of management at the University of New Orleans and Author of *How to Win Customers and Keep Them for Life*, takes it a step further and said, "A satisfied customer is the best business strategy of all."[230]

Undoubtedly, this is a powerful approach. To see this advocacy focused business strategy in action, I turned to Jesse Goldman, VP of Customer Success at Influitive.[231]

"Every team here at Influitive has some ownership of customer advocacy. Why? Advocacy plays a central role in enabling our growth and efficiency. Inspiring advocacy is at the core of our mission: we run advocate-first."

"The best designed advocacy programs are the ones which help amplify the success of important initiatives throughout the organization. Our most successful customers think cross-functionally and integrate their advocacy program into top organizational priorities. We do that too. The most

---

229 "12 Impactful Customer Success Quotes". 2018. Blog. *Mindtouch.*
230 Ganapathy, "The Power To Delight: Inspiring Quotes On Customer Success".
231 Eizips, Irit. 2017. "How To Focus Customer Success On Advocacy". Blog. *CSM Practice.*

mature organizations in this area truly do run advocate first, and that makes a big difference for them, as well as their customers."

"The key to a successful advocacy program is to align program metrics with the organization's top initiatives. Advocacy programs can amplify top objectives like new sales, retention, and product effectiveness. If the advocacy program is not aligned with top organizational objectives, there is a risk that the program will become isolated. In other words, it may not be clear how advocacy 'fits.'"

With such amazing impact and collaboration, it is no surprise advocacy is the place we want all customers to get to. The advocacy phase for the customer is about:

1. **Sharing their support**: Provide an avenue for customers to share their support for the product and to be rewarded for it, whether that is being a listening ear or starting a referral program.

2. **Joining in the journey**: Give your customer opportunities to join in your product's journey and add their brand to you, whether that is through ad hoc focus groups or structured customer advisory boards (CABs).

For customer success, the advocacy phase is about:

1. **Learning about key customers**: Identify and study your key customers by listening to those who have become invested and evangelists of your product.

2. **Building a brand**: Create a brand that you and your champions can be proud of!

By providing a venue for advocacy to happen, you can help set your customer success team and company up for long-term success!

FOR THE CUSTOMER: SHARING THEIR SUPPORT

Bo Bandy, Director of Marketing at ReadyTalk, wanted to create an avenue for her most enthusiastic customers to share their support and get rewards for doing so.[232]

"All we had to do to get customer referrals was 1) ask customers and 2) make it easy for them," said Bo. "They want to share the awesome experience that they've had with ReadyTalk."

"It's about making sure we're asking. Our customers are so willing to help us, to work with us, to step up and offer up their expertise. We just have to make sure we continue to ask. We're always trying different things within our 'hub.' We always try to maintain that kind of personal element of it with our advocates – the relationship piece has been really important."[233]

---

232 "5 Key Ingredients For A Successful Customer Referral Program". 2015. Blog. *Influitive*.

233 Reed, Jon. 2016. "Readytalk's Bo Bandy On Advocate Marketing, And Moving Beyond Vanity Metrics". Blog. *Diginomica*.

Within 10 weeks of launching the program, they saw 70 advocates opt to become sales references and 190 new referrals come in. Of those new referrals, a third of them were sold within two months, which is half their usual sales cycle of four months.[234]

Just as people want an avenue to share their grievances, people want an avenue to share their love for your product.

"What we've found in our research is that many people just want to be recognized for their efforts," said Craig Rosenberg, Co-Founder and Chief Analyst at TOPO Inc.[235] "Giving people a voice can be a great reward."

Creating this channel can be a super effective tool, as research shows:

- 83% of satisfied customers are willing to become an advocate and refer your company, but, on average, only 29% of customers do and only 7% were asked.[236] [237]
- Forrester Research found that 80% of leads now start with a referral, which are most often on Twitter.[238]

234 "Influitive Customers Readytalk, Bomgar Recognized For Successful B2B Advocate Marketing Programs". 2014. Blog. *Influitive.*

235 Monfette, Deb. 2013. "4 Steps To A Thriving Customer Advocate Program". Blog. *Content Triggers.*

236 Wood, Jillian. 2015. "6 Reasons Referral Programs Fail". Blog. *Influitive.*

237 Mitzenmacher, David. 2015. "Customer Referrals: The CSM Metric You Can't Ignore". Blog. *Gainsight.*

238 Iliff, Rebekah. 2014. "Marketing In The Age Of The Customer". *Inc,* 2014.

- According to *Harvard Business Review,* "84% of B2B buyers are now starting the purchasing process with a referral, and peer recommendations are influencing more than 90% of all B2B buying decisions."[239]
- McKinsey showed "Word of mouth is the primary factor behind 20% to 50% of all purchasing decisions. Its influence is greatest when consumers are buying a product for the first time or when products are relatively expensive, factors that tend to make people conduct more research, seek more opinions, and deliberate longer than they otherwise would."[240]
- Boston Consulting Group found consumers rely on word-of-mouth 2 to 10 times more than paid media.[241]
- Large corporations as HubSpot or Salesforce now generate 70% to 80% new customers through word of mouth.[242]
- 87% of frontlines sales reps, 82% of sales leaders, and 78% of marketers surveyed agree referrals are the best leads your business can get.[243]

---

239 Minsky, Laurence, and Keith Quesenberry. 2016. "How B2B Sales Can Benefit From Social Selling". *Harvard Business Review,* 2016.

240 Bughin, Jacques, Jonathan Doogan, and Ole Jørgen Vetvik. 2010. "A New Way To Measure Word-Of-Mouth Marketing". Mckinsey Quarterly. McKinsey & Company.

241 Patel, Sujan. 2018. "How To Set Up A Referral Marketing Program For Any Industry". Blog. *Sujan Patel.*

242 Userlane. n.d. "Important Factors That Led 14 Of The Top SaaS Companies To Success". Presentation.

243 Gains, Brandon. 2017. "17 Surprising Referral Marketing Statistics". Blog. *Customer Think.*

- Referrals from successful customers have a 37% higher retention rate, and according to the Wharton School of Business, the lifetime value for a new referral customer is 16% higher than non-referrals.[244] [245]
- CMO reported that loyal customers spend 67% more than new customers.[246]

Letting your customers share their support can come in many forms, from just asking to a community platform, to a referral program.

For those who are starting out and want to create a minimum viable version, identify those customers you have a good relationship with and ask them to refer their friends. Let these customers know you will happily be their friends' point of contact to answer any questions that they may have. Or more simply, ask them to leave a review for your product on a ratings site (ex. App Store or Google Play).

Another great avenue to allow customers share their support is through what I call community. Community is where you bring your key customers together (perhaps they get a cool name!) and they are showered with perks, exciting stories and news directly from your company. Customers within the community can also meet each other and

244 Guyadeen, Julia, and Chris Newton. n.d. "How To Turn Customer Success And Advocacy Into Retention And Growth". Presentation.
245 Gains, "17 Surprising Referral Marketing Statistics".
246 Boeckelman, Chris. 2018. "40 Customer Retention Statistics You Need To Know". Blog. *Get Feedback*.

share stories about their experiences and best practices of how they use your product. After all, hearing directly from another customer who has a similar pain point is a powerful way to develop a relationship with your product's brand. Two examples of communities out there right now include Yelp Elite and Salesforce Admins, whose advocate communities have really pushed other people to become fanatics as well.

Lastly, referral programs are one of the most popular forms of advocacy customer success, in conjunction with other teams, can lead. Here, customers can refer their friends and be rewarded with a nice perk or discount on a future purchase.

Referral programs can be tricky and I could write a whole book about it separately, however, here are the main parts:

1. *Create a program:* Understand what you are offering customers for referring their friends, understand how they can refer their friends, and determine how their friends can tell you that they have been referred

2. *Raise awareness of the program:* Now that you have this great program, tell your customers about it and make sure that they know how to refer and how their friends can let you know they have been referred

3. *Educate how to sell:* Once your customers know about your referral program, teach them how to best sell your product

4. *Track and reward:* Be sure that there is a strong positive feedback loop back to the customer when someone has been referred!

A strong example of a referral program is Evernote. They spent $0 in user acquisition to acquire 100 million users and achieve a 1 billion dollar valuation.[247] [248]

They achieved this by first building a world-class product that people raved about and then created a viral referral program to empower their first fans to share their love. They knew word of mouth would be their greatest marketing asset.

Their referral program was simple: refer a friend and they get a whole month of Evernote premium – free. In return, the referrer earns 10 points for the first three referrals, which equates to three free months of Evernote premium, and when their friend purchases premium, the referrer gets an additional 5 points.

With this referral program, more than 1 out of every 8 Evernote customers were referred by another user.[249]

Once you have a great referral program, remember to advertise it! Otherwise, people won't know about it. Sara

247 Brown, Morgan. 2014. "Evernote – The $0 Growth Engine". Blog. *Growth Hackers.*
248 Martin-Muir, Fiona. 2018. "6 Referral Program Examples (& The Strategies You Can Steal)". Blog. *Buyapowa.*
249 Aramyan, Pavel. 2016. "5 Examples Of Excellent SaaS Customer Referral Programs". Blog. *Incredo.*

Ostrowski, Customer Success Coach at Ambassador, shares one of her tips on how to promote a referral program.[250]

"Oftentimes, calls to action (CTAs) are the biggest missed opportunities for brands looking to promote their referral programs. For example, eCommerce clients can include a CTA to enroll in post-purchase confirmation emails. This is a moment of peak excitement for customers and, as a result, is the perfect time to ask for a referral. For B2B clients, including a CTA in regularly scheduled content, such as an email newsletter or blog post, may be a better fit."

Lastly, don't forget to also track the results of your referral program as well, as Jeff Epstein, Founder and CEO of Ambassador, cautions:

"Referral programs break at scale."[251]

"Without the right systems in place, tracking and rewarding referrals can be a nightmare. Without a clear approach to measurement and optimization, you'll fail to gather critical insight about customers and prospects that could improve your broader marketing strategy."

Some sample metrics to track include: participation rate, number of referral sales conversations, and impressions.

While all of this makes it seem like referral programs are a no-brainer, make sure you are creating it thoughtfully.

---

250 Chesnutt, Heather. 2018. "Developing A Client Referral Program: Professional Secrets Revealed". Blog. *Ambassador*.

251 Grabowski, Pawel. 2019. "4 Referral Program Metrics That Will Help You Boost Its ROI". Blog. *Cloudsponge*. Accessed January 6.

For example, understand what the goal of your program is, have a thesis for when the right time to ask a customer for a referral is, and determine enticing incentives.

For example, Sandra Lewis, Founder of Worldwide 101, created a referral program thinking it'd be an easy win especially since they already had customers who loved them.[252] They launched a program where a referrer would get a cut of the profit.

"Over the following year, we would try three different iterations on our referral program. All of them would fail, undermining our customer relationships and our brand. Only after offending a happy, loyal customer did we figure out how referral bonuses should really work for a premium brand like ours."

She found customers were referring leads that weren't qualified, which sucked a lot of time out of their team and also increased their churn rate.

"Taking stock of our rewards program after a full year, I declared it an utter failure. The quality of leads was horrible and the number of refunds we had to issue to unsatisfied referred customers increased."

"Of course, as our paid affiliate program was crashing and burning, we continued receiving unpaid, unsolicited referrals from happy clients. Since the quality of those referrals was top-notch, we began inviting clients to become

---

252 Lewis, Sandra. 2016. "From Bribing To Delighting: How A Referral Program Nearly Damaged Our Brand". Blog. *Startup Grind*.

affiliates. What better way to show our appreciation for spreading the word?"

"To my surprise, none of our clients accepted the invitation. In fact, one long-term customer emailed to say it had offended him:

Absolutely not. I am not interested in referring clients for a reward. I am happy with your service, and if ever I have friends who can benefit from it, I will let them know because I like to help my friends.

"His frank, jarring feedback convinced me that our entire approach to rewards was wrongheaded. We had designed our affiliate program to attract people who were detached from our company and who were in it for nothing more than the monetary reward. That might work for businesses selling an impersonal, commoditized product, but it was destructive for a premium, personalized service like ours."

"I immediately shut down the affiliate program."

She realized for a product such as theirs where their process is more high touch, a referral program didn't work in its current state. Their current program reinforces customer referral behavior by providing a discount to both the referrer and the referee after the new customer receives their first invoice.

Creating a thoughtful avenue for your customers to share their support is a vital first step to building advocates for your company.

FOR THE CUSTOMER: JOINING IN THE JOURNEY

"Customers feel a sense of partnership," says Carrie Weitzel, Head of Customer Success at LearnUpon.[253]

"They know that they contribute to the improvement of the learning management system (LMS). Our product roadmap is based on the features requested by customers. We use Trello to track how many requests we receive for every feature. It will run up the priority list if multiple customers request it. That's a big benefit of meeting with customer success. Your name gets on the list and impacts priorities. And a constantly improving LMS is a win-win for customers and LearnUpon."

Customers who love your product want to share in your journey. For the customer, the advocacy phase is also about being able to provide feedback and suggestions directly to the company to create a better product tailored to their needs.

You want them to feel more invested in your product and to get them as excited as you are. After all, you always hear people boast about how they were "one of the firsts" at a superstar company or how they inspired a feature within something their friends now also use – give them that satisfaction!

"My favorite clients aren't just the ones that are happy. They are the customers that push us to be the best

253 "Why Our Customers Love Customer Success". 2018. Blog. *LearnUpon*.

possible company we can become," says Nick Mehta, CEO of Gainsight.[254]

Those in the advocacy phase want the best for your company; after all, if you can help them succeed, they want to help you succeed in any way that they can.

Jesse Goldman of Influitive also noticed how more companies are using this phase of the customer journey to integrate feedback and strengthen the customer relationship.[255]

"We see a rise in leveraging advocacy to collect important feedback: product input, messaging, how we can improve, ideas that would help customers drive value."

"We hear from our customers that an often-overlooked benefit of a quality advocacy program is the speed at which they can get feedback. By launching a high-quality advocacy program, organizations can collect client feedback much more quickly. Instead of waiting weeks, they can now get feedback in as little as a few days or even hours."

One of those companies doing this is Blackbaud. Michael Beahm, Customer Advocate Marketing Manager for Blackbaud, talks about how he wanted to create an advocacy program that was a two-way relationship.[256] He called this group the "Blackbaud champions."

---

254 Mehta, Nick. 2018. "14 Things We Learned From 800 Survey Responses After Our 5,000 Person Event". Blog. *Gainsight.*

255 Eizips, "How To Focus Customer Success On Advocacy".

256 Reed, Jon. 2016. "How Blackbaud Turbo-Charged Referral Revenue By Upping Their Customer Advocate Game". Blog. *Diginomica.*

"You can't just go and ask for a referral. The reason we're able to grow by these percentages year over year is because we've spent eighteen months building relationships with a lot of these same people."

Through this program, he created professional development certification awards and offered blogging and speaking opportunities.

"It's a win-win, because they're building their professional brand, and they're also fueling our content. That's where it's at for me: when they love what they're getting, and then we totally get value from what they're giving us."

"Previously, our customers were engaging with us once a year at the conference or at a user group. But now, we're interacting with them all the time. The feedback and the testimonials being given through the program are fueling marketing campaigns… The customer sentiment has been just very positive."

"People just really enjoy participating and feeling wanted, and feeling like they are a part of your company. It's much more than paying money to go to a conference… the sky's really the limit in terms of what we can measure in terms of impact."

Beahm cites a boost in revenue from customer referrals, to the tune of $250,000 in 2014 to $500,000 in 2015.

"We've had really strong growth every year, and it's just continuing to build. Referrals are a strong point we've been able to take to our VP of marketing."

Chris Newton, VP of Business Development at Influitive, reports how Evan Jacobs, former Senior Manager of Customer Marketing and Advocacy at Rapid7, also used his advocacy program to engage his most enthusiastic users into training and product processes.[257]

"He educated customers on how to create content with the company through testimonials, blogs, videos, and webcasts via their advocacy program. He also offered program members opportunities to share feedback with the Rapid7 product development team, and then make 'Feature Friday' videos about newly released product features for other customers to watch."

"These videos encourage other customers to learn about new features and get more value from Rapid7 products. The customers who make the videos are positioned as experts in front of their peers, and they feel special for getting a sneak peek into the product development process. Some of the videos are also leveraged by sales to help bring in new prospects."

One popular way of structuring these discussions is creating a Customer Advisory Board (CAB), where a company has a group of key customers who provide feedback, usually in person, on their customer experience and future company developments.

---

257 Newton, Chris. 2018. "5 Ways To Mobilize Your Advocates To Boost Your Customer Success Function". Blog. *Customer Think*.

"We were able to email 10 of our customer advisory board members, give them mockups of the new feature and invite them for an hour of usability testing – we threw in Amazon gift cards as a reward – and the results were amazing," says Peter Kazanjy, Co-Founder of TalentBin.[258] "With a Customer Advisory Board, you essentially have a captive audience of folks who are fired up for your success, and who you can leverage on an ongoing basis to build the best product possible."

To create a strong Customer Advisory Board, be sure that you have a clear understanding of its purpose. Puja Ramani, Senior Director of Products at Gainsight championed the Customer Advisory Board effort at Gainsight.[259]

"No one would disagree that getting customer input frequently is extremely valuable, but it is important to align internally on what the purpose of the Customer Advisory Board is. It is possible that you have multiple goals."

"For us, we want to engage with our key customers on important strategic questions for the business, but we also want to be able to have an in depth discussion on our product roadmap. To support that goal, consider hosting multiple CABs that are broken out along customer characteristics.

258 "Start Up On The Right Foot – Build A Customer Advisory Board". 2019. Blog. *First Round*. Accessed January 6.
259 Ramani, Puja. 2018. "7 Tips To Run An Effective Customer Advisory Board". Blog. *Gainsight*.

That way you can target specific goals and hold the discussion that is most relevant to that group."

Furthermore, be sure you're including customers in your Customer Advisory Board who are aligned with the goal and can help provide sometimes hard to hear feedback in order to create a better product.

"You want people who are going to give you candid feedback – tell you when something is dumb," Peter continues. "And you need to help them do this, because people don't always want to. Make it clear to them that if they don't tell you when your ideas are dumb, you're going to build something dumb... and everyone will be sad."

"Make sure the composition of your CAB matches the challenges in front of you... Maybe you're having success going after a pretty uniform mix of SMB customers but you see an opportunity to go after an enterprise audience. You'd want to add 10 more enterprise buyers to your board to get their opinions... You want the people who love this stuff – people who get really excited having access to new technology and thinking through new problems."

Happy customers and customer success teams alike want the other to become successful. Build off that enthusiasm by engaging your customers – either informally or formally – and incorporating them into your company's journey.

FOR CUSTOMER SUCCESS:
LEARNING ABOUT KEY CUSTOMERS

"Developing a customer centric strategy is as much about honing in on your corporate identity as it is honing in on your customer's identity. The more you understand your company, the more you understand the type of customer you want to attract," says Kasen James, former Senior Marketer and Content Manager at Vertical Rail.[260]

"And vice versa – the more you understand the type of customer you are attracting, the more you will be able to strengthen your organization's identity by adjusting that which is not perceived the way you want it to be."[261]

During the advocacy phase, you want to let the customers do the talking. They are already ecstatic about your product so take the time here to learn more about them.

Michael Hinshaw, CEO of McorpCX, also shares how important this is for customer success and the company.[262]

"Ask yourself: Do customers love you? If they do, you're already beating your competition every day."

"When customers come into contact with your brand, they 'feel' a certain way as a result. Using tools such as customer listening and personas, you can better empathize

260 Stringfellow, Angela. 2018. "50 Expert Tips On Creating A Customer-Centric Marketing Strategy". Blog. *NGDATA*.
261 "Tips For Developing A Customer Centric Marketing Strategy". 2015. Blog. *Vertical Rail*.
262 Hinshaw, Michael. 2016. "7 Implications Of A Customer-Centric Strategy". Blog. *CMO*.

with and serve them. By being systematic in your efforts to make your customers truly enjoy – dare I say love? – your brand, you'll create connections your competitors can't begin to match."

Learn about your most enthusiastic customers so that you can circle that information back to the customer success team and to other internal departments. For example, if you learn that all enterprise customers use a particular page of the dashboard page and love it, you can then highlight that page during the onboarding of new enterprise customers.

Remember, these are the people who are super pumped about your product. They are in the overlap in the Venn diagram of what you think your target customer persona is and what your actual customer is. Use this exercise to better understand who may actually benefit the most from your product – which may change your perception of what your target person should be!

Through these conversations, you can also learn about pain points you may not have known you helped to solve or pain points you know you can help to solve only if it was messaged better as well.

Allison Pickens, COO at Gainsight, shares how her team has broken CABs down to a science.[263]

_____

263 Pickens, Allison. 2018. "How We Drive Advocacy At Gainsight". Blog. *Gainsight.*

"Our CSMs identify 'CSQAs' (Customer Success Qualified Advocates). These advocacy leads are customers who are interested in discussing the value they've achieved from Gainsight. Our CSMs provide those leads to Customer Marketing, who works with the customer on completing an advocacy event, such as a webinar, case study, or speaking engagement."

"We've created an 'Advocacy Potential' Scorecard to aid CSMs in identifying CSQAs. This measure averages the following different Scorecards that capture healthy usage, sentiment, value achieved, engagement, and willingness to advocate: habits, sentiment, success plan progress, community activity, NPS, 3rd party reviews, and advocacy history."

At Rosetta Stone, Katie Raeburn, Customer Marketing Manager, found by creating an advocate community she was able to help those who may have churned by connecting them with successful customers.[264]

"Customers would try to contact us for help, but in many instances, they either didn't know who to reach out to our large support team or where to find the materials they needed easily," says Katie.

She then tracked activity on this community and gave her client management team access to the backend. There, they could track advocate activity, collect user feedback data, and improve retention.

---

264 Newton, "5 Ways To Mobilize Your Advocates To Boost Your Customer Success Function".

"I let client managers know what's going on with their accounts to ensure that nothing falls through the cracks... Customer segments in our advocacy program have up to 58% higher renewal rates. And it's all because we're connecting with them more effectively and helping them succeed."[265]

The advocacy phase is a great way for your customer success team, and your company as a whole, to better understand your customers and learn how to better serve not only current customers but incoming ones as well.

FOR CUSTOMER SUCCESS: BUILDING A BRAND

"Nobody wants to buy from someone they hate," says Thomas Wachtel, Editor at Element Three.[266]

"If a customer believes in what a brand stands for, they like the brand's attitude and personality, or they feel like the brand is more local or just personable – rather than being a faceless corporate behemoth – they're likely to want to buy from that brand. Especially if buying from them allows the customer to feel like they're helping make the world better, whether that's through a brand's good works or simply supporting their own community."

---

265 "Preview Callout: Katie Raeburn". 2019. *Influitive*. Accessed January 6.

266 Wachtel, Thomas. 2018. "What Brand Loyalty Means For Your Business-And Why It Matters". Blog. *Element Three.*

Building a brand your company and your customers love is a powerful tool for the customer success team as well as the rest of the company. In the modern era, it is also increasingly a more important attribute for a company to have.

A Corporate Executive Board (CEB) study published by the *Harvard Business Review*, which included 7,000 consumers, showed that of those consumers who said they had a strong brand relationship, 64% cited shared values as the primary reason.[267] [268]

"We saw that emotional attachments to brands certainly do exist, but that connection typically starts with a 'shared value' that consumers believe they hold in common with the brand," said Aaron Lottonn from CEB.

Seth Godin, author and entrepreneur, sums this up perfectly when he said, "it's easier to love a brand when the brand loves you back."[269]

As much as your product and the way you present it determines your brand, your customers' brands also determine your brand. You have to consider – when these evangelists go out, how are they perceived within their communities and what are their brands?

---

267 "The Art Of Customer Loyalty". 2019. Blog. *Help Scout*. Accessed January 6.
268 Spenner, Patrick, and Karen Freeman. 2012. "To Keep Your Customers, Keep It Simple". *Harvard Business Review*, 2012.
269 Godin, Seth. 2012. "It's Easier To Love A Brand When The Brand Loves You Back". Blog. *Seth's Blog*.

Furthermore, you have to be cognizant about how to these people sell your product as well. Are they setting up the correct expectations for incoming customers? Are they providing accurate information? Customer success's role will be to help customers who do want to share the love, channel it in a productive way.

The stronger you build your brand here in the advocacy phase, the stronger the referral-marketing channel will be. This means the lives of both the sales team and the marketing team are easier, which makes your product easier to scale! By enabling this, your company will truly see the multiplicative effects of what customer success does.

If you go to Delighted's "Customers" page, you'll see the entire page is filled to the brim with glowing testimonials from household names – Bonobos, Slack, TaskRabbit, Staples. Jack Gerli, one of the first CSMs at Delighted, shares how building a strong brand has helped make his job smoother.

"Those testimonials are very short tidbits and stories given by customers who have had phenomenal experiences with us. We then have these brands build out content and best practices guides with us, which we then use as marketing materials."

"These testimonials, even if they are about our team, are amazing. Sometimes we hear about new leads and how they got to us and they cite their experience with me and Shawn. Our customers share how we have helped them align their products with their expectations and delivered well and thought out solutions to their problems."

"They'd say things like 'I heard about Delighted and I've just heard so much about your success team and about how they can help us realize the value of the purchase that I'm making.' It's hard to look at an NPS score and say, 'this is how many people have referred us', but seeing and tracking feedback like this helps to show our success team's value."

"It's a luxury that we can focus on being really passionate about our customers."

Justine Burns, Director of Customer Success at Jobber, has also felt how her team can help create a brand to bring in more business.[270]

"Customer success touches on every single part of the company, and it's what we're known for. If you look at our review sites, our customer success is what makes us stand out from other companies."

"Our customers know us, they feel comfortable getting ahold of us, and they know they are being listened to."

Nicolle Paradise, Senior Director of Customer Experience at ADP, also speaks to how by creating loyal customers, the customer success team can also build our brand and grow the company.[271]

---

270 Augustin, "Inside Customer Success: Jobber".
271 Paradise, Nicolle, Dave Blake, and Allison Pickens. 2018. Top Thought Leaders Discuss 2018 Customer Success and CX Trends Interview by Elyse Simek. In person. 27th February.

"There's an opportunity then to really action on listening to our customers and that action is how we understand the end-to-end experience of the client, empower not just our customer success teams but our culture, our culture at any company to say the center of what we do is our clients."

"When someone listens to us personally or professionally and actions on those pain points there is a level of loyalty and that loyalty leads to advocacy."

"They're going to go tell other clients, 'these folks listened to me and understand why I bought their product in the first place and what I'm spending money on,' and that advocacy then needs to loyalty and that loyalty and retention is how we drive efficiencies."

By creating a brand customers love, you can create the perfect environment for your advocates to thrive.

***

Advocacy is a phase we want to get all customers to and is an exciting part for the company particularly given its revenue potential. However, just because you are dealing with customers who are super excited about the product, that doesn't mean that customer success can relax in any way in this phase – if anything, customer success will be working just as hard to make sure customers in this phase are treated well and rewarded accordingly.

KEY TAKEAWAYS

The advocacy phase has four main objectives – two for the customer and another two for the customer success team.

For the customer:

1. **Sharing their support:** Provide an avenue for your customer to share their support for the product (and receive some love back for it!).
2. **Joining in the journey**: Allow your customer to join you and your company in your product's journey and empower them to add their brand to yours.

For the customer success team:

1. **Learning about key customers**: Identify and learn about your superstar customers and then double down on it.
2. **Building a brand**: Form and champion a brand that your customers would boast about.

By creating an environment where customers can advocate for you, the customer success team and the company overall will see multiplicative effects throughout the revenue funnel and company morale!

CUSTOMER FEEDBACK

—

"When a customer complains, he is doing you a special favor; he is giving you another chance to serve him to his satisfaction. You will appreciate the importance of this opportunity when you consider that the customer's alternative option was to desert you for a competitor."

– Seymour Fine, Author of *The Marketing of Ideas and Social Issues*

According to the White House Office of Consumer Affairs, for every 1 customer complaint, there are 26 unhappy customers who never speak up.[272] Furthermore, 91% of those

---

272 Aksu, Hulya. 2013. "Customer Service: The New Proactive Marketing". *Huffington Post*, 2013.

unhappy customers who never speak up will simple leave and never come back.[273]

"These are usually the ones who wait for you to contact them. But when you don't, they simply stop using your product," said Jawad Khan, an active consultant to several tech startups and SaaS companies in the U.S., Middle East, and Australia.[274]

"I once worked with an online B2B marketplace website, with more than 7 million registered users, which helped connect buyers and suppliers. A staggering 40% of their users had not logged into their accounts for more than 6 months. A deeper research revealed that many of them had defected to the company's closest competitors, Alibaba."

**

This is why customer feedback is such an important part of the customer success function. We are the eyes and ears of the company and with that comes the responsibility to properly collect and address feedback both within the company and with customers.

We are also the customer's liaison to the company. Whether your team is small or big – whether your accounts are huge or tiny – you're going to hear a lot of feedback from

---

273 Shaw, Colin. 2013. "15 Statistics That Should Change The Business World – But Haven't". Blog. *LinkedIn*.

274 Khan, "7 Signs That Your Customer Regrets Choosing You".

a lot of different types of customers. Managing all of this feedback effectively and efficiently will be critical for your team's success, your company's success, and your customer's success.

As Bill Gates famously said, "Your most unhappy customers are your greatest source of learning."[275]

At the beginning when your customer base is small, it is easier to respond to your client's requests and feedback. Bugs can be quickly addressed and new feature requests can almost be immediately considered. Every customer can get white-glove treatment!

However, when your customer base begins to grow, handling customers can become tough without the right processes in place – as a one-man team or even with a small group of people. Cases become more repetitive, you can't flag a bug to engineering every time it is brought up, and and the team can become overwhelmed.

Nevertheless, it is imperative every company values and puts their customers first. After all, how can you have a business without customers? To put customers first, it is vital to have strong customer feedback channels – both to the customer as well within the organization.

For me, customer feedback was my learning mechanism.

I was the student and they were my teachers. I learned about how they prefer to communicate, how they express

275 Gates, Bill. 1999. *Business @ The Speed Of Thought: Succeeding In The Digital Economy*. London: Penguin.

themselves, what they were hiding, and what they were proud of. I heard first-hand accounts of how our product improved their lives and how it disappointed them.

I had also learned early on that handling customer feedback wasn't easy. Not only from a response to feedback standpoint, but what happens to orchestrate the conversation and flow of information.

When I first started, if a customer called to voice a complaint, I'd figure out what their pain point was and offered a solution. However, once that call was over, the only evidence that it ever happened was anecdotal. There wasn't a recording of the call, no tally of what people were saying, and typically, other teams wouldn't hear much of it unless they saw me in passing. I had been so busy putting out fires that I didn't realize the treasure trove of information that I possessed.

As I gained confidence in my role and the fires became more familiar and manageable, I started organizing feedback in a table, then in slides I could share in the all-hands meeting, and then in reports I prepared for teams. I started Slack channels to disseminate information in a more digestible manner with a regular cadence.

While it's not in its final state by any means, by organizing the customer feedback that customer success receives, something amazing occurred. You see, I'd be presenting trends and themes I'd be hearing from the field – but when we added direct customer quotes to those documents, other teams ran with it. Direct customer quotes were found in other teams' presentations, in product specs, and in day-to-day conversation around the office.

This is customer centricity at its finest; we listened to our customers, and it's really made all the difference.

***

Customer feedback is important for both the customer as well as the organization.

The customer needs to feel heard when they have a concern or a suggestion. They want to make sure someone at the company values their business. This also helps to develop a level of trust so that they are more willing to reach out in the future. Furthermore, through customer feedback the company can keep a pulse on what happens to the customer – both bad and good – how customers are interacting with the product, what they like, what they don't like, and how often something frustrating happens.

When customers feel they have been heard, the interaction becomes magical. They will evangelize your product and use the product more. When customers don't feel they have been heard or that they have been scammed, this can hurt the business more than you'd think.

For the business, customer feedback is vital. First, it can help generate new ideas coming from the users themselves, which cannot only improve brand, but also give the company a competitive edge. Second, customer feedback is a great way to better understand customer pain points, even if they don't provide solutions. By being able to hear from the customer, the company can improve their product to serve their customers better down the line. Last, but definitely not least, customer feedback is a great way to see patterns and forecast renewals and churns.

There are four main steps to managing customer feedback internally:

1. **Receiving:** How do customers reach out to you?
2. **Organizing:** How do you take in what customers say?
3. **Parsing:** How do you process what your customers are saying?
4. **Presenting and distributing:** How do you share this information with others within the company to improve the product?

Each of these is a process within itself, but by executing them successfully, your company can reap multiplicative benefits.

RECEIVING CUSTOMER FEEDBACK

In 2013, Loni Spratt had just joined Entelo, a recruiting analytics software company, as a Customer Success Executive.[276] She was passionate and excited to help her customers

---

276 Abbott, Lisa. 2015. "Case Study: How Entelo Uses In-App Customer Feedback To Prevent Churn". Blog. *Wootric.*

get the most use out of the service. However, at the time, their customer feedback loop consisted of just one bi-annual survey sent via email.

This posed two issues for Loni. First, this process was time-consuming. Second, once the feedback came in, more often than not, it was too late to respond and address the customers' issues.

"We had a response rate of 22% each time we did it," said Loni. "How accurate can that survey really be? It wasn't a large enough sample size to get information that you could actually make decisions off of."

To address this issue, Loni used a third-party service to conduct in-app surveys. Instead of having to get an email, open an email, click on the survey, and then complete a survey, customers can now share their thoughts with a few simple taps within Entelo. Not only did response rates jump up to 50%, but the customer experience was smoother because responding to surveys didn't hinder her customers' flow.

"So simple but so powerful – customers can still do what they were doing and then go back to it if they need to finish the last thing they were about to do."

The biggest benefit Loni saw was how quickly her team could respond to customers once the feedback was submitted. Gone were the days of letting problems go unaddressed for months.

"Some of our customers are actually shocked at how fast we react when a negative comment comes in," Loni said.

"We've definitely received comments of, 'Whoa. I just did this an hour ago. Is this an automated thing?' They think it's really cool."

In fact, switching from a bi-annual email survey to an in-app survey saved a marquee customer for Entelo. Loni recounts a time when a user from one of her big accounts submitted in the survey a low satisfaction rating.

She looked into the account immediately. "We looped in one of my engineers, and we got it fixed," said Loni. "If we had to wait six months to be able to act on that, this person probably would have checked out and stopped using Entelo altogether."

As we see in Loni's experience, receiving feedback in a timely manner can make or break it for some deals.

Receiving feedback refers to how the customer provides the feedback. Whether it's a survey attached to the order receipt or asking for feedback during a monthly check-in call with the customer, the company should want to make this as seamless as possible.

To accomplish this, you will need to bake in two things into your feedback mechanism – 1) trust, and 2) ease-of-response. You need your customer's trust; otherwise, if the customer doesn't believe you will take their feedback seriously, they won't want to spend their previous time to give you the feedback. Furthermore, by reducing the friction to share feedback, your customer will have a better experience providing the feedback and the more feedback you will receive.

Furthermore, when you collect feedback, be present with the customer and keep your mind open and sharp. You want to make sure you show them you care, and can think on your feet for solutions you can share with them and/or with your internal team later on.

Monique Witt Araya, Customer Success Manager at Unbounce, adds a unique perspective.[277]

"Customer success involves both listening and scouting. Actively listening to your customers is a fine art. But truly active listening isn't as easy as it sounds. What about scouting – what does that mean? Think about the role of a scout on an expedition. The scout's job is to forge ahead of the group and report back on what can be anticipated or expected ahead. They play a proactive role that's pivotal to both helping optimize the journey and ensuring everyone avoids calamity."

"As your customer's scout, your job as a Customer Success Manager is to not only listen to what they say, but also pay attention to what they don't say. By forging ahead, you can provide relevant insights to business needs and problems your customers may not even be aware of yet."

Jesse Scharff, Startup Advisor and Senior Director at the Advisory Board Company, has been helping startups drive deeper client impact, sales, and renewals for years. However, in March 2017, one of his companies had trouble

---

277 Nica, "6 Pieces Of Career Advice From Women In Customer Success".

storytelling and establishing a meaningful customer feed-back process.

"I was trying to set up this customer success initiative within a research subscription based business. We publish articles on best practices for hospitals and health systems, so say if you're a health system executive, you get to purchase access to all these articles and then all of these on demand experts."

"We had tried and failed year after year to tell stories where research, both the white papers and expert consultations, had actually led to a meaningful business change or outcome. Part of it was that we went down the case study route where we would say, 'Find me a story where a customer used one of our resources to save a million dollars plus,' or 'Find me a story where we can go really in depth and see where they used our research to solve a problem they were having.'"

"Instead of trying to tell these really long and in depth stories, what we decided to do is focus on a volume of stories rather than the quality of the stories. So we were aiming to get dozens or hundreds of quick anecdotes instead. We can then comb through those and find the very best ones."

"To accomplish this, we set up essentially an email inbox internally at the company. Then we started a campaign where we asked people who had worked on a project with a client that is using one of our subscription resources or using one of our expert consultations: 'Describe what that project was like. What was the problem that the customer had? How did they use one of our resources to address that problem? And was there some sort of business outcome or meaningful impact?'"

"In the past, we were pretty good at describing what our customers' problems were and what we had done. This was the first initiative to follow back up with them and ask them how our product impacted them."

"So we ran this campaign for about six months with hundreds of our customers and we gathered 378 total stories by the second half of 2017. From there, I would say there were 30 or 40 stories that we fast tracked to be ones that we wanted to actually develop and publish them in a pretty powerful way through marketing and other means."

This feedback became instrumental in understanding their customers, hearing from them, as well as sharing more qualitative insights with the executives during the engagement and renewal phases.

"Creating this process was fairly scrappy in that it didn't take anything to set up an email address. It took one person reviewing the inbox and reading through the stories and then compiling them. Generation two of this effort would be actually opening it up to have our clients themselves be able to submit this stuff – we would love to get to a place where clients can submit the stuff on their own."

Jesse notes there were two key ingredients necessary to create a program like this: 1) ease of submission, and 2) customer/agent incentives to submit the stories.

"You are asking people to take time out of their busy day to do something. You have to give them a little bit of something in return to get them to be willing to take the time to do that. So you have to make the process super, super easy."

"We had toyed with the idea of a web form where you put your name, your organization, what was the subscription membership that you have and then a place to tell your story. But again, every additional click or drop down item that you ask them to go through is going to discourage people from taking the time to put it in. So we were wrestling with what's the easiest way to get all of this information in effectively."

"That was why the internal email inbox worked so well. We just told people, 'If you could submit it in this format, great. But if you want to total stream of consciousness type your feedback out, we'll take it too.' And that seemed to help a lot to get people to submit stories."

The second thing is to have the right incentives set up, whether monetary, status, or otherwise, so it would be worth the time to submit.

"You need something to motivate them to take their time to do it. Showing them the potential that something good's going to come out of their submission."

"What we thought through was creating a set of awards or something at the end of the year where we take our ten favorite client stories and publish them on our website. This got people to respond with things like, 'I thought this was a cool project that we did and it would be great if it got profiled.'"

"One thing that we did in the spirit of motivating people to submit their stories, I would send out an email once a month that tallied the stories submitted for every department and the stories submitted for the different types of subscriptions we offered. Then, I would also select three or four of my favorite client success stories and highlight them at the top of the email. I'd put the name of the client, the story, and pictures of each of the staff that submitted them. This email then went to all of the research department, all the client management department, and then a number of executives including our CEO who was really interested in this initiative."

"I think people also got motivated by both seeing how well their department was doing, but also the possibility that their story and their picture would be put on this email that goes out to the CEO and all of these department leaders."

There are many ways of collecting customer feedback, but what is important to remember is to make it something is operationalizable and is easy for your customers and agents to use.

ORGANIZING CUSTOMER FEEDBACK

Patrick Hansen is the VP of Customer Success at a technology review website, where buyers can read unbiased reviews of products and vendors can hear an authentic voice of the customer.[278]

---

278 Hansen and Govani, AMA with Patrick Hansen and Grishma Govani of TrustRadius.

Over time, they built a powerful customer feedback tool which helps them empower their customers to take actionable steps from the feedback they receive.

"When we started forming up our customer success team, I was a one-man band and our 'product' was a commitment to do certain things on behalf of our clients. You might call that vaporware!"

"From day one of generating our first dollar, our focus has been on working with vendors to scale their presence with us and leverage that VOC (Voice of Customer) across their sales and marketing programs. How we do that has changed dramatically now that we have a platform where our clients can do a lot of that work themselves. Our platform and the dedicated CSMs tied to it make it easy for our customers (and easier for us!) to get it all done."

Grishma Govani, Senior Customer Success Manager at the same firm chimes in. "To leverage review information and make sure it gets communicated back to our customer's internal teams, we will dissect every review. If the review has a rating of 7 or above, we will extract quotes for sales, marketing but also extract quotes for product, customer success, service feedback along with any upsell or cross sell opportunities."

"We create themes for each function. For example, for marketing and sales: we will create themes or tags based on benefits typically experienced by customers, or good responses from customers to help sales handle objections, quotes on feature benefits and many more. For product, we will create themes around specific features. Our platform allows us to tag quotes within reviews on all these different themes and sub-themes which then gets reviewed by different functions."

What systems such as the one Patrick and Grishma work for do is help organizing all of the customer feedback you receive in a more digestible manner.

Organizing refers to how the customer success team (along with any other customer facing teams) can record customer feedback. It is important all customer feedback is accessible from one place; otherwise, it will get much messier down the line as your customer base grows.

When you're just starting out, your organization tool could be a Google form which feeds into a Google Sheet or you can use third-party tools or a tagging system within your CRM. As long as there is a process everyone in the company can follow, this will help standardize and encourage more employees to share what they hear from the field.

For companies which are B2C (business to consumer) or where accounts may be smaller and therefore do not justify whole teams getting together to solve certain problems, the customer feedback process may be slightly different.

Superhuman, a premium email client startup, loves receiving customer feedback. One of their values is to create delight. This has helped them become ruthlessly customer-centric which means their customer feedback process is world-class. Vivek Sodera, their Co-Founder, describes how they created a customer feedback process with thousands of customers.

"We made the process of giving feedback to us incredibly simple. You can either do Cmd+K 'Feedback' or click the message bubble icon in the bottom. This opens up a pre-populated email where all the customer needs to do is add their feedback and click send."

"Once a customer sends us their feedback, our team created this tool where we just highlight the piece of feedback and right click to add the feedback and other metadata to our customer feedback database."

What's innovative here is that within this customer feedback database, each piece of customer feedback is tied to the account, tagged for categories, and even has a link to the original correspondence so you can read the whole message.

The greatest part about the system is now any team – product, sales, growth – can go into this database and look for anything they might need without needing to bother anyone else.

"I can go in at anytime and see how our customers are feeling and what they feel like we should work on next. Once we decide on what to work on next, our product team and engineers can also review word-for-word what our customers our saying so that they can build the best solution possible for them."

This has helped to keep their team relentlessly focused on the customer and their insane waitlist of over 5,000 people shows how attractive their product has become.

Slack is another company which organizing and operationalizing customer feedback in a creative way. In fact, they turned it around and organized their feedback as they were collecting it.

When Kenneth Berger joined Slack in June 2014 as their very first product manager, he found their team received a ton of feedback, however it was naturally hard to decipher.[279]

"The problem is not that startups lack feedback, it's that they don't know what do with it, or what they should react to."

"It's important to understand, for example, that your support requests are coming only from your most engaged users. If you're talking to people that are already engaged with the product by definition, you're excluding all of your potential customers who aren't engaged with the product."

"Quantitative data can tell you if something is wrong, and qualitative can tell you why."

"Early on, I sort of said to myself, 'Okay, if everyone on Twitter says this is the greatest thing since sliced bread, what am I here for? How am I supposed to add value?' It would have been so easy to just keep looking at the single source of feedback, which was so nice – everyone loved Slack! But that wouldn't have been good long-term."

279 "Slack's First Product Manager On How To Make A Firehose Of Feedback Useful". 2019. Blog. *First Round*. Accessed January 9.

Therefore, he had a different approach; start with a hypothesis and go out into the field and collect data to test it.

"My hypothesis was that we weren't serving those larger teams as well as we could. Within a week or two, I was out there with a set of questions that really were not focused around any particular problem, but just around understanding how those teams used the product."

"The easiest thing I can say is that your biggest conclusion will be obvious. A lot of people struggle with how to use qualitative data, because let's say you go out and do interviews with five people. You say, 'Well that's only five people. How do I know what to pay attention to, or whether this is important?' That's where all that preparation upfront becomes so important. You didn't just go to five random people. You thought about what your hypothesis was, and who the right people would be to go to and test that hypothesis."

Berger advises to tread carefully with this method. "Choose your hypothesis carefully, choose who you talk to carefully, and it will almost always be clear what to do next."

Organizing customer feedback so it is digestible is imperative for a customer success team to function efficiently.

PARSING CUSTOMER FEEDBACK

"People tend to focus on the wrong part of the feedback. Instead of focusing on the root cause or underlying issue behind the feedback, they focus on the *subject* of that feedback," said David Cancel, the CEO of Drift, a messaging app for customer success and sales.[280]

"For example, a customer might ask, 'How do I integrate this with Trello?' And if people hear that question enough times in feedback across their team, they'll start to say, 'We have a Trello problem. OK, let's add Trello features. We need more Trello features. I keep hearing about Trello.' So they'll run and rush to go fix the thing that they think is the subject: Trello."

David uses a framework he named the Spotlight Framework. Here, you listen carefully to what the customer is asking for and put them into one of three buckets: 1) user experience issues, 2) product marketing issues, or 3) positioning issues.

"Using this framework, we can see that a question like 'How do I integrate this with Trello?' fits into the user experience category. Because clearly the customer already knows that the integration is possible. It's not a discoverability thing. They're not asking if it's possible, they know that it's possible, they expect that it's possible, but they just don't know how to get it done."

"In contrast, customers could be asking, 'Hey, can you guys integrate with Trello?' or 'Can I integrate this part of your app with Trello?' Once again, the important part to focus on here is not the Trello part, it's the 'Can you ...?' or

---

280 Cancel, David. 2016. "A Simple Framework For Handling Customer Feedback". Blog. *Drift*.

'Can I …?' And what that tells you is that you have some level of product marketing issue. Because if you can integrate with Trello, the fact they're asking you that and that they don't know means that they weren't educated properly along some part of the sign-up or getting-started path."

"So that's how I think about user experience issues vs. product marketing issues. But there's also a third category in my framework: Positioning. Positioning issues are when someone gives you feedback, and they're usually trying to be nice, and they'll say something like, 'I'm probably not your target customer, but …' Now, if you know that person is your target customer, there's probably something wrong in your positioning that's leading them to believe they're not a good fit."

"The main thing is to categorize all of your feedback that you're getting. And then the action can be – depending on the cadence of your company – that every week or every month you look at the top user experience, product marketing, and positioning issues that you've categorized using the framework. From there, you can prioritize them and start making progress on them."

"We all need to do more listening. But then we need to take it one step further. We need to take what we've heard and categorize it."

***

Parsing refers to understanding and internalizing the feedback you've already organized to determine actionable takeaways just like David does at Drift.

As Jay Nathan, SVP of Customer Success at PeopleMatter, said, "Customer success leaders should also be able to provide input on strategy of the business given their proximity to and regular interactions with the market. They should serve as the eyes and ears of the market for the executive team and be able to massage massive amounts of data into useful information the company can use to make decisions."[281]

It may sound tedious, but it is important for someone to be combing through all feedback that is entered, tagging, assigning tasks, and running analytics. Furthermore, there are so many ways to organize and slice the data – by account, by CSM, by feature issue, by account size, by OS model – so to have a systematic way to understand what your customers are saying is vital to empowering your customers' voice at the company.

This analysis is particularly vital for 3 main reasons:

1. *Understanding frequency of events*: Without understanding how often an issue arises, it becomes harder to prioritize its fix or solution. For example, if a feature crashes 100 times but that only represents 1% of all users, it is important to know when deciding whether fixing that

---

281 McLaren, "14 Quotes On Succeeding In Customer Success Leadership".

would take priority over a tiny thing that inconveniences 50% of the user base.

2. *Delegating solutions*: Particularly if there isn't a known solution, it is important to assign CSMs to dive deeper and investigate feedback further. Sometimes this investigation uncovers a hidden bug no one else has been experiencing or a loophole sales needs to close!

3. *Demonstrating impact through data*: Without numbers, it becomes so much harder to make your case when you present! For example, say there is a small feature your team recently deployed; however, it helped your customers increase their revenue by 50% more than expected. Your company team should know that not only for boosting morale, but also so they can double down and continue to improve that feature in the future, instead of thinking "it's a small feature."

The customer feedback process may look different for every company; however, the themes don't change. For example, deal size could be an important factor when it comes to customer feedback. Feedback from a marquee client versus feedback from a smaller client should be weighed accordingly. Not because any feedback is more or less legitimate, but rather when it comes to prioritization, understanding the impact of the action (or inaction) is imperative.

For example, Jennifer Walker from Motivis Learning shared her steps for processing feedback. Motivis

Learning is an education technology company whose customers are educational institutions, like universities and school systems.

"I hear requests from customers all the time. My job is to be the liaison to build a use case for the thing that the customer is asking for and to work with the product team. It can be rough, but diplomacy is key. Also, knowing when is the right time to escalate something is really important."

"So let's say – the customer says, 'I want you to make everything purple.' Well when one customer says it, it sounds a bit crazy! Why would we do that? But, after I hear 'we want everything to be purple' over and over again across customers, it is my job to go to the product team to say that we are hearing a groundswell of support to change everything to purple."

"To organize all of this information, we use an Atlassian product called JIRA. However, the intake and discussion around the feedback is very narrative. I have an account meeting where we pull all stakeholders together and we talk about the customer experience one for one."

Once she feels there is enough response from customers, she'll bring the data to the product team.

"I'll ping the [product managers] and say, 'I'm hearing this. We want to look into this. Can we set up a meeting so that you can hear it from them?'"

Jennifer also adds the importance of knowing when to take in the feedback yourself and when to act as a connector.

"Try to facilitate a conversation that will allow your company to make the right decision and for the customer to be heard and to feel acknowledged. There's a balance of efficiency when acting as a liaison to the customer. There is also a moment to step aside and connect the customer to the right people at the company to be heard. There's only so much that you can do and it shouldn't always be a game of telephone."

"Sometimes the job isn't always to absorb everything, but it's to connect people. So there is something to be said for not hashing it out – the back and forth like 'I think the customer thinks...' and then the product team will say 'Well, what about this?' and I'll say 'I don't know I didn't ask them that yet.' It's better to put everyone in a big room so that they can extemporaneously talk about ideas together.

"This also has two great benefits – A) the customer feels valued. They can see that we want to hear their thoughts, and B) the product team is hearing straight from the horse's mouth the requirements from the customer and can iterate on ideas together. For example, 'even if it's not purple, what if it was like a really really dark blue?' This is a way for the customer success and product teams to figure out what is at the heart of what the customer is asking for and to also determine whether something else could satisfy their requirement in a way that would also satisfy other customers' requirements."

Allison Pickens, Chief Operating Officer at Gainsight, also adds how when it comes to organizing, you sometimes will need to think beyond the words the customers are saying to get to the root of the feedback.[282]

"Is the customer always right? No, but customer feelings are always right."

"Feelings aren't necessarily right or wrong, but they are always there. The debate comes on how we can make these feelings positive."

Julia DeWahl, General Manager, Trade-Ins at Opendoor who has been at the company working with customers since the beginning adds to this conversation.[283]

"Instead of 'customer is always right' we say, 'the customer pain is real.' We spent a lot of time really understanding the pain's root cause and then from there, thinking – how can we design the best solution for this pain."

"Our late checkout program is a great example. Sellers were selling their houses on Opendoor and they wanted the proceeds to go to the down payment on to their next house. However, they wanted to move in one day – after all, coordinating the moving trucks, etc. is just easier to get it all done at once. From this, we created the late checkout program where the seller would sell to us, and then we would rent the home back to them for two weeks so that they have more flexibility."

"No one told us to create this late checkout solution, but we listened to their pain point and came up with this solution."

---

282 Pickens and DeWahl, "#Techtalks: All About The Customer".
283 Ibid.

Lastly, it is also in this stage where we better understand company focus and prioritization. Once you better understand the impact of the bug or feature request, you will also need to find the confidence to say "no" and have that conversation with your internal team as well as with your customers. Rick Perreault, the CEO of Unbounce, shares his experience from his company's early years.[284]

"It's especially tough when you're bootstrapping, and you're Ramen profitable, and you start getting recognized brands calling you up saying hey, if you just build this feature, we'll buy. It's so tempting, but it's also a huge distraction. We fumbled around for two years trying to do everything for everyone, and it took a lot of discipline to get focused."

Lincoln Murphy, Founder of Sixteen Ventures, adds, "It seems odd to have to say this out loud, but if you do whatever it takes to please the customer (like never saying 'no' to customization requests), but you do so to the detriment of your company, this is not customer success."[285]

Organizing customer feedback isn't easy, but it is a crucial step to truly understanding what your customers are saying and figuring out what are the best next steps for your customer and your business moving forward.

---

284 Turnbull, Alex. 2015. "My First $100K In Monthly Revenue: Rick Perreault, CEO Of Unbounce". Blog. *Groove*.
285 Harvey, Kate. 2015. "SaaS Customer Success: The Secret To Reducing Churn And Increasing MRR". Blog. *Chargify*.

PRESENTING AND DISTRIBUTING
CUSTOMER FEEDBACK

Hiten Shah, the founder of Crazy Egg and KISSmetrics, and the author of the Hitenism newsletter, asked his readers to share their biggest product problems, and in more than 100 replies, customer feedback was one of the top two themes of problems product teams experienced.[286]

"Having a regular cadence of customer interaction to develop insights and product intuition."

"My main problem is to get to know our audience and talk directly to them."

"In product, we're expected to be customer-centric. We're supposed to get feedback and talk to customers all the time. It's literally our day job. But that's on top of making sure we're focused on building the right things and helping our teams ship too."

Product, along with other teams, should be working hand in hand with customer success to address problems like those that Hiten's readers posed. Once all of the feedback is organized, the customer success team now has the duty to distribute the content appropriately.

Presenting refers to how the customer success team presents or shares the feedback with the rest of the company – primarily the product team, but also the sales, operations, and marketing teams. This is the "action item" from the

286 DeMeré, Nichole. 2018. "How To Tackle The #1 Problem Product Teams Face: Customer Feedback". Blog. *Wootric*.

database and it is important everyone in the company is aware of the customer feedback database existence as well as use cases.

For example, product may have filtering access so when they need to brainstorm something, they can read directly what customers are saying instead of having to set up a meeting with the customer success team. Or having a bi-monthly meeting where customer success and product could review what customers are saying and hear about what's in the pipeline and how these things are being addressed.

According to McKinsey, this is one of the major value-adds that customer success can bring to an organization.[287]

"One hallmark characteristic of a strong customer success organization is that customer insights are shared across the entire organization. In that way, the customer success organization becomes the company's 'learning engine' – relaying their findings from the field to the sales, product, and marketing teams. This feedback loop is critical in allowing for the overall product, value proposition, and delivery model to improve."

In a 2015 study, McKinsey also found that while 44% of companies surveyed focus resources primarily on customer experience rather than the product, only 13% feel they effectively identified their customers' decision journeys and

---

287 Miller, Allen, Ben Vonwiller, and Peter Weed. 2016. "Grow Fast Or Die Slow: Focusing On Customer Success To Drive Growth". McKinsey & Company.

know where to focus marketing, and thus have difficulty delivering growth.[288]

Furthermore, 46% of respondents said they base marketing decisions on data rather than qualitative metrics, but only 10% believed they were effective in using insights in customer behaviors and feeding them back into the organization to improve performance. This is why distributing customer feedback properly within an organization can really differentiate a company from its competitors.

With customers expecting quick turnarounds for answers and with internal teams – such as product and marketing – needing feedback constantly on the dime to make sure the company is providing the best possible features and improvements to our customers, customer feedback management really becomes a beast.

I spoke with Tim Raftis, Head of Customer Success at Affinity, about how he handles customer feedback, particularly at the beginning stages when they were still iterating on their core product and getting feedback from early users.

"I created an email distribution list called Customer Feedback. So, anytime I get an email from a customer – good, bad or ugly – or a great compliment, I just immediately forward it to this distribution list.

---

288 Edelman, David, and Jason Heller. 2015. "The Marketer Strikes Back". McKinsey & Company.

"If you talk to the employees at Affinity, they will tell you that there's a steady stream of constant feedback directly from the customer."

"And when our customer calls and says, 'Something's really broken' and we can confirm it on the customer success side. I'll literally just go out to the floor and grab the engineer that built the feature. Less so 'fix this' but more so 'look how painful this is when we do this to our customers.'"

"We do it this way because I'm a big believer in pushing information down or across the organization because if you hire really smart people they'll make the right decisions."

"It's important that there isn't some boss telling engineers what to do, but actually letting engineers – and everyone else on the team – to understand the problem from the customer's perspective. I don't want to make the decision, but rather want to give people the information they need and have them understand the why behind what we're doing to help them make better decisions."

Jo Massie, Head of Customer Success at Slido, takes it a step further and operationalizes how she and her team present customer feedback.[289]

"Sharing customer feedback and data with other departments is our success team objective for this quarter actually! We realized that our customer facing teams didn't feel like they were able to have a big enough impact on our roadmaps

---

289 Massie, AMA with Jo Massie of Slido.

and they were missing the understanding of how/why these were developed … and our product team were missing it from the other side."

"Our CX team are owning this and they collect insights in two different ways – our support tool and Slack. In Slack, we have three different channels: #customer-insights, #customer-pains, #customer-love"

"Everyone who interacts with a customer posts the information including the why and background into those channels which anyone in the company can join – next step is figuring out how to scale this as we continue to grow."

"It's really important for our CEO and Head of Product/product managers to be able to see those there and respond. The CX team then provide weekly and monthly reports which track how much things are appearing and what we should focus on fixing/having in our next roadmap."

"So far it's working really well. We polled our team on Tuesday and 60% of them feel they're already influencing the product even though we started in September of 2018."

Julie DeWahl adds how you can incorporate this feedback-friendly culture to your organization.[290]

"Early on, we had three customers. So the entire company would all go into a conference room and every single person talked to all three of the customers."

---

290 Pickens and DeWahl, "#Techtalks: All About The Customer".

"Now that we're much bigger, some people in the company are quite distant from the customer. This is where customer storytelling really comes into play. To do this, every new hire that comes on needs to understand the company's vision and how the company got started. Furthermore, each new hire that joins Opendoor is required to join these three Slack channels – #customers, #review, and #nps."

"I highly recommend that customer success has more meetings with everyone. Become buddies with the engineering manager and with product! Have someone from the field share a story every meeting! We had weekly CX meetings and included a special guest team join us every time, so that – for example – the brokerages team could learn more about CX and vice versa."

"It's about creating those spaces where feedback can happen and for people to learn about the customer."

Jesse Colligan, Director of Customer Success at Neoway Business Solutions, also shares how bringing in a layer of data and personability can help elevate the conversation.

"A challenge that my organization has right now is aligning other departments. Having to explain the same thing a million times over is exhausting and not always effective. So instead, have some source of truth that other people can come to better understand what customers are feeling or experiencing."

"The ultimate source of truth usually is whether or not a customer renewed – and why. If they renewed, great – let's better understand how we made them successful; if not, let's get a sense of why they didn't renew and start to track it. This is a really important step and will only strengthen your internal advocacy efforts."

"It's one thing to say, 'Hey, customers are upset because of x.' It's another thing to say, 'Hey, we're losing $10,000 a month at this stage of recurring revenue because we haven't resolved this issue.' Having the data to back up your conclusions will make your life a million times better."

"Lastly, to empower those that aren't customer facing to become more customer centric, I believe it starts from the moment a new employee enters the company. You should have a thorough onboarding process that allows new employees to absorb who customers are and what they care about. The challenge is most startup team leaders don't feel it's a valuable use of time to put their new engineer in this type of thing for a month – it's all about *I need help right now or the company may fail* type mindset."

"The 'customer' isn't an abstract concept – it is a real person. That face time is in my view absolutely critical."

Presenting customer feedback effectively and efficiently is how the customer success team can help bring all teams together and to keep beating the customer drum. After all, all teams must work together to help the customer succeed.

Dave Blake, CEO of ClientSuccess, summarizes this sentiment well.[291]

"It's not just one department that's in charge of customer success. It's all departments. Whether it's sales, marketing, product, support, or customer success, they have all touched the customer in some way, either directly or indirectly, and so you need to have them each plugged in and aligned with the proper cross-functional accountability and empowerment for each."

***

For all teams, regardless of Product Complexity or User Complexity Scores, customer feedback is vital to any organization. It provides a pulse of how customers are feeling and how we can better serve them. By instituting clear processes for handling customer feedback, your company will not only reap the benefits but also provide better service.

As Justine Burns, Director of Customer Success at Jobber puts it, "Customer success is a highly valued team because they know our customers best."[292] So let's ensure that both our teams and our customers benefit!

---

291 Alder, Burke. 2019. "Building Out Your Customer Success Department: 3 Do's And 3 Don'Ts". Blog. *ClientSuccess*. Accessed January 9.
292 Augustin, "Inside Customer Success: Jobber".

KEY TAKEAWAYS

There are four main steps to managing customer feedback:

1. **Receiving:** Make it easy for your customers to share feedback with you! This also includes building a sense of trust between you and your customers so that you can get that honest and raw feedback.

2. **Organizing:** Record feedback in an easily accessible way, ideally in one place!

3. **Parsing:** Process what your customers are saying in a digestible manner.

4. **Presenting and distributing:** Share this information with others within the company to improve the product.

By systematizing your customer feedback, you can create a customer success organization that can scale efficiently while staying customer-centric.

PART IV

BEYOND
SQUARE ONE

Now that you have the basics of what the customer success role does and how you can apply it to your company, it is now time to look beyond. Let's now understand how the increasing demand for customer success employees affects you, on how to improve yourself and your customer success strategy, how to scale your team, how to help other departments within your company, and how to work with tough customers.

PRIORITIZATION AND PLANNING AHEAD

———

"To be a successful customer success leader you have to see everything as a journey. Customers will not do what you need right away; they will always have questions and areas for improvement. A customer success team will never be smoothly running; there will always be another hurdle to overcome or new thing you can be doing to improve. As a customer success leader, you therefore have to guide your customers and team through a journey, step by step, to achieve your goals."

– Jessica Weisz, Chief Client Officer at Soapbox

"Start small," says Keri Keeling, Head of Customer Success Enablement at Oracle.[293] [294]

"Elephants don't get eaten in one bite. Great customer success is nothing more than 'small ball.' To come out of the gate, swinging at the fence, it can feel very, very intimidating – and it is – because it's a lot! That's where you will feel like you're at the bottom of the mountain."

"Pick your battles, choose your true North and nibble away at where you want to go. You're going to feel very quickly – especially at smaller organizations – whether something is working or is not working. And you'll be able to iterate accordingly."

"It's a series of little things that you do each day to improve the relationship, loyalty, and adoption with your customers. Develop a plan that focuses on the things you can do today – surveys, adoption campaigns, product road map, great onboarding experiences/fast time to first value, etc."

"Once you have the small things mastered, continue to add other small things that you can do today and increase your plan and bring on other things that you can that are of a bit larger scope – such as customer journey mapping, quarterly business reviews, customer success team development,

293 Harvey, "16 Ways To Master Customer Success From Industry Leaders".
294 Planhat. 2017. *Keri Keeling, Oracle's Head Of Customer Success Enablement & Quality.* Video.

etc. – and keep growing your efforts in small steps with each planning exercise."

"Before you know it, you will have an award winning customer success team and a well-baked strategy!"

Perhaps one of the most common phrases I hear among my peers in customer success is that there isn't enough time to get everything done and to treat all of our customers the way we want to treat them. They've taken too big a bite to chew. However, we want the best for our customers, so we work hard to make sure that they are satisfied.

According to a 2015 Preact Survey on Customer Success Priorities, only 35% of customer success teams feel they're firefighting and a fourth of that – 9% – are feeling in control.[295]

You may think – well if you map everything out well and create the correct processes, you should be able to manage everything effectively, no? Well, unfortunately it's not that simple.

I remember when I first had everything set up. I had presented and implemented my initial thesis for our onboarding, engagement, renewal, and advocacy strategies. I was very proud of it! It was a great first start, but little did I know how much work I had set myself up with. After all, back then, I was still a team of one.

I started getting to know our customers: hopping on calls with them to understand their pain points, letting them air

---

295 Goodbary,"Dissecting Preact's Customer Success Priorities Report".

their grievances about our service, and showing them how their children could get more value out of our service. I knew this was by no means scalable, but I wanted to learn more about our customers.

So far so good – I was able to keep a solid onboarding schedule, calendared all of my engagement campaigns, had a game plan for renewals, and was excited to start building a community for advocacy.

However, one by one, each of the initiatives became deprioritized. My days began filling up with fighting fires and meetings around fighting those fires.

"The app isn't working and I've restarted it two times already."

"I want to talk to someone now about my kid's latest test grades."

"I thought my daughter would have been using this for at least five hours a week, and she's only used it for two hours so far – what's happening?"

I remember thinking there were some days where I finished fighting all of the fires for the day, and I would look at the clock: 4:45pm. I knew being in this role was going to be a learning process, but it became much harder to learn when the majority of my time was spent responding to customers.

What made it harder was I was told to focus on getting more referrals. A very worthy cause, but it was hard to get a referral engine going when I was still struggling to get customers to adopt the product properly. Furthermore, by making my top priority getting more referrals, I couldn't focus on revising my onboarding or support processes to help save time and to keep our customers from being frustrated.

Ultimately, I realized my number one focus should be my team and the value my team could bring to both my customers and my colleagues. I started by providing timely feedback to internal departments so they could become more customer-centric. I started setting goals and priorities for each quarter and then broke them down into weeks. I started prioritizing scale and proactiveness, rather than waiting for people – customers or other individuals – to tell me what should be my focus. It was a huge learning and leadership opportunity for me, and I know the journey isn't over yet.

It reminded me of what Chase Clemons, Support Pro at Basecamp, once said: "It's tempting to sacrifice yourself on the altar of customer success. Ideas like 'the customer comes first' and 'the customer is always right' leads to a company elevating customers over the team. But that's an unhealthy perspective. It'll leave you looking for any escape route you can find."[296]

"You come first. You have to put on your oxygen mask first. You can't help others if you're gasping for air yourself."

---

296 Harvey, "16 Ways To Master Customer Success From Industry Leaders".

Through this process, I learned how to grow as a customer success leader; understanding that while things pile on, focus and planning ahead is vital.

As customer success, you will constantly be adapting your processes. You'll hear feedback from your customers and their evolving pain points. You'll hear about new product initiatives your team can use to upsell or increase engagement within accounts. As your customers and your product evolve, so must your customer success team. They must quickly adapt their systems and processes to the changing landscape; whether that is creating new systems or even hiring a new team member.

Once you have your processes set up, it will become painfully clear there is a lot of work to do, but not enough time to do it. To ensure you are developing as a customer success function, make sure that you are always doing these three things:

1. **Understand your priorities**: Give yourself space to see the bigger picture and to understand what your team should be tackling first. As much as we'd like to do everything, we can't; so understanding priorities will be key.

2. **Manage your time wisely**: Because customer success is a combination of strategy and execution, manage your time wisely so that you have time to be proactive and time to address fires in case they appear.

3. **Plan ahead to frequently reevaluate and adapt**: As your company and customer base grows, you will need to

constantly reevaluate your goals and strategies to make sure that you are continuing to help customers succeed even as things evolve.

By keeping these three top of mind, you can maintain a healthy and growing team that can become more proactive and better cater to customer's needs.

UNDERSTANDING PRIORITIES

"When I was a CSM, I often could only plan 24 to 48 hours in advance, since I was always putting out fires," says Nils Vinje who runs Glides Consulting and previous VP of Customer Success at Rainforest QA.[297]

"That's a crazy short scope – especially for someone whose ultimate goal is long-term customer success. Of course, there was all kinds of proactive stuff that *needed* to be done. It just was always left on the back burner."

"CSMs need to focus on the long term. And *they get there by focusing on process goals, not product goals.* There's a really crucial difference here, and one that's easy to forget in the heat of a crisis."

"Product goals are about ultimate outcomes like customer renewal, company growth, healthy NPS numbers. Process goals are about how you get there. They're about doing what

---

297 Vinje, Nils. 2016. "Customer Success Time Management: How To Stop Firefighting And Start Managing Your Time As A CSM". Blog. *Glide Consulting.*

you know is right on a day-to-day basis, even if it means not following your gut instinct to put out fires as they crop up. You might have a goal to do one proactive thing per day, or reach out. Think of them as repeatable activities or actions that, when done over and over again, will help you reach your product goals."

"'I want to lose 10 pounds' is a product goal. 'I want to exercise every day' is a process goal. You reach your product goals through your process goals – but only if you actually stick to them. If your goal is to lower your churn rate to 3%, your process might be to be proactive and reach out to 10 customers a day. When one customer threatens to leave, you might remember that the product goal is to prevent churn at all costs. But if you sacrifice the process for the outcome, you end up with other unsatisfied customers, which hurts your overall churn."

Step one to organizing any chaos is to understand your priorities. In Part I, we discussed the overall focus of the customer success function. The next step is to break down the focus into goals that your customer success team wants to reach and creating projects around those goals. By understanding your core priorities, you can then determine out of all of the daily tasks – which of your daily or weekly tasks directly relate to the core priorities and what do not.

Dwight Eisenhower once said, "What is important is seldom urgent and what is urgent is seldom important." While he was referring to war and politics, the sentiment still applies to customer success. Urgent things, like checking emails or responding to phone calls, are things that we react to; whereas important things are those that add to long-term strategy.

He had a strategy now called the Eisenhower Matrix or the Eisenhower Box.[298] Here, we would eliminate tasks that weren't urgent or important, delegate tasks that were urgent but not important, schedule tasks that weren't urgent but important, and then do the tasks that were important and urgent now. This is a powerful tool to help us focus on what matters the most.

For DocSend, a document management solution, they saw that they needed to sometimes sacrifice the urgent for the important.[299]

"From the very beginning, we've operated in two very distinct modes: 1) high touch or 'white glove' customer success management for our strategic accounts, and 2) automated outreach paired with passive monitoring for our long tail of lower value customers," says Ari Klein, former Head of Customer Success at DocSend.

"Because we have so many individuals and small teams using DocSend, there's a constant stream of feedback, requests, and questions to address. In the early days, it was

298 Clear, James. 2019. "How To Be More Productive And Eliminate Time Wasting Activities By Using The "Eisenhower Box"". Blog. *James Clear*. Accessed January 9.

299 Klein, "A Push System For Customer Success".

easy to fall into the trap of working out of our inboxes. Dual wielding fire extinguishers, one in each hand, putting out one small fire after another."

"But that meant that we weren't setting aside time for proactive monitoring, relationship building, and account growth activities that drive value for our strategic customers. In short, we were sacrificing the important for the merely urgent."

To address this situation, they restructured the customer success organization such that there were specialized roles within the team, from adoption focused to renewals focus.

"As we shifted away from being in firefighting mode, the importance of proactively driving value with our key accounts came into focus."

By understanding their priorities and focusing people on them, DocSend was more efficiently able to scale their team. However, how do you manage time and priorities within each of these teams? To learn more, I spoke with Maranda Dziekonski, VP of Customer Success at Pared. She spoke about how she's able to manage her time even with all of these ideas and priorities.

"It's tough. Some days are 8 hours long and some days are 12 hours long. But when it comes to prioritizing my time, I love the OKR framework."

OKRs, or Objectives and Key Results, is a well-known framework for defining goals and tracking progress and outcomes. It is an approach to goal setting first introduced at Intel in mid-1990s and is most famous for helping Google get from 40 employees to more than 60,000 today.[300] The formula this approach uses is breaking down goals into an objective – a qualitative description of what you want to achieve – and key results – the metrics that you will use to measure progress on that objective. For example, "Customer success will improve the customer onboarding experience as measured by improving adoption rates from 60% to 75% and by improving new customer NPS from 36 to 45."

"I've used OKRs now for a few years," says Maranda, "I like to look at where we need to be at in a year and then I break it down into quarters. That way, they are palatable chunks. Then, I break those quarters down into months and then days. Now I have a better understanding of what we need to do daily to achieve the month's or the quarter's goals and what metrics I should be focusing on."

"This makes things really palatable so that you're not so overwhelmed."

"Breaking down these big projects into smaller tasks is helpful. For example, last year I had a personal goal to write one customer success article a month. Now if I would have thought about that, I was like, 'Oh that should be easy. Right? 12 articles, no big deal.'"

"But then when I started on my first couple of months I'm like, 'Oh my gosh, this is going to be hard.'"

300 Castro, Felipe. 2019. "The Beginner's Guide To OKR". *Felipe Castro*. Accessed January 9.

"To make this goal more manageable, I wrote a whole list of article topics and then I assigned a month to each topic. Afterwards, I broke each of the topics down and then started working a little bit here and a little bit there. This process made it less daunting and easier to start."

"It's the same kind of thing that I have my teams do at work. I ask them to first determine our goals, then from there figure out what projects would best address those goals. Then from the projects, we can figure out the tasks and to do's from there."

"Instead of looking at customer success and your metrics as a big chunk, break it down."

In customer success, it will at times feel like you have so many things to do you lose track of priorities. By focusing your efforts, you can better manage your team's workload and keep in mind what is best for the customer.

MANAGING TIME WISELY

"The cornerstone of customer success management is the proactive nature of the work. The holy grail of any CSM is to be 100% productive and strategic all of the time," says Phil O'Doherty, Senior Manager, Customer Success at HubSpot.[301]

"Unfortunately this not realistic. The best CSMs I work with embrace this fact and allow flexibility in their schedule for 'stuff to happen.' As a rule of thumb I would say any CSM

---

301 O'Doherty, Phil. 2018. "Boosting Your Day To Day Productivity As A CSM". Blog. *Amity.*

who is 80% proactive and 20% reactive is hitting the mark. If you fail to realize this fact and completely schedule your calendar with customer meetings, training, onboarding sessions and strategic planning you will be overwhelmed when ad hoc situations occur."

One of the many challenges with being in customer success is we're balancing execution and strategy. Though we may not always be at the front lines in terms of customer complaints and support, we are definitely there to hear our customers out – both when something goes well and when something does not go well. However, outside of interacting with customers directly, we also are behind the scenes – working cross-functionally to make sure the product is the best possible, but also within our own customer success team to become more proactive and save customers from any future frustrations.

This makes it tough to budget time.

To investigate this more, Nils Vinje, the Founder of Glide Consulting who we met earlier, surveyed over 700 CSMs and found the top frustration was "time management."[302]

"Some have almost resigned themselves to this fact, and see a reactive schedule as part of the job description. In order to please customers, they think it's impossible to manage their time well. They have become accustomed to the stress of living without a schedule. It doesn't have to be that way."

302 Vinje,"Customer Success Time Management: How To Stop Firefighting And Start Managing Your Time As A CSM".

"If you're always ready to drop everything you're doing to put out the biggest fire, you'll never take care of the smaller tasks on your to-do list."

One way to combat this is to become more resourceful, says Nils. While we always want to help our customers out the best we can, sometimes it's better to help them help themselves.

"Even though it sounds like the most important trait for a CSM to have, *too much empathy can really hurt you.*"

Nils then reflected on key best practices from Des Traynor, Co-Founder at Intercom.

"Empathy often makes people wind up doing their peers' work. Imagine this scenario: you're on the phone with a customer who is having a hard time inputting data into your product. You know that the problem is with the formatting of their CSV file, but they don't know how to fix it. Empathy is what will cause a Customer Success Manager to say, 'I know exactly the problem. It's absolutely with your CSV file; it's not with Intercom. Send me the CSV file; I will fix it for you and I'll give it back to you. You can import it and that will get you to your end goal.' If you're too empathetic, you wind up doing too much work, which means you don't have any time for your own tasks."

"Here's a better quality to have when delegating: resourcefulness. Resourcefulness involves getting creative and choosing the best possible solution from all the ones possible. It's way more powerful than empathy because it protects your time and still gets the job done. An empathetic CSM might take that CSV file and fix it. A resourceful one might have the educational material on hand to give the customer so that they can learn to do it themselves."

Maranda also shared more about how strategy, particularly around time management, was for her at HelloSign, where she was the VP of Customer Operations.

"At HelloSign, we had a team of two at the beginning when we first started customer success there. To be able to get through everything on a daily basis, that's a lot of work to do even with two people. Not to mention, also provide product feedback, marketing feedback, etc."

"So it really is making sure you leverage your partners within the company. It's tough to do, but for example, if an issue keeps coming up with a customer and is very reactive, introduce that customer to your support team after a certain amount of time because otherwise they're going to always want to call you up! By doing this, that frees your time up to be more strategic and to really add the value that you need to add."

"This can be a tough conversation with the customer, but they start getting trained after a little bit. For example, if they're calling you to reset their password or they're calling you for something that typically technical support or customer support could help them with, inform them that they need to call support."

"In regards to prioritization, I look at two main buckets of things – one of things that are really simple and provide a little bit of bang for the buck, and a second bucket of things that are going to be longer term but are going to add so much more value."

"So every quarter when I do my planning, I try to make sure that I pepper in a little bit of both and not be too heavily weighed on things that are so overwhelming that everyday I come in and I'm like, 'Oh my gosh, how am I going to accomplish this?' For example, have a few things that you can just check off – such as answer a few of those emails that are weighing you down or pick up the phone and respond to whatever it is you need to respond to. Everybody loves having some quick wins!"

To balance the quick wins, Maranda also schedules time to think of meatier projects which have a larger impact.

"For those longer term value-adds, for example, I think about who am I going to get a referral for sales. I know sales has this big customer that they are talking to soon and they might need a customer reference. Who would be a good candidate for referral?"

This exercise of figuring out who would be the best referral candidate for her sales team is what actually inspired her to start the Voice of the Customer program over at HelloSign. In this program, every quarter the customer success team would try to identify a couple of customers who would talk to the entire organization. Without managing her time wisely, Maranda may have never created such an impactful program.

"Those are the bigger things that provide so much value and impact to the entire organization."

Nevertheless, even with all of this planning, customer success still has to do some firefighting – hopping on calls with upset customers or dealing with the support tickets and disgruntled executives when things go awry.

Maranda notes it is imperative to include this in your calculations.

"You do need to include firefighting into your plans."

"You just can assume that 50% of your day is probably going to go to firefighting, and if you do that when you're building out your quarterly plan, you're not going to be so stressed and setting yourself up for failure. Especially in the customer-facing world, I think 50% is pretty good and it's probably going to be more than that some days, but less than that other days. So it'll balance itself out."

I spoke with other customer success people and most others ballpark the time that they spend firefighting around 50% as well. For example, Jennifer Walker of Motivis Learning cites it at around 40%.

Maranda continues as to how this then informs her daily schedule. "I try to carve out four hours a day just for all of the reactive stuff I need to do. Then, the other 50% will be trying to do more proactive strategies."

"I wish it was a science, but it's an art. It's going to depend on the product. It's going to depend on the customers. If you have heavy enterprise customers or you have heavy small business customers, your days are going to look really different. So it really depends on your overall customer portfolio as well."

"There's just no way in a customer facing world that fire-fighting would be any less."

"In the customer success world, we all talk about being proactive, driving value, and proving time to first value and all of those buzz phrases and words used in this industry. But the reality is we still have to do work; we still have to do our job every day."

"You go to these conferences and you hear people talk about the importance of being proactive. It's absolutely important to be proactive, but you have so many reactive things that you have to do every day and they're not going to go away. So there isn't some magical moment where you can say, I have achieved 100% proactivity."

Managing time can be tough as a CSM even when we have our priorities straight. While we may never reach 100% proactivity, we should always look for ways to manage and plan our time more effectively so we can grow our teams.

PLANNING AHEAD, REEVALUATING, AND ADAPTING YOUR STRATEGIES AND PRIORITIES FREQUENTLY

Brian Hall is President of Carema Consulting, and has more than 20 years of leadership experience in building and leading scalable customer success teams at B2B companies. A common mistake within customer success teams he advised was that they weren't periodically reevaluating their strategy.

"As a leader in any function within an early or growth stage B2B software company, really challenge yourself if your team is composed properly and compensated in a way that is promoting the behavior that you want to see. You should be reinventing the team every twelve to eighteen months because after all, customer success is all about being proactive so you cannot get too comfortable. If something worked in the past three to six months, that doesn't mean that the strategy will work in the future."

"What I've come to learn through my experiences working with companies and what I coach my clients on, is that when it comes to account allocation, customer segmentation, and overall compensation, look at things – especially if you are small – from a growth hacking perspective. You are treating everyone like you can't lose them, but when you grow, you have to consider a low touch method and a reactive model for some customers so that you can focus more time and resources on those accounts that have the biggest opportunities to grow and provide negative churn."

"This means that every other quarter, good customer success leaders need to look at their team and challenges themselves to be thinking ahead – whether it's segmentation or automation, and then you should staff (or hire) the people in the right roles accordingly."

As important as prioritizing and managing time properly is, the step most customer success people forget is planning ahead and constantly reevaluating their plans. Customer success is constantly evolving. To ensure that you are keeping up, create space and time to pause, breathe, and reflect on what your priorities and plans are.

Jennifer Walker, Director of Customer Success at Motivis Learning, had a similar approach to budgeting time and prioritization so she could balance her execution and strategy work. She also took it a step further by extrapolating how planning these things out can also inform other decisions, such as hiring.

"What I did when I first started was I developed a 3-year plan. I knew that couldn't do everything so I validated it with my managers and said, 'Okay, if we're going to do three things each year, year one is going to look like this, year two is going to look like this, and year three like this.'"

"Then, have a hiring plan to go with it. So, you need to call out to leadership – in order to get to year three, here are the resources that I think I'm going to need. Obviously, it's subject to change because you don't know until you've gotten there so state that you are assuming some things. Then, depending on what your product value proposition is, develop the possibilities for your hit list of activities based on that."

"I'll give you an example. For some, it's really important that there's a community of users connecting with each other. So maintaining, curating, and monitoring your online community of users might be a huge part of your time. And you say 'Okay, because I'm spending 70% of my time there, I'm going to spend 10% of my time on writing and maintaining support articles and therefore I'm only focusing on top twenty articles. And then case management is the other 20% of my time.'"

"So you are breaking it down and saying out of the gate, 'We need these things year one,' and then year two you tack on more resources."

"For example, there are a lot of possibilities for what one can do in customer success. You could send quarterly newsletters from customer success about best practices and how to succeed. Or maybe this is already happening in your communities and you want to blow that out more. Or you could send literal thank you gifts to customers who have done referrals or who you're trying to build a longer relationship with. Projects like these take research. Therefore, they have to be mapped back to what you're trying to accomplish at the company and get validation from your leadership team by telling them, 'Here is what I have planned.'"

She notes how important it is to lay out the plan to our company, despite how busy we can get.

"I always say, 'I'm so busy,' but it's really important to lay our plans out for them. Leadership is not going to project or be able to draw from your expertise unless you tell them. They can't give you what you need unless you develop the plan with them. You owe it to yourself. You owe it to them to be very clear and articulate and say 'this is what this company needs.'"

Burke Alder, Customer Success Strategist at Client-Success, also shares how planning is not only important for helping our customers but also keeping our teams accountable.[303]

"Whether your customer success team is in its infancy or more established, it's important to have a strategy in place to ensure your team's success as they approach a new quarter. With about a month to go until quarter's end, it's a great time to reset the dials, take a step back, and ensure you (and your customers) are prepared for the upcoming quarter."

"Unfortunately, many organizations put new quarter preparation at the end of their to-dos and it certainly does feel that way for CSMs. It's crucial to have a game plan in place to set both you and your customers up for success."

303 Alder, Burke. 2019. "3 Techniques To Ensure Customer Success As You Start A Quarter". Blog. *ClientSuccess*. Accessed January 9.

He recommends reviewing your customers' goals and whether they are changing in the next quarter, and if so, how can you help set them up for success. This way you can also start preparing for the upsell or renewal conversations!

"Reviewing those now will ensure you're helping your customer hit the ground running in achieving those goals. Often times, this means reviewing how they are currently using your product or service, asking questions about what could be better or why members of the team are not more engaged. Dig deep into use cases and help them identify new and innovative ways to use your product or service to see the most value and return so they are sure to renew when the time comes."

Furthermore, he recommends doing the same introspection within your own team.[304]

"Quarterly reviews aren't just for sales teams. These built-in review periods are a great way to step back and determine what is working and what needs to be re-tooled."

"This is also a great way for other members of the department to learn best practices and tips from their peers. Holding a QBR will add customer value because it ensures all members of a customer success team are aligned on critical objectives and goals. It can also open up new doors and ideas to increase customer satisfaction and sentiment."

304 Alder, Burke. 2019. "5 Customer Success Strategies To Complete To Prepare For A New Quarter". Blog. *ClientSuccess*. Accessed January 9.

Planning ahead is something that can get lost in the weeds when you're in customer success. However, it is vital to your team's growth and sanity to strategize long-term so you and your customers can find success.

**

"Do not try and make every customer happy all the time. Prioritize programs that generate tangible business outcomes for their team. When you focus on making the customer successful with your product or service, things like retention and renewal become an easy conversation," says Omer Gotlieb, Co-Founder and Chief Customer Officer at Totango.[305]

Customer success cannot help make customers successful unless they can prioritize their goals, budget their time intelligently, and plan effectively. As your customer base and team grow, establish healthy practices within your team to make sure your team can also see success!

KEY TAKEAWAYS

Customer success can seem like a lot of work – especially at the beginning. The key here is to:

1. **Understand your priorities**: There will be a lot going on, so focus your efforts on what your team's core priorities

---

305 Zhang, Elisha. 2018. "Time Management For Customer Success Managers". Blog. *Wootric.*

are and then manage your schedule and projects around that.

2. **Manage your time wisely**: Though firefighting may always be a part of a customer success team, it doesn't have to take over your schedule! Focus your efforts on the priorities that matter and be smart with how you budget your time.

3. **Plan ahead and reflect on your plans regularly**: Approximately once a quarter or once every other quarter depending on your sale cycle, sit down with your team and plan ahead. Reflect on what worked well and what didn't, and evolve your strategies accordingly.

By doing these things, you can set up your customer success team – and subsequently your customers – for long-term success.

CUSTOMER SUCCESS TEAM MATURITY

———

"As you mature, it's important to keep in mind that "one size does not fit all." Think about the outcomes the solution you are selling needs to deliver for the end customer. By understanding where you are today, you can evolve faster by investing in and implementing customer success best practices where needed."

– Grant Clarke, Senior Vice President, Global
Customer Operations at Service Source

"Growing capacity without growing capabilities means you'll end up with a team of disorganized, heterogeneous individual CSMs doing everything differently and without a common end goal. Growing capabilities without adding on the capacity you need will lead your customer success team to operate too rigidly to handle the various situations they may face," says Mathilde Augustin, former Digital Marketing Manager at Amity and who has written over 50 articles about customer success.[306]

"The only viable way to adapt your customer success team as your company experiences growth is by taking the middle path – adjusting capacity and capabilities simultaneously."

"As your company grows, you need to focus on specializing your CSMs' areas of expertise – domain expertise vs. process expertise, for example, lend themselves particularly well to different roles and businesses. That same expertise should be cultivated and encouraged with your CSMs throughout their career – the more value they can deliver to the customers, the more successful they will be."

Your customer base will be the biggest driver for your customer success team's growth. Whether that is the introduction of different types of customers (ex. expanding into new international markets), the transition in pricing that changes the makeup of the customers (ex. selling to SMB versus selling to large enterprises), or just the sheer volume of customers, customer success must be nimble to these business changes.

306 Augustin, Mathilde. 2017. "Maintaining Proactive Customer Success In A Fast-Growing Startup". Blog. *Amity*.

One of the easiest ways for your team to respond to these changes is to hire more headcount. After all, a growing customer base warrants a growing customer success team!

When it comes understanding when would be a good time to hire another CSM, the ratio most used among the customer success community was popularized by Jason Lemkin, Founder of SaaStr.[307] He suggests, "$2 million dollars in annual recurring revenue (ARR) per Customer Success Manager is a solid model to scale with. In fact, if you can afford it, you may even want to take the hiring to the next level, and hire one CSM per $1 million per ARR or so, if you are growing reasonably quickly."

However, this will look different at every company. A 2015 survey found that in practice, this number ranged from $15,000 to $17.5 million in ARR per CSM.[308] Dan Steinman, General Manager of Gainsight EMEA and former VP of Customer Success at Marketo, said in 2015 that his ratios differs based on how much you needed to work with customers.[309]

"At Marketo, I ran the customer success management organization on a 1-to-$8M ARR ratio largely because we didn't actively manage customers but just worked with

307 Lemkin, Jason. 2013. "The $2 Million Dollar Man/Woman: How To Think About Scaling Your Customer Success Team". Blog. *SaaStr*.
308 Satrix Solutions. 2015. "2015 Customer Success Industry Trends Report". Scottsdale.
309 Steinman, Dan. 2015. "How To Determine The Best Customer Success Manager Ratio". Blog. *Gainsight*.

at-risk accounts. Conversely, here at Gainsight, I'm running below $1M as we over-invest with early customers to ensure success."

Whatever the CSM to ARR ratio looks like at your company, which will again depend on your Product Complexity and User Complexity scores, it is important to invest purposefully and intelligently in your new customer success hires to best suit your company's strategy and your customers' needs.

At my company in 2017, we shifted customer success's focus from selling to schools (B2B) to selling directly to parents (B2C). While I never lost ownership of my school accounts, I was now also in charge of the hundreds of parent accounts – with more on their way as our new sales team ramped up.

The contract value between the two were drastically different. Furthermore, because core stakeholders and customer champions of both account types were different, my customer success strategy had to be different.

For example, my B2B accounts were typically schools who had purchased licenses for our product for anywhere from one classroom of 25 students to thousands of students. Typically, these accounts saw success when they saw enough students engaging with the product, even if it wasn't all of the students. Furthermore, they saw the value we could bring to those students they could not normally reach. Due to the size of these accounts, the biggest challenge was user adoption. This typically meant the school administrator needed to onboard the math department chairs, who needed to onboard the teachers, who needed to onboard the students.

On the other hand, my B2C accounts were typically parents who enrolled one of their children to our service. They measured success solely on their one kid's performance in school, whether it was their homework scores or their overall grade. Unsurprisingly, this meant they were more sensitive to mishaps and needed more handholding throughout their customer journey.

Taking care of both proved a struggle especially as the number of accounts grew. After all, I was the only person on the customer success team at the time! I was then able to make the push to hire someone for my team to help build and grow our parent onboarding and engagement initiatives. Though we have a long way to go, the feedback from our parents so far has been positive because of our teams' increased focus on what our customers need.

Naturally as your customer base evolves and your company's needs evolve, the customer success team must stay nimble to address any changes which may affect current customers and stay proactive to prepare for any new customers. This means that at times you will need to reorganize your team so your team is best set up for success and your customers can get the best care possible.

As your customer success team matures and your company's strategy evolves, your team's structure must also evolve with it.

There are two drivers which affect your team's organization:

1. **Company top-of-the-funnel strategy**: When either your customers' companies mature and/or your company's marketing strategy targets a different customer base, your customer success team needs to adapt accordingly to fit new customer needs.

2. **Efficiency due to an expanding customer base**: As your customer base grows, not everyone can be a generalist CSM. Specialize your CSMs so that you can run a more efficient operation!

By adapting your customer success team properly as it matures, you can adequately and strategically cater to a growing and evolving user base in an efficient and effective manner.

COMPANY-DRIVEN CUSTOMER SUCCESS TEAM GROWTH

"One customer that had been an early and longtime Zendesk customer was a popular marketing and ad software platform. We initially aligned really well, as we were both fast-growing tech companies, and we had strong relationships across executive teams," Sary Stefanki, Senior Director of Global Customer Success at Zendesk, recounts how

Zendesk's lack of a customer success team almost cost them an account.[310] As Zendesk's customers matured, the customer success function failed to mature with them.

"Because they had self-implemented Zendesk at the beginning, they thought they were on their own, and thus didn't think about adapting or how else to use the product – they just assumed they had outgrown us and it just wasn't a good fit any longer."

"The beauty of the cloud is that, in theory, we can flex right with them as they grow and evolve, but we didn't have anyone guiding this process."

Zendesk then created a customer success team who discovered they needed to understand better how their clients would evolve going forward so they could retain them as customers for life.

"We documented strategies, benchmarked metrics, and created a plan to move their goals forward. It resonated well, but looking back, it was a very dicey time. We had to help mature their whole experience with us – we had, essentially, started with them in elementary school, watched them mature into a teenager, but let them still use their crayons when they should have been using graphing calculators."

Companies, startups in particular, can change go-to market strategies swiftly and sometimes your customers' may

310 DeMeré, Nichole. 2016. "An Early Customer Thinks They've "Outgrown" Your Product: A Customer Success Close-Call". Blog. *Wootric*.

also evolve, as we saw in Sary's case. This can be a growing pain for many companies and the unprepared may find their customer success programs back at square one. Relax and remember why you have been brought in – to champion the customer. Learn what the new environment is and adapt your customer success strategies accordingly.

"The decision to move up-market and re-position your product for Enterprise customers is one that should not be taken lightly: Treat it as a full-scale pivot of the business," said Ed Shelley, Director of Product at ChartMogul.[311]

"When you move upmarket, expect to offer higher-touch support, particularly onboarding, when working with Enterprise customers. They're paying a premium so they'll want things to simply 'get done.' Customer success may also need to take on some of the bespoke integration work that can't feasibly be done by Product and Engineering."

Jeffrey Doucet, CEO of CareerJSM, shifted his focus to enterprise and his team subsequently became more high-touch and interacted with customers more, which ultimately was better for their company.[312]

"We took a bit of a contrarian approach with our SaaS company. Most startups don't go from smaller, simpler

---

311 Shelley, Ed. 2017. "How To Move Up-Market Without Losing Your Soul". Blog. *ChartMogul.*

312 Blaskie, Erin. 2017. "4 Lessons Learned From Going Upmarket In A SaaS-Based Business". Blog. *L-Spark.*

clients to one bigger customer but we've found that it's been a fantastic move for us for a number of reasons."

"While a lot of startups focus on a growth strategy that encourages them to focus on reaching a high volume of customers quickly, we have found that working closely with a large enterprise allows us to focus on product market fit innovate together."

He found that when working with larger companies as a startup, you must own that you are a startup and manage expectations properly with your clients.

"We've found that our large, enterprise clients appreciate our transparency and openness and it's allowed us to go above and beyond on areas like customer success as they know we're small and we have a lot to prove."

Through oversharing data with his clients by involving them at every step of the process, Doucet found that he was able to make this transition upmarket easier on his team.

"We involve our customer at every point. It helps us to build better software and it brings the customer along for the journey. We see tremendous buy-in from our customers when we do this as they feel like they are a part of the product development process."

However, sometimes the strategy is to cater to both smaller and larger customers. Todd Eby, Founder and CEO of SuccessHacker and former Vice President, Professional

Services at Five9, shares his observations and experiences regarding this.[313]

"When it comes to delivering value, the single biggest difference between SMB and enterprise comes not necessarily in what they need, but in determining what they believe success or value looks like."

"What I've found is that, more often than not, SMB customers require more time on the definition of success, on identifying what value they are truly looking for, than the enterprise does. This is not because they don't know what they're doing, far from it. The problem is often that they are so busy doing it that they don't have time to stop and instrument what they're doing so that they can measure their success. It's the 'go-go-go' environment and mindset that leads to the SMB accounts typically having only a general picture of success. And this is where the SMB Onboarding Team has to really work to dig in and get down to the specifics – the measures and KPIs that would usually just be there in the enterprise simply aren't."

"On the team front, I favor specialization. And because of that, I recommend that a dedicated team be built for each market. If you try and take the ironman approach – one team to do it all – you'll quickly see that the expected efficiencies are not going to materialize, and that, because of the effort needed to context switch effectively between the two worlds,

313 Krackeler, Tom. 2014. "Look Both Ways: Customer Success That Spans Enterprise & SMB". Blog. *Frontleaf*.

you're actually negatively impacting your ability to scale and deliver a streamlined experience based on the market segment of the customer."

"As both teams mature and build experience, begin to cross-pollinate in order to share best practices and lessons learned. This approach really enables you to build the critical core knowledge and competencies necessary to truly serve a given market, while enabling you to leverage the learned best practices that cross the market boundaries once they have been developed and recognized."

"At Five9, we learned a great deal as we moved upmarket. Our platform was designed to be very simple and flexible from the outset. However, we found that, despite our best planning, the enterprise market still had unexpected curveballs to throw at us. What has made us successful and able to handle the curveballs coming our way as we moved up-market was the investment in success and product that we made at the outset."

"We recognized that in light of moving upmarket we needed to aggressively pursue a more proactive approach to success. We invested heavily in the front end of the lifecycle, building an onboarding program that focused on understanding what success looked like to our clients and delivering that value to them from the outset."

"We know that our ultimate success is only achievable if our customers are successful, and we strive each and every day to deliver that success for our customers. I think it's that type of mandate, one that transcends markets, that ultimately got us where we are today and will continue to guide us as we seek to grow in both the SMB and enterprise spaces."

Business strategy changes happen, and in response, customer success must be nimble to adapt to their customers and to be able to set them up for success. Continue to vouch for your customers and show your company the value that your customer success team brings!

EFFICIENCY-DRIVEN CUSTOMER SUCCESS TEAM GROWTH

Shreesha Ramdas, CEO and Co-Founder of Strikedeck, shares a mistake that he sees often among customer success teams: efficiency. As your company grows, staying efficient and effective within your customer success team is vital.

"A big mistake that I see is that companies think that you can just throw bodies at the problem and that all you need is a larger customer success team."

"That is not efficient. You need to create the right processes and the right playbooks so that you can achieve the same goals with less people. A mistake that I see is having a CSM assigned to an account and they are just talking and answering questions. They aren't walking the customer through a structured process and then are just taking the problems they are facing to product and engineering. These CSMs can be providing so much more value!"

"To combat this, train CSMs as they are hired on the steps that they need to take and the steps to watch out for. Particularly when it comes to the onboarding process, which is 60% of the customer experience, you want to have customers start off on the right foot and that starts with having a good CSM who is bringing value to your organization and your customers."

"Once the number of customers start increasing, it's worth considering appointing different CSM for high-touch and low-touch clients."[314]

"High-touch customers expect white glove treatment; they demand quick fixes of issues and rapid addition of features. In an attempt to keep high-touch customers happy, CSMs can barely find time to monitor low-touch clients. As a result, lower-revenue customers tend to churn at a higher rate. Therefore, it's important to assign a separate CSM to serve low-touch customers. Since the requirement is limited interaction, the same CSM can work with multiple low-touch customers at scale."

"In the end, it's not so much about the high or low-touch, but about being proactive and consistent in the quality of service that a customer success team puts in to solve a customer's problems."

As your company grows, your customer base will grow too, which means your customer success team will need to

314 Ramdas, Shreesha. 2018. "Should There Be Different CSMs For High Touch & Low Touch?". Blog. *Strikedeck.*

keep up. While hiring more people is one method of combating the problem, another is to segment your customers and assign CSMs accordingly so they can focus on the type of service that they provide.

Jim Jones, VP of Customer Success at ISI Telemanagement Solutions, has seen a lot of growing customer success organizations and has had a lot of experience advising companies on how to create customer success properly at an organization.

"Some of the organizations that I've helped already had customer success organizations but they had been built and designed by people that didn't really understand what customer success was. By redesigning these organizations, we were able to fit in best practices and become more efficient."

"I worked for a company based in Chicago for about five years who has since been bought out and I inherited the CSM team. Each of their CSMs had almost a 100 accounts assigned to them and it was everything from really small accounts to the enterprise level accounts."

"The CSMs basically got pulled into it in a very reactive way like, 'Hey, this customer is at risk – go make them happy' or 'They've got an escalation' or a technical issue. Because of this, the CSMs were just running around trying to make their customers happy. It was not efficient nor effective."

This company Jim worked with in the Chicago area at the time was a B2B company dealing with a myriad of customers from large enterprise, to mid-market, to SMB;

whereas the CSMs were working with whichever accounts they were assigned – not necessarily segmented by type of customer. This created too many mindset shifts between the CSMs, which reduced their effectiveness and focus.

"But there's a different skill set for managing enterprise customers versus mid market versus SMB, or however else a company splits them. These are all separate tiers."

"And so I said, 'What we're going to do at this company is we're going to have these people be the Enterprise CSMs and they're only going to cover five accounts each. This guy's the mid-market CSM, he's going to provide good service, but not do all the same things that the Enterprise people did. And then the SMB CSMs, they are going to reach out to these customers primarily through technology, not through live touch. This way, these SMB CSMs can work at scale.'"

Sam Brennand, former VP of Customer Success at Uberflip, spoke about how segmentation was able to bring their customer success team to the next level by setting up his CSMs to be more effective.[315]

"At the beginning, our customer success roles were generalist roles. We were doing anything and everything under the sun: onboarding new customers, scheduling regular check-ins, putting out fires on the tech support side, handling renewals, and driving upsell."

---

315 Augustin, "Inside Customer Success: Uberflip".

"We quickly realized that by doing everything we were doing nothing."

"We got to a point where we were fortunate that the team had grown enough that we could start to specialize. We made the decision to split the team into onboarding, coaching, support, and eventually, to add a services component. We now have two full-time Onboarding Specialists, three full-time Customer Success Coaches, three Tech Support Specialists, and three members of our services team."

"Segmentation has definitely been our team's biggest advantage. Role specialization is something that I would advise other customer success leaders to do if they have the bandwidth and budget."

Justine Burns, Director of Customer Success at Jobber, also found that by splitting and specializing the team, she was able to get more accomplished.[316]

"Up until last year, we were a single team of about 10 people and we realized we could start making things more efficient by branching out some of the duties, and that's where Tier 2 Support came into place. Tier 2 is taking all of the day-to-day technical stuff off of the support team's plate."

"Then, we noticed that product coaching impacted our abandon rate greatly. We decided to dedicate two people to full-time product coaching."

---

316 Augustin, "Inside Customer Success: Jobber".

"Our customer success funnel starts with the sales team identifying qualified leads and ensuring there's a good fit. Once the customer enters their credit card information, we send them over to Product Coaches and give all of them some one-on-one training."

"After that, we monitor usage and activity and reach out proactively to increase adoption. Once we know they're going to stick, it's in the support team's hands to answer any technical questions or issues that might come up."

However, segmentation like this isn't for all teams. Michelle Garnham, Senior Vice President of Customer Success at infinity co shares how specializing her team wasn't for her organization at her state.[317]

"Specialization from my perspective is probably a luxury of a larger organization. That said if you have operational roles like training, onboarding and support as part of your customer success org you will definitely need to look at specialization or you risk 'slave to many master of none' and confusion for CSMs on what they are expected to do. We have stayed away from being completely verticalized because I find it creates too narrow a view on best practices. But there is definitely some benefit to doing it and collaborating together."

While your customer success team grows, it is also important to evaluate whether your team should specialize

---

317 Joseph and Garnham, AMA with Michelle Garnham of infinity co and Adam Joseph of CSM Insight.

for efficiency. By doing so, your CSMs can better focus on one aspect or type of customer and can therefore provide better service.

***

As your customer success team grows and matures, it still needs to be efficient and resilient to change. Regardless of what is thrown at your team, it is important to keep the customer top of mind and evolve into what is best for your team and your customers in the long-run.

KEY TAKEAWAYS

As the customer base grows or the company's strategy evolves, there are two drivers here that affect your team's organization:

1. **Company top-of-the-funnel strategy**: Here, your customers may be maturing so you should mature with them so that you can serve them long-term; or your company may decide to target a different market altogether, which means that customer success strategy should change accordingly.

2. **Efficiency due to an expanding customer base**: As customer volume increases, the customer success team still needs to stay efficient. The most common way to do so is to specialize your team (ex. adoption specialist or all

healthcare accounts) so that they can better focus on serving a specific set of customers.

Through these changes, customer success must be able to adapt to these changes so they can best serve their customers.

WHAT'S NEXT FOR CUSTOMER SUCCESS

———

"To succeed in customer success leadership, I think you need four customer success superpowers: courage, creativity, concentration, and clairvoyance."

    – Ellie Wilkinson, Senior Digital Marketing Manager at Highspot and former Manager of Customer Success at Moz

In writing this book, I've had the unique privilege of speaking with dozens of leaders in customer success. In our journey so far, we've covered best practices that ensure your success today.

However, customer success isn't just about succeeding today. To enable your customers to really succeed, you're always thinking about their future.

And to best serve your customers' future needs, you also need to think about the future of customer success as well.

Since customer success is still such a young field, there are huge opportunities for growth and evolution across multiple axes. Let me share a couple of these trends with you, and empower you to set the foundation for a robust customer success function – one that sits at the heart of your company and in the hearts of your customers.

So, customer success is not going anywhere. In fact, it will quickly become the most integral parts of the business organization.

If you go online and search "customer success," you'll be overwhelmed with a plethora of surveys, best practices (and "best practices" that don't say much), whitepapers, and stories. It's exciting, but painfully clear there's more learning we need to do as a whole – from understanding how we can better work cross-functionally with other teams as to how to better identify, entice and develop future CSMs even before they join the workforce.

Over the past ten years, customer success has demonstrated its value to stakeholders, the basics of what makes a good customer success experience, and has built a community filled with amazing, giving people who are ready to help whomever whenever possible.

Over the next ten years, customer success will be focused on these three things to help take the industry to the next level.

1. **Customer success leadership evolution**: Now that the industry has a good thesis for what a customer success function does, we next need to understand best practices to lead a customer success function.

2. **Customer success team evolution**: To match a growing customer success team size and growing customer expectations around quality of service, we will also need to create, adapt, and establish roles to support and augment Customer Success Managers' jobs.

3. **Customer success technology evolution**: As we solidify best practices, we can automate them and use technology to provide us with more insights. We will need to continue to encourage and engage with customer success technologies that can both help us better cater to our customers' long term needs as well as fit within our budgets.

By focusing on these three things, customer success as an industry can help set up future generations of customer success for success.

EVOLUTION OF CUSTOMER SUCCESS LEADERSHIP

"Search for 'Top Traits for a CSM,' and you get all kinds of answers," says Ellie Wu, Senior Director of Customer Success at SAP Concur.[318] "However, type in 'Customer Success Leadership Traits' – even different permutations like 'CSM Director Traits' – and all I can find are a subset of the CSM Trait results."

"With the growing need, our industry leaders have an incredible responsibility to determine what is next and shape the future of customer success. Invest in your A players and be the best path for continuous growth and go back to your active network for your next group of champions."

"As we continue to experience this hyper-growth of customer success and scale, let's get intentional about adding layers of leadership, not just management."

Customer success as an industry already has a pretty decent grasp over what its main role is and how to interact with customers.

However, because it's such a young and fast growing industry, there aren't necessarily a lot of "seasoned leaders" like there are in marketing or sales who can teach the ropes and lead the way for future generations of customer success leaders. This has created two unique issues – first is the lack of experience overall within customer success leadership, and second is the lack of resources for those who are in customer success leadership positions.

I spoke to Maranda, VP of Customer Success at Pared, to learn more.

---

318 Wu, Ellie. 2017. "Top Traits Of A Customer Success Leader". Blog. *PictureCS*.

"Because as an industry customer success hasn't had a lot of time to mature, I don't think that we're getting the leadership component 100% right yet."

"For example, I see people who have been doing customer success for a year now and all of a sudden they are promoted to become Directors and VPs of Customer Success. They could be the company's most talented individuals, but I think that we need more time to mature to really have some powerful, powerful leaders in the organization."

"We don't know what we don't know as a customer success industry. We haven't been doing it long enough to have tried and true customer success and to know and develop theories and strategies out there to have this many leaders in a leadership position."

"Going forward, I really would love to see more content for leaders, more training for leaders and individuals who have been in it for seven to ten years."

Maranda then adds what she sees as the top attributes a great customer success leader has which have helped her become the leader she is today.[319]

"The first attribute is passion – passion to help your team succeed, passion to help your customers be awesome, passion for the business and product you're working with. Personally, I don't just think of customer success as a job. I also write about customer success, I speak, I go to networking events,

---

319 Chiu, *What You Need To Know When Building A Strategic Customer Success Team*.

so to me, a great customer success leader has to be passionate because it is such a new industry, therefore it is up to us to evangelize it and help shape it as it evolves. Another attribute is desire – the desire to learn, teach, and dig in. We are still trying to figure this industry out, and in order to be a successful leader, just don't have the fear to admit what you don't know!"

Jason Noble, Director of Customer Success at Goodlord, agrees customer success leadership struggles due to the industry's infancy.[320]

"With this growth, the need for very good customer success leadership is becoming more and more critical, to ensure we're delivering the necessary outcomes for and growing value to our customers."

"There are some amazing customer success leaders internationally and I'm lucky enough to know a good number of them, but there are some big challenges that we're facing. For example, lack of customer success experience. It is a new and fast changing area, and there just aren't leaders around with long track records in this world called customer success. That's not to say there aren't leaders with solid world class experience in customer-facing roles but it can make finding the right person more of a challenge and require a wider search. This can be seen especially when we need more strategic thinking and planning."

---

320 Noble, Jason. 2018. "Customer Success Leadership As We Move Into 2019". Blog. *KUPR*.

"Another challenge is short tenures... Many customer success leaders have had to move around in different organizations and whilst this has given a solid benefit of broad experience, it can be seen as an issue. I'd always encourage good conversations with my customer success leader candidates to understand the drivers behind different positions and moves, and not simply put this as a blocker which it often is."

However, as I have learned as well, there is an amazing customer success community that is eager and enthusiastic to help one another to grow its leaders.

"We're a very strong community. Generally, if you reach out to anybody and you want help, we're going to jump right in," Maranda says.

In addition, we should be helping one another! It costs nothing to give, but is priceless. Regardless of who you are, VP of Customer Success, Onboarding Specialist, or the Customer Success Manager that just started two weeks ago, there is always more to learn and new perspectives to consider. By helping one another, we can lift our entire industry up and help more companies become more customer-centric.

Elakkiya Sivakumaran of Amity affirms, "As a growing industry, we have to help each other. Share the results of your customer success experiments and practices with colleagues, in a blog, and at local meetup groups. These are not only great ways to share the wealth, but they also allow us to learn from one another and share tips with fellow CSMs. There has already been so much progress in this up-and-coming industry over the past years, so by working together we can grow at a more accelerated rate."[321]

Customer success may be young, but our leaders are budding. In the coming years, we will see customer success leadership evolve through the help of mentorship, resources, and of course, each other!

EVOLUTION OF CUSTOMER SUCCESS TEAMS

According to a 2016 UserIQ Survey, 75% of teams are staffed with five or fewer people.[322]

Liz Alton, a B2B technology and marketing writer, observes in 2018 there is a strong trend to not only increase headcount in customer success, but also to diversify customer success roles.[323]

"A major trend on the horizon is a spike in the number of customer success positions. As companies recognize the value of what customer success teams can add to their bottom line, they are investing in hiring executives, managers, and agents to staff up these departments."

"We're not just saying everybody's a Customer Success Manager," says James Scott, General Partner at

---

321 Sivakumaran, Elakkiya. 2018. "6 Tips And 5 Predictions For The Customer Success Industry". Blog. *Amity.*

322 UserIQ. 2017. *The State Of Customer Success And Trends For 2017.* Video.

323 Alton, Liz. 2018. "5 Customer Success Trends For 2018". *Marketing Daily Advisor,* 2018.

SuccessHacker adds.[324] "We're actually realizing that customer success requires a whole different assortment of skills and that's going to look different from company to company."

This reflects a shifting trend in not only an increased number of people working within customer success, but also the need to create new roles to fulfill the needs of a scaling team and industry.

Currently, there are multiple ways to model and design a customer success team. Because each company is different and serves a different audience, there is no magical formula for what your customer success team must look like. For a general breakdown, you'll typically see customer success broken into Customer Success Managers who take care of accounts and professional services teams who take care of onboarding and maintenance. Some companies will also hire a referrals focused team or some may also include support.

However, customer success relies greatly on other internal teams and third party tools to execute their objectives which can slow them down. As the industry grows and develops, customer success will need resources dedicated solely for their team. That's why we see the creation of entirely new customer success roles such as customer success engineers, customer success marketers, and customer success operations.

---

324 Sivakumaran, "6 Tips And 5 Predictions For The Customer Success Industry".

Jo Massie, Head of Customer Success at Slido, shares how they began adding more roles to their team.[325]

"I realized earlier this year that some of our CSMs were spending up to 50% of their week doing internal tasks! It really broke my heart."

"To resolve this, we introduced two new operations positions. First, an Advisory Operations person – her mission is to maximize the amount of time our CSMs can spend talking to customers. The second is the Regional Operations role – they look after all the people stuff and ensure we're working effectively in the various regions."

In fact, these sorts of operation roles are becoming more and more popular. Currently, according to the 2018 Coastal Cloud Report, only 12% of companies have a Customer Success Operations role.[326] However, they found the biggest operations challenge for customer success teams right now is lack of data and reporting, so we should expect this number to rise in the coming years.

"Every customer success team of over ten people will have a dedicated Customer Marketing and/or Customer Success Operations role," James Scott predicts for 2018 and 2019.[327]

---

325 Massie, AMA with Jo Massie of Slido.
326 Coastal Cloud, "2018 Customer Success Industry Report."
327 Sivakumaran, "6 Tips And 5 Predictions For The Customer Success Industry".

Matt Myszkowski, VP of EMEA Customer Success at SAP Digital Business Services, also noticed this trend.[328]

"A trend that I see for 2019 is a greater investment in customer success operations. This is a dedicated customer success operations teams are increasing productivity and consistency of a wider customer success organizations."

"This is one of those changes that has been sneaking up on me over the past two or three years. It's only really this year that I've seen it become prominent in all types and sizes of customer success organizations. What's interesting is that we aren't questioning the role of a sales operation function and the benefits to a sales organizations, and I think we're applying that logic now to our customer success organizations."

Back in 2015, Nick Mehta, CEO of Gainsight, had already started to see this trend.[329] [330] "We got a lot of interest in helping to shape that job category of customer success operations. They can definitely help Customer Success Managers become more effective and we think that's a good trend."

"I remember the days when you used to have to convince leaders to hire Sales Operations. 'Why do I need Sales Operations? Here's the phone book – start calling!'"

---

328 UserIQ. 2018. *Reflection & Predictions: Customer Success From 2017-2019*. Video.

329 English, Rachel. 2015. "Customer Success Is Eating The World". Podcast. *Customer Success Radio.*

330 Mehta, Nick. 2018. "The CEO's Guide To Under-Budgeting For Customer Success And Destroying Shareholder Value In The Process". Blog. *Gainsight.*

"As they learned the benefits of consistent process, automation, enablement, and data, companies started realizing that Sales Operations is a critical part of Sales. In fact, I recently talked to the president of a rapidly growing public company who budgets 0.2 FTEs in Sales Operations for every one Account Executive."

"In customer success, we're still in the old 'phone book' world. CSMs work in spreadsheets, live with bad data, have no consistent processes, and get very little training. Meanwhile, their aggregate headcount cost dwarfs a relatively small amount of spend on operations."

"Some companies might say, 'Oh, we let the CSM team share resources from Sales Operations.' However, look at the name of the team. It's 'Sales Operations,' so obviously at the end of the day the priority is going to be new sales."

Allison Pickens, COO at Gainsight, also adds to this conversation.[331]

"Interestingly, most CEOs don't ask VPs of Sales to justify hiring a Sales Operations lead; they simply assume that they'll have to hire someone after the sales team reaches a certain size. The question is 'when' – not 'whether' – the hire should be made."

"We take it for granted that these Sales Operations responsibilities are valuable; we should attribute equal value to those same responsibilities in the customer success realm."

331 Pickens, Allison. 2018. "The Value Of Customer Success Operations". Blog. *Gainsight.*

"Even so, it's not surprising that many customer success teams don't have customer success operations leads yet. Sales Operations is an older (and therefore more trusted) function, having originated when CRM software made it possible to design, manage, and report on processes. Still, given the recent development of customer success software, companies now can design, manage, and report on processes in post-sales as well, presenting an opportunity for an Ops lead to drive tremendous value for customer success teams."

"For example, customer success operations can help determine the timing and content of touch points for CSMs along the customer journey, to drive optimal adoption and high net promoter score, track leading indicators of renewals and upsell, and analyze them to understand what's going well and what's not, or coordinate cross-functional processes (with product, engineering, support, services, and sales) that help meet renewal and upsell targets and deliver on customers' needs."

"Once you have about 5 CSMs, you'll need to start developing smart processes for running your team. That's when you'll want to make your first Operations hire."

Customer success operations is a great example of how customer success as an industry is starting to mature. By developing new roles as we scale, customer success teams can become more efficient and can better help our customers.

EVOLUTION OF CUSTOMER
SUCCESS TECHNOLOGY

"Within the last decade, technological advancements have pushed the customer success industry forward by leaps and bounds," says Burke Alder, Customer Success Strategist at ClientSuccess.[332]

"CSMs no longer have to rely on telephone calls, paper surveys, or even tedious spreadsheets that house account information. Cloud-based platforms and solutions now provide a central, holistic place for all customer data to be housed, allowing CSMs and customer success leaders to be able to quickly and easily access all data and information. CSMs never have to be unprepared for meetings or update calls, and leaders are always up-to-date regarding how their department is performing and how satisfied (or not) their customers are."

According to a 2015 Preact survey, 39% of customer success teams have CSM productivity tools and 22% have a customer success platform.[333] However, only 4% list as top priority for the upcoming year; nonetheless, the sentiment is shifting as the industry matures.

---

332 Alder, Burke. 2019. "4 Current Trends Affecting Customer Success". Blog. *ClientSuccess*. Accessed January 9.

333 Preact and Service Excellence Partners, "2015 Customer Success Priorities Survey".

In fact, Technology Services Industry Association has identified three main layers within the customer success technology stack:[334]

- *The customer-facing layer*, which includes conferencing tools and usage tracking tools
- *The productivity layer*, which includes knowledge base and search functions
- *The infrastructure layer*, which includes marketing automation systems and CRMs

Together, these layers can help streamline a customer success team's job so that they help customers more efficiently and effectively.

"To be successful in customer success leadership you need to have the correct systems and automation in place so you can grow your customer base at a faster rate than your team," says Vinay Patankar, CEO of Process Street.[335]

"What that means is using technology to achieve efficiency so that your customer success reps can ensure customers are receiving everything they need for a great experience, every time, and you are well on your way to enabling your team for success at customer success."

---

334 Nanus, Phil, and John Ragsdale. 2017. "2017 Customer Success Technology Stack". Technology Services Industry Association.

335 McLaren, "14 Quotes On Succeeding In Customer Success Leadership".

Along with the growth of a team is the growth in options and use of automation tools and other technologies for Customer Success Managers. As the customer success technology industry also evolves, customer success can be better empowered to help their customers. In the meantime, stay efficient by being resourceful with the many third party product options currently available.

"A data-empowered CSM stays ahead of issues by leveraging customer intelligence to help drive business outcomes with her customer. However, with the evolution of customer success comes the realization that simply hiring people to proactively manage customers won't scale," says Catherine Blackmore, Head of SaaS Customer Success at Oracle.[336]

"While a high-touch model may still make sense for customers that pay six or seven figures, it certainly doesn't if they only pay three or four. It is time to marry customer data with programs, technology, and automation. We're entering a new era of customer success: the Age of the Technologist."

"We now have not only the data, but also the technology that allows us to score risk and flag issues that could lead to churn or identify early signals of customer advocacy. Customer usage or non-usage can be fed into digital programs. These programs are much more intelligent as new information – such as if a customer has logged in after training – are

---

336 Blackmore, Catherine. 2016. "Customer Success Evolves To Deliver Customer Satisfaction, At Scale". *CMSWire*, 2016.

designed to drive a different intervention depending on the highs and lows of the customer journey."

One of the biggest technology trends for customer success has been content automation.

The team at Custify shares, "Automation is now so big that it has its own trends for 2018 – and you'll likely see them popping up in discussions of customer success, too. Many customer success tactics, like sharing useful content, providing information on product updates, and checking in to see how things are going, can be completely automated."[337]

"The most familiar form of automation is probably the onboarding email series. When you sign up for a free product trial, you get an email thanking you for checking out the product and suggesting a few useful resources. The next email will recommend ways to further customize the experience. The final one might encourage you to upgrade to a paid plan. But there are tons of other ways that automation can help your customer success outreach. Provide onboarding or implementation tips. Keep people updated with relevant blog posts from your company based on their buyer persona. Catch people who signed up but haven't started using the product and get them back on track."

Jim Jones, VP of Customer Success at ISI Telemanagement Solutions, has seen a lot of growing customer success organizations and has had a lot of experience advising

337 "The Biggest Customer Success Trends In 2018-And How You Can Take Advantage Of Them". 2018. Blog. *Custify.*

companies on how to create customer success properly at an organization. He breaks down what he sees are the tools that a customer success team needs.

"There are four tools that you need to be successful with starting a customer success team even before you get onto a formal platform. 1) A CRM to manage your accounts and also automate the renewals process, 2) marketing automation to automate success for your smaller customers, 3) a data visualization tool so that you can build your dashboards and 4) a self help service technology to help your company provide users with answers and insight on how to use your products while reducing costs."

However, not all technology that customer success adopts needs to be third-party. Ashley Minogue, Director of Growth at OpenView Venture Partners, notes how she sees a trend in integrating the technology directly into the product and using that to augment customer success initiatives.[338]

"A broader trend that we are noticing is that more and more companies are adopting product led growth strategies, so thinking about how they can put their product more at the forefront of user acquisition, user retention and ultimately that user expansion which obviously impacts customer success."

"I think companies are trying to get smart about what can be productized in terms of customer success and where can

---

338 UserIQ, *Reflection & Predictions: Customer Success From*   .

customer success reps and managers also play an important role and how can the two really work together."

Technology is an important and powerful lever for customer success teams to use to improve efficiency as the team scale. Furthermore, as customer success matures, the technologies we use and the way we use them will also mature.

***

Customer success is still a very young industry, but one which has an incredibly bright future. Over the next decade, we will hope to see evolution in the way customer success as an industry views its leadership, its team composition, and its use of technology for the team.

KEY TAKEAWAYS

Over the next ten years, customer success will be focused on these three things as the industry matures.

1. **Customer success leadership evolution**: The customer success industry is still very young; however, with the power of community and passion for customer success, we can develop a generation of customer success leaders to come.

2. **Customer success team evolution**: As customer success teams grow, the roles within the team will become more specialized. Most notably, the customer success

operations role will grow to help empower CSMs to become more data driven and efficient.

3. **Customer success technology evolution**: To maintain efficiency, customer success will need to use technology to augment their processes as they scale. From marketing automation to data analytics, in the next decade, we will see a rise in the use of customer success tools.

Each of these levers will help customer success become more efficient as our companies scale.

CONCLUSION

—

"There isn't one way to do customer success," says Junan Pang, Director of Customer Success at Optimizely.[339]

"So, as a leader, you were not hired to come in and run a playbook that you ran at a previous company. That doesn't work. You are there because you are capable and because you know which levers to pull to help your customer success team succeed."

"To me, the big word here is balance: Can you balance the strategy versus the tactics? Can you balance the business versus the needs of your team? Can you balance all of the things that make you a strong leader?"

"Customer success is so multifaceted that you have to continuously be passionate about it. Go out and learn about

---

339 Chiu, *What You Need To Know When Building A Strategic Customer Success Team.*

the different things that you've heard in the industry and figure out how you can quickly shift gears depending on your company needs. Keep learning about customer success."

Customer success is a powerful tool for any company. By streamlining customer experiences, improving adoption and engagement, properly managing renewals, and reducing churn, the customer success team can help increase your company's bottom line and help focus and steer your company's efforts towards creating a product and an experience your customers will love and share with everyone.

Once your company has adopted a customer success mindset, you will have unlocked your most effective driver to grow your business.

Customer success can take many different shapes and sizes. What customer success looks like at your company will be different from what it looks like at mine. However, regardless if your company is large or small, brand new or established for a decade, what holds true is our passion to champion the customer at our companies.

It can be daunting, but you don't need a million tools to champion your customers. All you need to know are the basics and understand how you can apply them to your situation.

In this book, Part I was all about focusing your customer success functions based on the complexity of both your product and your user. Part II gave you approaches for building your customer success team. Part III drilled down into the four phases of the customer journey, cultivating a customer success culture, and creating a strong feedback process. Part IV emphasized the importance of the customer success team growing and maturing with the customer, as well as the future of customer success.

Starting customer success can be overwhelming, but take it step by step. You now understand what you need to do to build a customer success function at your company from:

- Working with your company to develop a customer success function
- Laying out the groundwork for a solid customer journey and success strategy
- Understanding how feedback ties in to your strategy
- Learning about the exciting new developments in the customer success industry and how they can help your team and company

There is a lot to digest and learn, but this is an incredibly exciting time to be in customer success and to champion our customers.

The customer success community is really special, and this book can help add to the success of our industry. We are all here for each other, so if you ever want to chat, feel free to reach out. I'm excited to see you embark on your journey into customer success, and I can't wait to hear your stories!

ACKNOWLEDGEMENTS

I've been so humbled by the amazing support I've received throughout this journey.

First of all, thank you to my family, friends, and coworkers. Your support, patience, and enthusiasm throughout this endeavor is something that I'll be forever grateful for. Special thanks to Naguib Sawiris for his encouragement since the beginning and for believing in me, and to Clement Kao for sharing in the joys and challenges of the writing process.

Thank you to my interviewees for taking the time out of their busy schedules to share their stories and to give me advice on how I can grow as a customer success leader. Your passion, generosity, and grit inspires me everyday and I hope those who read this book can be inspired too by the insights you have shared. I am super excited to help grow the customer success industry with you all.

Last but not least, thank you to everyone at New Degree Press for helping me to turn my dreams into a reality and for cheering me on throughout this undertaking. Writing a book is just as hard as it sounds, but you all made it less painful and – dare I say – fun.

This was an incredibly challenging and rewarding experience and I couldn't have done this without you all. Thank you again to everyone who joined me and I'm looking forward to when our paths cross again.

WORKS REFERENCED

———

INTRODUCTION

Bishop, Todd. 2015. "10 Years Later, Amazon Releases Every Prime Number – Except The One Everyone Cares About". *GeekWire*, 2015.

Carpenter, Hutch. 2010. "Model For Employee Innovation: Amazon Prime Case Study". Blog. *Cloudave*.

Duryee, Tricia. 2015. "Amazon's 40 Million Prime Members Spending $1,500 A Year On Average". *GeekWire*, 2015.

Greene, Jay. 2015. "10 Years Later, Amazon Celebrates Prime's Triumph". *The Seattle Times*, 2015.

Lashinky, Adam. 2012. "Amazon's Jeff Bezos: The Ultimate Disrupter". *Fortune*, 2012.

Marcus, Wohlsen. 2014. "Amazon Prime Was Too Good To Be True After All". *Wired*, 2014.

Reilly, Katie. 2018. "Amazon Has More Than 100 Million Prime Subscribers, Reveals Jeff Bezos". *TIME*, 2018.

Seward, Zachary. 2014. "The Very Unscientific Tale Of How Amazon First Set The Price Of Prime". *Quartz*, 2014.

Siu, Eric. 2016. "5 Things Digital Marketers Can Learn From Amazon Prime's 35 Percent Growth". *Entrepreneur*, 2016.

Soto Ouchi, Monica. 2005. "Wall Street Slaps Amazon On Costs". *The Seattle Times*, 2005.

Temkin, Bruce. 2017. "Customer Obsession Lessons From Amazon.Com's Bezos". Blog. *Experience Matters*.

CUSTOMER SUCCESS AS A MINDSET

Basu, Tyler. 2019. "The Top Customer Success Strategies Used By Successful Companies (Complete Guide)". Blog. *Thinkific*. Accessed January 2.

du Toit, Gerard, Rob Markey, Jeff Melton, and Frédéric Debruyne. 2017. "Running The Business Through Your Customer's Eyes".

Forrester Research, Inc. 2016. "72% Of Businesses Name Improving Customer Experience Their Top Priority". *Media Center*.

Ganapathy, Shankar. 2016. "The Power To Delight: Inspiring Quotes On Customer Success". Blog. *Mindtickle!*.

Goodbary, Brooke. 2017. "Hiring For Customer Success Teams". Blog. *Medium*.

Google Trends. 2019. "Explore: "Customer Success"". *Google Trends*.

Niv, Dana. 2017. "Choo Choo: How To Get On The Social Customer Care Train". Blog. *Oktopost.*

Walker Information, Inc. 2013. "Customers 2020: A Progress Report".

HISTORY OF CUSTOMER SUCCESS

Customer Success Association. 2019. "The History Of Customer Success – Part 1". *Customer Success Association.* Accessed January 2.

"Customer Success: A Brief History | Customergauge". 2015. *Customergauge.*

Pine, B. Joseph, and James Gilmore. 1998. "Welcome To The Experience Economy". *Harvard Business Review,* 1998.

Zorzi, Stefano. 2015. "Service As A Software". Blog. *Medium.*

WHEN TO START CUSTOMER SUCCESS

Augustin, Mathilde. 2017. "10 Leaders Share Their Customer Success Career Paths". Blog. *Amity.*

Augustin, Mathilde. 2018. "Inside Customer Success: Jobber". Blog. *Amity.*

Augustin, Mathilde. 2017. "Inside Customer Success: Loopio". Blog. *Amity.*

Frye, Lauren. 2015. "What Our Customer Success Team Taught Us About Referral Marketing". Blog. *B2B Marketing Blog.*

Johnson, Eric. 2019. "17 Strategies From Customer Success Experts". Blog. *Typeform.* Accessed January 2.

MacDonald, Steven. 2018. "How To Create A Customer Centric Strategy For Your Business". Blog. *Superoffice*.

McKinsey & Company. 2017. "Customer Experience". McKinsey & Company.

McLaren, Matthew. 2016. "14 Quotes On Succeeding In Customer Success Leadership". Blog. *Amity*.

Mura, Andy. 2018. "The Status Quo Of Customer Success In SaaS: Stats, Facts, Data, And Japanese Restaurants". Blog. *Userlane*.

Pickens, Allison, and Julia DeWahl. 2018. "#Techtalks: All About The Customer". Presentation, Opendoor, 2018.

Rogynskyy, Oleg. 2016. "Why You Need Customer Success Early". Blog. *Gainsight*.

Steinman, Dan. 2018. "How To Map The Customer Journey With Engagement Models". Blog. *Gainsight*.

Thompson, Bob. 2016. "Take A Tip From Bezos: Customers Always Need A Seat At The Table". *Entrepreneur*, 2016.

York, Christian. 2017. "Client Success 101: Building Strong, Personal Relationships". Blog. *Amity*.

HOW TO GET BUY-IN FOR CUSTOMER SUCCESS

Burns, Megan. 2013. "The Customer Experience Index". Forrester Research, Inc.

Corthout, Jeroen. 2018. "Guilherme Lopes Of RD Station". Blog. *Founder Coffee*.

Crandell, Christine. 2015. "2015 State Of The Customer Success Profession". *Forbes*, 2015.

Farris, Paul, Neil Bendle, Phillip Pfeifer, and David Reibstein. 2014. *Marketing Metrics: The Definitive Guide To Measuring Marketing Performance.* Upper Saddle River, N.J.: Pearson Education.

Goodbary, Brooke. 2015. "Dissecting Preact's Customer Success Priorities Report". Blog. *Medium.*

Hayes, Emily. 2017. "How To Save The Day And Convince Your Executives To Adopt Customer Success". Blog. *Access Development.*

Khan, Jawad. 2019. "7 Signs That Your Customer Regrets Choosing You". Blog. *Hiver.* Accessed January 3.

KPMG International. 2017. "Customer First: How To Create A Customer-Centric Business And Compete In The Digital Age". KPMG International.

Lawrence, Alex. 2012. "Five Customer Retention Tips For Entrepreneurs". *Forbes*, 2012.

Lopes, Guilherme. 2017. "Sharing Customer Success Experiences". Blog. *Medium.*

MacDonald, Steven. 2018. "The Secret Ingredient To Increasing Revenue". Blog. *Superoffice.*

McKinsey & Company. 2016. "The CEO Guide To Customer Experience". McKinsey & Company.

Moon, Garrett. 2019. "There's Only One SaaS Sales Strategy You Really Need". Blog. *Neil Patel.* Accessed January 3.

Mura, Andy. 2018. "The Status Quo Of Customer Success In SaaS: Stats, Facts, Data, And Japanese Restaurants". Blog. *Userlane.*

Nanus, Phil, and Allison Pickens. 2016. "Building A Business Case For Customer Success". Presentation, 2016.

Nica, Irina. 2018. "6 Pieces Of Career Advice From Women In Customer Success". Blog. *HubSpot.*

Odden, Lee. 2013. "100+ B2B Content Marketing Statistics For 2013". Blog. *Top Rank Marketing.*

Philip, Paul. 2016. "The Why, What And How Of Customer Success". Blog. *Amity.*

Preact, and Service Excellence Partners. 2015. "2015 Customer Success Priorities Survey". Presentation, LinkedIn, 2015.

Reichheld, Fred. 2019. "Prescription For Cutting Costs: Loyal Relationships". Bain & Company, Inc.

Temkin, Bruce. 2018. "ROI Of Customer Experience". Temkin Group.

WHO TO START CUSTOMER SUCCESS

Augustin, Mathilde. 2017. "10 Leaders Share Their Customer Success Career Paths". Blog. *Amity.*

Augustin, Mathilde. 2016. "Inside Customer Success: Typeform". Blog. *Amity.*

Augustin, Mathilde. 2016. "Inside Customer Success: Uberflip". Blog. *Amity.*

Blake, Dave. 2015. "5 Hurdles To Clear For Effective Customer Success Management". Blog. *OpenView.*

Blake, Dave. 2019. "Hiring For Customer Success". Blog. *ClientSuccess.* Accessed January 3.

Crandell, Christine. 2015. "2015 State Of The Customer Success Profession". *Forbes*, 2015.

Kosmowski, Christina, and Rav Dhaliwal. 2017. "We Are The Champions: Inside The Customer Success Org Of Slack, The Newest Billion Dollar Unicorn". Presentation, London, 2017.

Lynley, Matthew. 2018. "Slack Hits 8 Million Daily Active Users With 3 Million Paid Users". *Techcrunch*, 2018.

Martin, Cory. 2017. "What Is The Best Way To Start A Customer Success Program In A SaaS Startup?". *Quora*.

Mura, Andy. 2018. "The Status Quo Of Customer Success In SaaS: Stats, Facts, Data, And Japanese Restaurants". Blog. *Userlane*.

Pigford, Josh. 2017. "How To Transition From Customer "Support" To Customer "Success"". Blog. *Founders Journey*.

Sutarno, Gabriella. 2018. "Inside Customer Success: Densify". Blog. *Amity*.

Totango. 2015. "2015 Customer Success Salary & State Of The Profession Report". Totango.

Vinje, Nils. 2017. "Hiring That First Customer Success Manager". Blog. *Glide Consulting*.

Vinje, Nils. 2019. "The Importance Of Hiring For Customer Success Early". Blog. *Glide Consulting*. Accessed January 3.

"Why Our Customers Love Customer Success". 2018. Blog. *Inside Learnupon*.

CULTURE

Abbott, Lisa. 2017. "How SaaS Companies Hire & Scale Customer Success: Perspectives From Leaders At Jobscience & Brightwheel". Blog. *Wootric.*

Atkins, Charles, Shobhit Gupta, and Paul Roche. 2018. "Introducing Customer Success 2.0: The New Growth Engine". McKinsey & Company.

Augustin, Mathilde. 2018. "Inside Customer Success: Jobber". Blog. *Amity.*

Bowley, Rachel. 2018. "LinkedIn Data Reveals The Most Promising Jobs And In-Demand Skills Of 2018". Blog. *LinkedIn Official Blog.*

Burrell, Lisa. 2018. "Co-Creating The Employee Experience". *Harvard Business Review*, 2018.

Calendly. 2016. "Salesloft's Katie Rogers On Scaling Customer Success To Support 2000% Growth". Blog. *Calendly.*

Chiu, Edward. 2018. *What You Need To Know When Building A Strategic Customer Success Team.* Video.

Coastal Cloud. 2018. "2018 Customer Success Industry Report."

Freshour, Eric. 2018. "Human Powered: Empowering Employees To Deliver Great Experiences In A Digital Age". Presentation, San Francisco, 2018.

Harvey, Kate. 2016. "16 Ways To Master Customer Success From Industry Leaders". Blog. *Chargify.*

Hayer, Kristen. 2018. "5 Ways To Get Your Best CSMs To Stick Around". Blog. *The Success League.*

Kelly, John. 2019. "Hiring, Developing, And Retaining Your Customer Success Team". Blog. *Natero*. Accessed January 5.

Lemkin, Jason. 2017. "What Is The Best Way To Start A Customer Success Program In A SaaS Startup?". *Quora*.

Martinak, Lukas. 2018. AMA with Lukas Martinak of Kentico Interview by Lauren Olerich. In person. Slack.

McClafferty, Alex. 2015. "Customer Success: The Best Kept Secret Of Hyper-Growth Startups". *Forbes*, 2015.

McLaren, Matthew. 2016. "14 Quotes On Succeeding In Customer Success Leadership". Blog. *Amity*.

O'Doherty, Phil. 2015. "How To Hire For Customer Success Teams". Blog. *Keep | Grow*.

VentureSCALE. 2018. "EIR Spotlight: Brian Hall". Blog. *VentureSCALE*.

ONBOARDING

Agrawal, Pulkit. 2019. "How The Aha Moment Unlocks Successful User Onboarding". Blog. *Chameleon*. Accessed January 5.

Alder, Burke. 2019. "Fives Steps To Establish A Successful Knowledge Transfer Between Sales And Customer Success". Blog. *ClientSuccess*. Accessed January 5.

Azevedo, Aline. 2018. "Cliente Insatisfeito: Como Prever Um Churn + Bônus". Blog. *Tracksale Satisfação De Clientes*.

Brandall, Benjamin. 2018. "14 Top SaaS Companies Reveal Their Customer Success Process". Blog. *Process.St*.

Chen, Andrew. 2019. "New Data Shows Losing 80% Of Mobile Users Is Normal, And Why The Best Apps Do Better". Blog. *@Andrewchen*. Accessed January 5.

Coastal Cloud. 2018. "2018 Customer Success Industry Report."

Dixon, Matthew, Karen Freeman, and Nicholas Toman. 2010. "Stop Trying To Delight Your Customers". *Harvard Business Review*, 2010.

Expertus. 2008. "Research By Expertus And Training Industry, Inc. Delves Into Motivation For Customer Training."

Forrest, Conner. 2015. "Huddle Brings Clarity Back To Enterprise Content Collaboration". *Techrepublic*, 2015.

Graham, Paul. 2013. "Do Things That Don't Scale". Blog. *Paul Graham*.

Gupta, Kishan. 2016. "The 21-Step Checklist For Bulletproof Mobile User Onboarding". Blog. *Sitepoint*.

"How 3 High-Growth Companies Think About Scaling Customer Success". 2016. Blog. *Calendly*.

"How To Train Your Customers". 2012. Blog. *Chief Learning Officer*.

Huddle. 2011. "Huddle Announces Industry-First, 100 Per Cent Adoption Guarantee."

Joseph, Adam, and Michelle Garnham. 2018. AMA with Michelle Garnham of infinity co and Adam Joseph of CSM Insight Interview by Lauren Olerich. In person. Slack.

MarketWired. 2012. "Huddle On Track For Future IPO, Leading Enterprise Content Collaboration Market."

Martinak, Lukas. 2018. AMA with Lukas Martinak of Kentico Interview by Lauren Olerich. In person. Slack.

Massie, Jo. 2018. AMA with Jo Massie of Slido Interview by Lauren Olerich. In person. Slack.

McKenzie, Patrick. 2012. "Designing First Run Experiences To Delight Users". Blog. *Inside Intercom.*

Munger, Nate. 2016. "Day Zero: A New Way To Define Customer Success". Blog. *Inside Intercom.*

Murphy, Lincoln. 2019. "SaaS Customer Retention Is The Key To Long-Term Profitability". Blog. *Customer Success-Driven Growth.* Accessed January 5.

Nanus, Phil, and Allison Pickens. 2016. "Building A Business Case For Customer Success". Presentation, Webinar, 2016.

Nayak, Arnab. 2019. "7 Types Of SaaS Customer Churn You May Not Be Aware Of!". Blog. *CustomerSuccessBox.* Accessed January 5.

O'Connell, Caitlin. 2017. "24% Of Users Abandon An App After One Use". Blog. *Localytics.*

Pickens, Allison, and Julia DeWahl. 2018. "#Techtalks: All About The Customer". Presentation, Opendoor, 2018.

Pope, Vikki. 2016. "Three Steps To Building An Effective Client Success Plan". Blog. *Gainsight.*

Price, Shayla. 2019. "Customer Onboarding: Your Secret Sauce To Reducing SaaS Churn". Blog. *Neil Patel.* Accessed January 5.

Puhm, Kia. 2017. "Customer Success Plan: Motivation And Focus For Adoption And Expansion". Blog. *KIA CX Consulting.*

Puhm, Kia. 2017. "Customer Success Plans Unplugged: How To Use Them To Drive Adoption And Expansion Part I". Blog. *KIA CX Consulting.*

Schroeder, Peter. 2019. "Six Steps To An Effective Customer Onboarding Program". Blog. *Northpass.* Accessed January 5.

Shelley, Ed. 2018. "Lock-In Vs. Stickiness In SaaS: Retaining Customers The Right Way". Blog. *ChartMogul.*

Smartsheet. 2019. "The Advanced Guide To Customer Onboarding". Blog. *Smartsheet.* Accessed January 5.

Sutarno, Gabriella. 2018. "Inside Customer Success: Densify". Blog. *Amity.*

"The Three Leading Causes Of Customer Churn". 2015. Blog. *Retently.*

Turnbull, Alex. 2015. "How We Measure And Optimize Customer Success Metrics In Our SaaS Startup". Blog. *Groove HQ.*

UserIQ. 2018. "User Adoption Expedition: Camp San Francisco". Presentation, San Francisco, 2018.

ENGAGEMENT

"75 Customer Service Facts, Quotes & Statistics". 2019. Blog. *Helpscout.* Accessed January 6.

Brandall, Benjamin. 2015. "Why Is Customer Success Important? A Guide For SaaS Companies". Blog. *Process.St.*

"CSAT Stat Of The Month". 2019. Blog. *CustomerThermometer.* Accessed January 6.

DeMeré, Nichole. 2016. ""I Almost Lost A Customer When Our Champion Left": A Customer Success Story From Zuora". Blog. *Wootric.*

DeMeré, Nichole. 2017. "How To Start A Customer Success Program From Scratch". Blog. *Wootric.*

Hansen, Patrick, and Grishma Govani. 2018. AMA with Patrick Hansen and Grishma Govani of TrustRadius Interview by Lauren Olerich. In person. Slack.

Massie, Jo. 2018. AMA with Jo Massie of Slido Interview by Lauren Olerich. In person. Slack.

McLaren, Matthew. 2016. "14 Quotes On Succeeding In Customer Success Leadership". Blog. *Amity.*

Medina, Manny. 2015. "Uncomfortably-Close Customer Success". Blog. *Outreach.*

Murphy, Lincoln. 2018. "The Power Of The Quarterly Business Review – QBR". Blog. *Gainsight.*

Patel, Sujan. 2018. "7 Lessons From 90 Days In Customer Success". Blog. *Sujan Patel.*

Pickens, Allison, and Julia DeWahl. 2018. "#Techtalks: All About The Customer". Presentation, Opendoor, 2018.

Pickens, Allison. 2018. "The Be Brave Campaign". Blog. *LinkedIn.*

Pickens, Allison. 2019. "The Essential Guide To Quarterly Business Reviews". Blog. *Gainsight*. Accessed January 6.

Sutarno, Gabriella. 2018. "Inside Customer Success: Densify". Blog. *Amity*.

Szundi, George. 2019. "Designing Customer Health Scores". Blog. *Natero*. Accessed January 6.

UserIQ. 2018. "User Adoption Expedition: Camp San Francisco". Presentation, San Francisco, 2018.

Wiesenfeld, Justin. 2019. "Why We Choose To Make Customer Success Our Priority". Blog. *Piktochart*. Accessed January 6.

RENEWALS

Abraham, Jay. 2018. A Q&A with Jay Abraham: Strategies from Creating $21.7 Billion in Growth Interview by Adam Siddiq. Radio. The Soulfully Optimized Life.

American Express. 2017. "#Wellactually, Americans Say Customer Service Is Better Than Ever."

Benjamin, David. 2017. "Customer Success: It's Not About Changing Your Product, It's About Changing". Presentation, London, 2017.

Bernazzani, Sophia. 2018. "Why Customer Success Matters". Blog. *HubSpot*.

"Customer Success: Unlocking Growth From Existing Accounts In SaaS Companies". 2019. Blog. *JMSearch*. Accessed January 6.

Doyle, Matt. 2018. "4 Steps To Take Before Asking A Client To Renew". *Inc*, 2018.

Farkas, Daniel. 2018. "A Practical Guide To Renewals, Upsells And Customer Success". Blog. *Heresy*.

Gallo, Amy. 2014. "The Value Of Keeping The Right Customers". *Harvard Business Review*, 2014.

Gangwani, Haresh. 2017. "A 3-Step Guide To Making Renewals Happen". Blog. *Bolstra*.

Given, Blake. 2019. "10 Companies Mastering Customer Success". Blog. *Tenfold*. Accessed January 6.

Goh, Gareth. 2014. "4 Tips To Perfect The Art Of The Upsell". Blog. *Insight Squared*.

Goodbary, Brooke. 2015. "6 Strategies For Building Customer Trust". Blog. *Medium*.

Hasija, Nikhil. 2018. "3 Ways To Drive More Upsells That Every CSM Needs To Know". Blog. *Gainsight*.

Ismail, Kaya. 2018. "Enterprise SaaS Churn Rates: What's Acceptable?". *CMSWire*, 2018.

Johnson, Eric. 2019. "Customer Success". Blog. *Typeform*. Accessed January 6.

Klein, Ari. 2019. "A Push System For Customer Success". Blog. *Natero*. Accessed January 6.

Kolsky, Esteban. 2015. "CX For Executives". Presentation, Las Vegas, 2015.

Kuznia, Adam. 2017. "Stop Focusing On Renewals". Blog. *OUTCOMES: The Customer Success Community*.

Markidan, Len. 2015. "10 Customer Retention Strategies To Implement Today". Blog. *Groove HQ.*

Mura, Andy. 2018. "The Status Quo Of Customer Success In SaaS: Stats, Facts, Data, And Japanese Restaurants". Blog. *Userlane.*

Murphy, Lincoln. 2019. "Customer Success: Who Should Handle Upsells?". Blog. *Customer Success-Driven Growth.* Accessed January 6.

Murphy, Lincoln. 2019. "SaaS Churn Rate: What's Acceptable?". Blog. *Customer Success-Driven Growth.* Accessed January 6.

Nanus, Phil, and Allison Pickens. 2016. "Building A Business Case For Customer Success". Presentation, LinkedIn, 2016.

Pickens, Allison. 2018. "Renewals & Expansions: A Primer". Blog. *Gainsight.*

Poirier, Greg. 2018. "The 5 Steps For A Successful SaaS B2B Renewal". Blog. *CloudKettle.*

Powers, Ed. 2017. "The Customer Success Trust Framework". Presentation, Webinar, 2017.

Powers, Ed. 2014. "Why Trust Matters For Customer Success". Blog. *Service Excellence Partners.*

Preact, and Service Excellence Partners. 2015. "2015 Customer Success Priorities Survey". Presentation, LinkedIn, 2015.

Reichheld, Fred. 2001. "Prescription For Cutting Costs: Loyal Relationships". Bain & Company.

Rouser, Jacob. 2018. "Building A Customer Success Framework: How To Delight Customers And Drive Renewals". Blog. *Codescience.*

Samuels, David, Robert Asscherick, and Sean Cox. 2014. "How To Prep For And Drive Renewals". Presentation, LinkedIn, 2014.

Seebacher, Noreen. 2016. "CMSWire's Top 10 Customer Experience & Marketing Stories Of 2016". *CMSWire,* 2016.

Simek, Elyse. 2018. "6 Surefire Strategies To Increase Customer Retention". Blog. *Userlane.*

Skok, David. 2015. "2014 Pacific Crest SaaS Survey – Part 2". *forEntrepreneurs.*

"Tech Customer Success Programs Focus On Increasing Product Usage, Cutting Churn". 2018. Blog. *Marketing Charts.*

Toder, Blake. 2017. "The Voice Of The Customer". Blog. *LinkedIn.*

Tunguz, Tomasz. 2015. "The Innovator's Dilemma For SaaS Startups". Blog. *Tomasz Tunguz.*

Tunguz, Tomasz. 2014. "Why Customer Success? Why Now?". Blog. *Tomasz Tunguz.*

UserIQ. 2018. "User Adoption Expedition: Camp San Francisco". Presentation, San Francisco, 2018.

van Biljon, Ryan. 2018. "How Customer Success Creates Product Stickiness For SaaS Companies". *Forbes,* 2018.

van Biljon, Ryan. 2018. "Using 'Land And Expand' To Drive Revenue". *Forbes,* 2018.

Virgillito, Dan. 2015. "10 Actionable Ways To Reduce SaaS Churn Rate". Blog. *Elegant Themes*.

Whitehead, Jason. 2014. "Customer Success Management And The Critical Path To SaaS Renewals". Blog. *OpenView*.

Whitehead, Jason. 2017. "User Adoption & The 20-Year Renewal". Blog. *Amity*.

York, Joel. 2019. "SaaS Revenue | The Beauty Of Upselling And Upgrades". Blog. *Chaotic Flow*. Accessed January 6.

ADVOCACY

"5 Key Ingredients For A Successful Customer Referral Program". 2015. Blog. *Influitive*.

"10 Quotes On The Power Of Being Customer-Focused". 2013. Blog. *OpenView*.

"12 Impactful Customer Success Quotes". 2018. Blog. *Mindtouch*.

Aramyan, Pavel. 2016. "5 Examples Of Excellent SaaS Customer Referral Programs". Blog. *Incredo*.

Augustin, Mathilde. 2018. "Inside Customer Success: Jobber". Blog. *Amity*.

Boeckelman, Chris. 2018. "40 Customer Retention Statistics You Need To Know". Blog. *Get Feedback*.

Brown, Morgan. 2014. "Evernote – The $0 Growth Engine". Blog. *Growth Hackers*.

Bughin, Jacques, Jonathan Doogan, and Ole Jørgen Vetvik. 2010. "A New Way To Measure Word-Of-Mouth Marketing". Mckinsey Quarterly. McKinsey & Company.

Chesnutt, Heather. 2018. "Developing A Client Referral Program: Professional Secrets Revealed". Blog. *Ambassador.*

Duris, Sue. 2016. "Five Key B2B Customer Experience Trends For 2017". Blog. *M4communications, Inc..*

Eizips, Irit. 2017. "How To Focus Customer Success On Advocacy". Blog. *CSM Practice.*

Gains, Brandon. 2017. "17 Surprising Referral Marketing Statistics". Blog. *Customer Think.*

Ganapathy, Shankar. 2016. "The Power To Delight: Inspiring Quotes On Customer Success". Blog. *Mindtickle.*

Gerke, Grant. 2015. "Tesla Model S In Insane Mode On German Autobahn". Blog. *Teslarati.*

Godin, Seth. 2012. "It's Easier To Love A Brand When The Brand Loves You Back". Blog. *Seth's Blog.*

Grabowski, Pawel. 2019. "4 Referral Program Metrics That Will Help You Boost Its ROI". Blog. *Cloudsponge.* Accessed January 6.

Guyadeen, Julia, and Chris Newton. n.d. "How To Turn Customer Success And Advocacy Into Retention And Growth". Presentation.

Hanley, Steve. 2016. "Bjørn Nyland Wins Second Tesla Referral Contest". Blog. *Teslarati.*

Hanley, Steve. 2015. "First 'Winner' Of Tesla's Referral Program Confirmed By Musk". Blog. *Teslarati.*

Hinshaw, Michael. 2016. "7 Implications Of A Customer-Centric Strategy". Blog. *CMO.*

Iliff, Rebekah. 2014. "Marketing In The Age Of The Customer". *Inc*, 2014.

"Influitive Customers Readytalk, Bomgar Recognized For Successful B2B Advocate Marketing Programs". 2014. Blog. *Influitive*.

Lewis, Sandra. 2016. "From Bribing To Delighting: How A Referral Program Nearly Damaged Our Brand". Blog. *Startup Grind*.

Luckerson, Victor. 2015. "Tesla's Elon Musk Responds To Consumer Reports Model S Criticism". *Fortune*, 2015.

Martin-Muir, Fiona. 2018. "6 Referral Program Examples (& The Strategies You Can Steal)". Blog. *Buyapowa*.

McClafferty, Alex. 2015. "3 Startup Experts Reveal Their Customer Success Secrets". *Forbes*, 2015.

Mehta, Nick. 2018. "4 Reasons You'Ll Miss Your Number Without Customer Success". Blog. *Gainsight*.

Mehta, Nick. 2018. "14 Things We Learned From 800 Survey Responses After Our 5,000 Person Event". Blog. *Gainsight*.

Minsky, Laurence, and Keith Quesenberry. 2016. "How B2B Sales Can Benefit From Social Selling". *Harvard Business Review*, 2016.

Mitzenmacher, David. 2015. "Customer Referrals: The CSM Metric You Can't Ignore". Blog. *Gainsight*.

Monfette, Deb. 2013. "4 Steps To A Thriving Customer Advocate Program". Blog. *Content Triggers*.

Newton, Chris. 2018. "5 Ways To Mobilize Your Advocates To Boost Your Customer Success Function". Blog. *Customer Think*.

Nyland, Bjørn. 2015. *News Update: Tesla Referral Program And Model X*. Video.

Paradise, Nicolle, Dave Blake, and Allison Pickens. 2018. Top Thought Leaders Discuss 2018 Customer Success and CX Trends Interview by Elyse Simek. In person. 27th February.

Patapoutian, Talia. 2019. "Case Study: Tesla's Customer-Centric Referral Program". Blog. *Swell*. Accessed January 6.

Patel, Sujan. 2018. "How To Set Up A Referral Marketing Program For Any Industry". Blog. *Sujan Patel*.

Pickens, Allison. 2018. "How We Drive Advocacy At Gainsight". Blog. *Gainsight*.

"Preview Callout: Katie Raeburn". 2019. *Influitive*. Accessed January 6.

Ramani, Puja. 2018. "7 Tips To Run An Effective Customer Advisory Board". Blog. *Gainsight*.

Reed, Jon. 2016. "How Blackbaud Turbo-Charged Referral Revenue By Upping Their Customer Advocate Game". Blog. *Diginomica*.

Reed, Jon. 2016. "Readytalk's Bo Bandy On Advocate Marketing, And Moving Beyond Vanity Metrics". Blog. *Diginomica*.

Spenner, Patrick, and Karen Freeman. 2012. "To Keep Your Customers, Keep It Simple". *Harvard Business Review*, 2012.

"Start Up On The Right Foot – Build A Customer Advisory Board". 2019. Blog. *First Round*. Accessed January 6.

Stringfellow, Angela. 2018. "50 Expert Tips On Creating A Customer-Centric Marketing Strategy". Blog. *NGDATA*.

"The Art Of Customer Loyalty". 2019. Blog. *Help Scout*. Accessed January 6.

"Tips For Developing A Customer Centric Marketing Strategy". 2015. Blog. *Vertical Rail*.

Toledano, Eyal. 2016. "How Tesla's Magnetic Referral Program Delivered Over 40X ROI In Q4 2015". Blog. *Business 2 Community*.

Userlane. n.d. "Important Factors That Led 14 Of The Top SaaS Companies To Success". Presentation.

Wachtel, Thomas. 2018. "What Brand Loyalty Means For Your Business-And Why It Matters". Blog. *Element Three*.

"Why Our Customers Love Customer Success". 2018. Blog. *Learnupon*.

Wood, Jillian. 2015. "6 Reasons Referral Programs Fail". Blog. *Influitive*.

CUSTOMER FEEDBACK

Abbott, Lisa. 2015. "Case Study: How Entelo Uses In-App Customer Feedback To Prevent Churn". Blog. *Wootric*.

Aksu, Hulya. 2013. "Customer Service: The New Proactive Marketing". *Huffington Post*, 2013.

Alder, Burke. 2019. "Building Out Your Customer Success Department: 3 Do's And 3 Don'ts". Blog. *ClientSuccess*. Accessed January 9.

Augustin, Mathilde. 2018. "Inside Customer Success: Jobber". Blog. *Amity*.

Cancel, David. 2016. "A Simple Framework For Handling Customer Feedback". Blog. *Drift*.

DeMeré, Nichole. 2018. "How To Tackle The #1 Problem Product Teams Face: Customer Feedback". Blog. *Wootric*.

Edelman, David, and Jason Heller. 2015. "The Marketer Strikes Back". McKinsey & Company.

Gates, Bill. 1999. *Business @ The Speed Of Thought: Succeeding In The Digital Economy*. London: Penguin.

Hansen, Patrick, and Grishma Govani. 2018. AMA with Patrick Hansen and Grishma Govani of TrustRadius Interview by Lauren Olerich. In person. Slack.

Harvey, Kate. 2015. "SaaS Customer Success: The Secret To Reducing Churn And Increasing MRR". Blog. *Chargify*.

Khan, Jawad. 2019. "7 Signs That Your Customer Regrets Choosing You". Blog. *Hiver*. Accessed January 6.

Massie, Jo. 2018. AMA with Jo Massie of Slido Interview by Lauren Olerich. In person. Slack.

McLaren, Matthew. 2016. "14 Quotes On Succeeding In Customer Success Leadership". Blog. *Amity*.

Miller, Allen, Ben Vonwiller, and Peter Weed. 2016. "Grow Fast Or Die Slow: Focusing On Customer Success To Drive Growth". McKinsey & Company.

Nica, Irina. 2018. "6 Pieces Of Career Advice From Women In Customer Success". Blog. *HubSpot*.

Pickens, Allison, and Julia DeWahl. 2018. "#Techtalks: All About The Customer". Presentation, Opendoor, 2018.

Shaw, Colin. 2013. "15 Statistics That Should Change The Business World – But Haven't". Blog. *LinkedIn*.

"Slack's First Product Manager On How To Make A Firehose Of Feedback Useful". 2019. Blog. *First Round*. Accessed January 9.

Turnbull, Alex. 2015. "My First $100K In Monthly Revenue: Rick Perreault, CEO Of Unbounce". Blog. *Groove*.

PRIORITIZATION AND PLANNING AHEAD

Alder, Burke. 2019. "3 Techniques To Ensure Customer Success As You Start A Quarter". Blog. *ClientSuccess*. Accessed January 9.

Alder, Burke. 2019. "5 Customer Success Strategies To Complete To Prepare For A New Quarter". Blog. *ClientSuccess*. Accessed January 9.

Castro, Felipe. 2019. "The Beginner's Guide To OKR". *Felipe Castro*. Accessed January 9.

Clear, James. 2019. "How To Be More Productive And Eliminate Time Wasting Activities By Using The "Eisenhower Box"". Blog. *James Clear*. Accessed January 9.

Goodbary, Brooke. 2015. "Dissecting Preact's Customer Success Priorities Report". Blog. *Medium*.

Harvey, Kate. 2016. "16 Ways To Master Customer Success From Industry Leaders". Blog. *Chargify*.

Klein, Ari. 2019. "A Push System For Customer Success". Blog. *Natero*. Accessed January 9.

O'Doherty, Phil. 2018. "Boosting Your Day To Day Productivity As A CSM". Blog. *Amity*.

Planhat. 2017. *Keri Keeling, Oracle's Head Of Customer Success Enablement & Quality*. Video.

Vinje, Nils. 2016. "Customer Success Time Management: How To Stop Firefighting And Start Managing Your Time As A CSM". Blog. *Glide Consulting*.

Zhang, Elisha. 2018. "Time Management For Customer Success Managers". Blog. *Wootric*.

CUSTOMER SUCCESS TEAM MATURITY

Augustin, Mathilde. 2018. "Inside Customer Success: Jobber". Blog. *Amity*.

Augustin, Mathilde. 2016. "Inside Customer Success: Uberflip". Blog. *Amity*.

Augustin, Mathilde. 2017. "Maintaining Proactive Customer Success In A Fast-Growing Startup". Blog. *Amity*.

Blaskie, Erin. 2017. "4 Lessons Learned From Going Upmarket In A SaaS-Based Business". Blog. *L-Spark*.

DeMeré, Nichole. 2016. "An Early Customer Thinks They've "Outgrown" Your Product: A Customer Success Close-Call". Blog. *Wootric.*

Joseph, Adam, and Michelle Garnham. 2018. AMA with Michelle Garnham of infinity co and Adam Joseph of CSM Insight Interview by Lauren Olerich. In person. Slack.

Krackeler, Tom. 2014. "Look Both Ways: Customer Success That Spans Enterprise & SMB". Blog. *Frontleaf.*

Lemkin, Jason. 2013. "The $2 Million Dollar Man/Woman: How To Think About Scaling Your Customer Success Team". Blog. *SaaStr.*

Ramdas, Shreesha. 2018. "Should There Be Different CSMs For High Touch & Low Touch?". Blog. *Strikedeck.*

Satrix Solutions. 2015. "2015 Customer Success Industry Trends Report". Scottsdale.

Shelley, Ed. 2017. "How To Move Up-Market Without Losing Your Soul". Blog. *ChartMogul.*

Steinman, Dan. 2015. "How To Determine The Best Customer Success Manager Ratio". Blog. *Gainsight.*

WHAT'S NEXT FOR CUSTOMER SUCCESS

Alder, Burke. 2019. "4 Current Trends Affecting Customer Success". Blog. *ClientSuccess.* Accessed January 9.

Alton, Liz. 2018. "5 Customer Success Trends For 2018". *Marketing Daily Advisor*, 2018.

Blackmore, Catherine. 2016. "Customer Success Evolves To Deliver Customer Satisfaction, At Scale". *CMSWire*, 2016.

Chiu, Edward. 2018. *What You Need To Know When Building A Strategic Customer Success Team*. Video.

Coastal Cloud. 2018. "2018 Customer Success Industry Report."

English, Rachel. 2015. "Customer Success Is Eating The World". Podcast. *Customer Success Radio*.

Massie, Jo. 2018. AMA with Jo Massie of Slido Interview by Lauren Olerich. In person. Slack.

McLaren, Matthew. 2016. "14 Quotes On Succeeding In Customer Success Leadership". Blog. *Amity*.

Mehta, Nick. 2018. "The CEO's Guide To Under-Budgeting For Customer Success And Destroying Shareholder Value In The Process". Blog. *Gainsight*.

Nanus, Phil, and John Ragsdale. 2017. "2017 Customer Success Technology Stack". Technology Services Industry Association.

Noble, Jason. 2018. "Customer Success Leadership As We Move Into 2019". Blog. *KUPR*.

Pickens, Allison. 2018. "The Value Of Customer Success Operations". Blog. *Gainsight*.

Preact, and Service Excellence Partners. 2015. "2015 Customer Success Priorities Survey". Presentation, LinkedIn, 2015.

Sivakumaran, Elakkiya. 2018. "6 Tips And 5 Predictions For The Customer Success Industry". Blog. *Amity*.

"The Biggest Customer Success Trends In 2018-And How You Can Take Advantage Of Them". 2018. Blog. *Custify.*

UserIQ. 2018. *Reflection & Predictions: Customer Success From 2017-2019.* Video.

UserIQ. 2017. *The State Of Customer Success And Trends For 2017.* Video.

Wu, Ellie. 2017. "Top Traits Of A Customer Success Leader". Blog. *PictureCS.*

CONCLUSION

Chiu, Edward. 2018. *What You Need To Know When Building A Strategic Customer Success Team.* Video.